PURE STRATEGY

This book is animated by the recurring question of whether there are enduring principles of strategy. In the process of isolating and interpreting the fundamentals of strategy, the reader is confronted with a startling realization: the concept of strategic victory must be summarily discarded. This is not to say that victory has no *place* in strategy or strategic planning. The outcome of battles and campaigns are ever-present variables within the strategist's plan, but victory is a concept that has no *meaning* there. The pure strategist accepts that war is but one aspect of social and political competition, an ongoing interaction that has no finality. Strategy therefore connects the *conduct* of war with the *intent* of politics. It shapes and guides military means in anticipation of a panoply of possible coming events. In the process, strategy changes the context within which events will happen.

Pure Strategy is thus an inquiry into the fundamental *truth* of strategy; its purpose, place, utility, and value. It places the classic works of strategy into a framework informed by the modern physical and biological sciences as well as the military ones. While it is more properly a philosophy of strategy than a utilitarian investigation, and is meant to be heuristic rather than deterministic, it is nonetheless intended for practicing strategists. Ultimately, *Pure Strategy* makes a case for an innovative approach to security policy decision-making, one that reverberates into issues of space weaponization, information operations development, and key methods for waging an international War on Terror.

This book will be of interest to advanced undergraduate and postgraduate students of strategic theory, security studies, and twenty-first century politics.

Everett Carl Dolman is Associate Professor of Comparative Military Studies at the US Air Force's School of Advanced Air and Space Studies. His published works include *Astropolitik: Classical Geopolitics in the Space Age* and *The Warrior State: How Military Organization Structures Politics*, and he is co-founder and editor of *Astropolitics: The International Journal of Space Power and Policy*.

CASS SERIES: STRATEGY AND HISTORY
Series Editors: Colin Gray and Williamson Murray

This new series will focus on the theory and practice of strategy. Following Clausewitz, strategy has been understood to mean the use made of force, and the threat of the use of force, for the ends of policy. This series is as interested in ideas as in historical cases of grand strategy and military strategy in action. All historical periods, near and past, and even future, are of interest. In addition to original monographs, the series will from time to time publish edited reprints of neglected classics as well as collections of essays.

MILITARY LOGISTICS AND STRATEGIC PERFORMANCE
Thomas M. Kane

STRATEGY FOR CHAOS
Revolutions in military affairs and the evidence of history
Colin Gray

THE MYTH OF INEVITABLE US DEFEAT IN VIETNAM
C. Dale Walton

ASTROPOLITIK
Classical geopolitics in the space age
Everett C. Dolman

ANGLO-AMERICAN STRATEGIC RELATIONS AND THE FAR
EAST, 1933–1939
Imperial crossroads
Greg Kennedy

PURE STRATEGY
Power and principle in the space and information age
Everett C. Dolman

THE RED ARMY, 1918–1941
From vanguard of world revolution to US ally
Earl F. Ziemke

BRITAIN AND BALLISTIC MISSILE DEFENCE, 1942–2002
Jeremy Stocker

THE NATURE OF WAR IN THE INFORMATION AGE
Clausewitzian future
David J. Lonsdale

STRATEGY AS SOCIAL SCIENCE
Thomas Schelling and the nuclear age
Robert Ayson

WARFIGHTING AND DISRUPTIVE TECHNOLOGIES
Disguising innovation
Terry Pierce

PURE STRATEGY

Power and principle in the space and information age

Everett Carl Dolman

FRANK CASS
LONDON and NEW YORK

First published 2005
by Frank Cass, an imprint of Taylor & Francis
2 Park Square, Milton Park, Abingdon, Oxon OX14 4RN

Simultaneously published in the USA and Canada
by Frank Cass
270 Madison Ave, New York, NY 10016

Frank Cass is an imprint of the Taylor & Francis Group

Transferred to Digital Printing 2005

Typeset in Times by GreenGate Publishing Services, Tonbridge, Kent

British Library Cataloguing in Publication Data
A catalogue record for this book is available from the British Library

Library of Congress Cataloging in Publication Data
Dolman, Everett C., 1958–
Pure strategy: power and principle in the space and information age/Everett
Carl Dolman.–1st ed.
p. cm.– (Cass series–strategy and history; 6)
Includes bibliographical references and index.
1. Strategy. I. Title. II. Series.

U162.D65 2005
355.02–dc22

2004017855

ISBN 0–7146–5605–4 (hbk)
ISBN 0–7146–8498–8 (pbk)

To the students, faculty, and staff of
the School of Advanced Air and Space Studies.

Modern War

American Modern War

CONTENTS

ILLUSTRATIONS

Figures

Tables

ACKNOWLEDGMENTS

The US Air Force's elite School of Advanced Air and Space Studies (SAASS) is unpretentiously located in a wing of the Fairchild Library on sleepy Maxwell Air Force Base, Alabama. It seems almost fanciful to imagine that in this modest little corner of the American landscape, some of the most far-reaching and vital preparation for the nation's future is taking place. Each year, up to 40 students from the Air Force, Army, and Marines are selected from among the service's most promising field grade officers and subjected to an academically brutal year of intense instruction in the history, theory, and application of air and space strategy. These incomparable men and women, chosen for their proven leadership skills and demonstrated proficiency as pilots, navigators, engineers, and operational specialists, read more than 400 assigned texts, prepare dozens of papers and presentations, and produce a master's thesis in just over eleven months. For all of this hard work, they are rewarded with more work. They are assigned to the most important and challenging positions in the services, most with palpable national security requirements and pressures that chew up and spit out the best of military officers. To a person, the graduates of SAASS have contributed mightily and fearlessly to the national defense. I am proud to have played a small part in this process. This book is for the magnificent students, faculty, and staff of SAASS, with whom it has been my distinct honor and privilege to serve.

A great many persons contributed to my intellectual development on the subject of strategy, many of whom will be forced to deny any knowledge of or participation in this book, so as not to scuttle their credibility. Moreover, while I am ultimately responsible for the words herein, none of them would have been possible without the endless hours of discussion, debate, rants, diatribes, heated and cordial argument, knife fights, drunken brawls, and other assorted scholarly interactions that take place daily at the School. In other words, while I take full responsibility for the following work, there is plenty of blame to go around.

First, I owe a great debt to the students of SAASS, who are the future of the United States Air Force. They are, by extension, the future of this great nation. They will not disappoint. They are smart, driven, practical, and absolutely dedicated to their service. Many are heroes from our nation's conflicts. All have had brilliant careers and are currently in (or will be assigned to) some of the most vital jobs in service to their country. To the men and women of Classes XI, XII, and 'Lucky' XIII, thank you.

While all of the students in these three years have contributed to my strategic education, more than I could have possibly contributed to theirs, I would be remiss if I did not single out those with whom I spent the most time (and, usually, effort). Raymond 'Krypto' O'Mara, dashing jet pilot extraordinaire and bona fide deep thinker, who more than anyone deserves reproach for setting me on the path that led to this book. Douglas 'Stick' Stickle, whose breathtaking ability to leap logically through any argument while brewing a perfect pot of coffee left me, well, breathless. Stephen Whiting, space advocate and gentleman, taught me the power of the quiet, reasonable, and relentless approach to making a difference. Scott 'Dutch' Murray, whose ceaseless efforts to tie morality to strategy inspired many of the inductive leaps that led to fresh new thoughts herein—at least new to me. Brian 'Freddie' Fredriksson and Stanford 'Stan' Kekauoha, a one–two punch of space power advocacy who spent a year patiently listening to and critiquing my increasingly unorthodox views. And, finally, to Douglas 'Stroker' Cox, for no reason in particular.

For those among the faculty of SAASS to whom I undoubtedly will one day have to make amends, hopefully not as part of a twelve-step program, the following acknowledgments are presented. Dr Steven Chiabotti, who, as Dean in 2001, still is not sure what divine intervention or cosmic meddling influenced his decision to hire me, but who has unflaggingly supported my academic efforts anyway. Dr Thomas Griffith, who as the current Dean continues a tradition of not firing me, and who gives me all the rope I need to venture out on new paths (or to hang myself, only time will tell). Dr Hal Winton, the soul of SAASS and my personal benefactor, mentored my early teaching duties at SAASS and introduced me to the fullness of classical military theory. Dr David Mets, the treasure of SAASS, whose personal knowledge of Air Force operations goes not to the beginning of powered flight, as some might believe, but far enough back to constantly fascinate and regale with insight and humor. Dr John Terino, the heart of SAASS, whose razor wit is defiled by his innate civility, most especially for his encouragement and opportune assistance in making sense of all the issues herein. Dr Peter Hays, now at the National Defense University in Washington, for timely inputs and an equally timely and uncanny ability to know when it was time to take a break and 'do' lunch. Professor Denny Drew, SAASS curmudgeon-in-residence, whose constant reminders to make this work practical were not heeded enough. Dr Ed Westermann and Dr Thomas Hughes, true academic scholars whose example I consistently try to emulate, and of whom I inevitably fall short. Dr Gary Schaub, who graciously pointed out the really awful parts of this text, and offered numerous—though unquestionably too few—constructive fixes. Dr Richard Andres, whose skepticism about my wildest tangents kept at least part of this work grounded in reality, and Dr Jim Forsyth, whose extraordinary recollection of 60s' and 70s' rock album covers is always worth mentioning. Last, to Dr Karl Mueller, brilliant space theorist now at RAND, for being decent enough to vacate the position I now hold.

Particularly heartfelt thanks go to Sheila McKitt and Sandy Smith, the incredibly supportive core of the SAASS support staff. Their ability to get everything I need done, and to keep my spirits up while doing so, has been a priceless gift. To Frank 'The Neighbor' Mileto and local man Jay 'THBT' Wiemuth, for whom no point was too trivial to challenge nor any statement too obvious to debunk, who helped me work out the finer points of theoretical applications while drinking beer and watching Monday Night Football. Of course, for my lovely wife, Denise Dolman, who as my copyeditor read over every word at least three times and for that alone deserves a commendation of meritorious service, a special thank you for your love and patience throughout this process.

Last, I must single out Dr Thomas Ehrhard, military savant and possibly the most talented strategist I have ever met. Tom is a spigot of genuinely original and heuristic genius, which, to my knowledge, has never been turned off. I think he has solved more than half the problems that have plagued this world, and nearly all that have beset the Air Force. If he ever gets the time to write them down, there may be little for the rest of us to do. So invaluable were his insights, I asked Tom to co-author this book. Had he been foolish enough to accept, it undoubtedly would have been much better. Therefore, Tom, I offer not only the largest acknowledgment, but my sincerest apology and deepest condolences for misinterpreting many of your ideas and making them, in some cases, unrecognizable.

1

THE PATH OF PURE STRATEGY

We soldiers are mostly alchemists, and many of us more than military sorcerers.

J.F.C. Fuller, *The Foundations of the Science of War*[1]

Pure Strategy began as an attempt to answer a pair of questions that have been at the core of long-standing debate in military studies. Can there be an operational theory of war? If so, what is the utility of culling from a broader theory of war a unique and meaningful operational one? I wanted to determine, specifically, if air and space warfare were innately different from other operational-level forms, and if so, what value might be gleaned from the explanation. The difference had to be substantial, enough to clearly separate air and space warfare from at least ground and sea war, but at the same time not so exceptional as to separate it from the general theory of war in which, with the others, it must reside. I wanted the effort to be scientific, empirical, and above all, useful. In due course I found, as have so many who grapple with these issues, that a meaningful exploration of the tenets of war and strategy requires more than rigorous mathematical analysis and complete rationality of purpose. It requires revelation, insight, steadfast commitment, and faith, for strategy is not a pure science. It cannot be. There are, of course, tools, tricks, rules of thumb, and innumerable models that will assist the planner bold enough to make strategy. None by themselves will suffice, however, and all of them together are not enough. Strategy is not a *thing* that can be poked, prodded, and probed. It is an idea, a product of the *imagination*. It is about the future, and above all it is about change. It is anticipation of the probable and preparation for the possible. It is, in a word, alchemy; a method of transmutation from idea into action.

The odd angle of entry into this debate caused me to look at the primary issues of strategy in a manner quite different than most previous analyses. In the main, war theorists have (quite rationally) tended to define strategy in a way that makes cogent a comparative examination of historical victories and defeats. The effort is undertaken to provide decision makers with a rationale for why events unfolded in the manner they did, and more importantly, to serve as a manual or guide for future decision-making. The method varies, but the intent is constant. That the latter is explicit or implied matters little. As an examination of strategy, it is always at the fore. Actions are presumed to determine outcomes, and so a careful analysis should be able to tie outcomes to their determining cause. Analyses that connect favorable outcomes with momentous and decisive actions are preferred, as these should provide an economical guide for future actions. The goal is laudable, and the analysis thoroughly encompassing. Lamentably, however, no universally reliable guide has been achieved.

Part of the trouble is to be found in the malleability of key terms and methods. Whether strategy is first defined and then historical examples are brought in to demonstrate the robustness of the interpretation, or a careful comparison of like situations is studied so as to draw out the key tenets in order to define it, the propensity has been to make the concept of strategy rather broad and quite acquiescent. To accommodate such breadth, strategy is typically redefined for each theorist and each application, leading to a great deal of confusion and misconception about the place and purpose of strategy.

More constraining to the effort to find the foundational laws and principles of strategy, such comparative and historical analyses have tended to share a common set of constitutive conjectures. First is an assumption that battles and wars are won or lost, a premise so obvious it is not even stated, but one that becomes increasingly problematic for the pure strategist. Second, the outcome of conflict, be it victory or defeat, can be traced *directly to the actions and decisions* of key figures, usually at crucial moments or turning points, but also in the routines and processes of preparation for war. The common-sense import is that an alternative outcome would have occurred if the key decisions had been different. Agent-centered action as the primary cause of favorable outcomes is thus the second base assumption. Individual choice is the key variable of study. While this is an obvious characteristic of tactics, it is not so clear at the level of strategy where structure and aggregate decision-making have far more impact than individual choices, no matter how timely or profound. For this reason, much of *Pure Strategy* concerns the necessary discrimination of tactical and strategic decision-making.

Third, and because the overriding intent is to determine the keys to victory, the results of analysis are tainted by pre-establishing good cases (victories) and bad ones (defeats). The first is desirable; the latter is to be avoided. While such a bias appears reasonable, tying the dependent variable a priori to the independent one is theoretically flawed. When posed as a question, the bias becomes clear. We know the United States was victorious in World War II: what decisions and actions by its leadership made it so? Again, a manual of success is sought, a recitation of essential judgments that can be repeated in like situations.

A more neutral approach, one that is too rarely connected to an analysis of decision-making, is to determine the criteria on which the outcome was judged a victory first, and *then* assess which side prevailed. Chester Wilmot did just this when he argued shortly after the start of the Cold War that it was Stalin who truly won World War II.[2] By the Bretton Woods talks in 1943, conducted by the Allies to design post-War international trade, monetary, and banking systems, it was no longer an issue of which side would prevail. After the invasion of mainland Italy later in the year (making an Allied Balkan campaign unlikely) it was not much of a mystery how the war would play out.[3] Tactical victory at Stalingrad and the collapse of Paulus's Sixth Army further meant that the danger of a potentially ruinous peace between Hitler and Stalin had evaporated.[4] In retrospect, the signs are plain, but it was Stalin who most clearly grasped the importance of the geopolitical structuring of the coming peace. By the end of 1943, he transformed the focus of his efforts from military victory to continuing political dominance. The 1944 Anglo-American landings in Normandy and southern France merely made obvious the coming military defeat of Germany, which had been envisioned and preliminarily dissected at Casablanca. As the German Ardennes counter-offensive slowed the anticipated American advance, Stalin seized the moment. Recognizing that capturing and holding Berlin was the key to his visions of redrawing the political map of Europe and northern Asia, he pushed to occupy the German capital quickly. In so doing, he ensured that all of the territorial gains realized with the secret pre-War Ribbentrop–Molotov Pact would be legitimized, and more. Eastern Europe came under Soviet sway in a vision unimagined to anyone but Stalin. Without firing a shot, he manipulated the peace negotiations so as to receive Sakhalin Island and effective control of northern China and Korea. At every turn, it seems, Stalin saw past the end of hostilities and looked outward to the post-War settlement. In a recent book by Anthony Beevor, one gets the impression that Stalin had completely mastered the strategic situation.[5]

It may be centuries before it is truly determined who won World War II. The boundaries of cause and effect on a global scale are lengthy indeed. Nonetheless, at the tactical level the issue of deciding a victor is relatively straightforward. Tangible objectives such as relative casualties, physical control of territory, and public sentiment can be measured, and under these pre-established criteria, a victor assigned. At the strategic level, one quickly loses faith in such calculations. It is quite possible to win the battle and lose the war. It is moreover possible to win the war and lose the strategic advantage. In an attempt to disentangle these contradictions, the twin notions of victory and defeat are critically assessed, and the case is made that planning based on achieving one and avoiding the other is detrimental to clear strategic thinking.

Fourth, there is a widely recognized assumption that although wars and battles can never be repeated—at a minimum the details of any given battle or conflict will never be precisely matched—an examination of roughly similar events is expected to yield the essential elements of future action. This is a more than reasonable approach, and has proved valuable for the customary activities of managing war. It is the essence of training and preparation, for example, the foundation of doctrine and war planning. Yet at the strategic level, this assumption, too, will ultimately be rejected. Whereas standard operating procedures and doctrine are efficiency maximizers for tactical decision makers and operational planners, there is no comparable utility in such handbooks for strategists. There are only principles and norms, analytic techniques, analogies and metaphors, personal experience to include the advice of mentors, and innate judgment for the strategist to draw on. These are tapped for insight, not for answers.

And so here is found the crucial difference between strategists and tacticians. The tactical thinker seeks an answer. And while coming to a conclusion can be the beginning of action, it is too often the end of critical thinking. The strategist will instead search for the right questions; those to which the panorama of possible answers provides insight and spurs ever more questions. No solutions are possible in this construct, only working hypotheses that the strategist knows will one day be proven false or tossed aside. Strategy is thus an unending process that can never lead to conclusion. And this is the way it should be: *continuation* is the goal of strategy—not *culmination*. Actions taken and actions to be taken are weighty factors in the strategist's thinking, of course, but they are elements to be shaped and manipulated, not strict lessons leading to instructions that must be followed. This perhaps counterintuitive assessment animates several discussions on the value of history and social sciences for studying war and strategy, the relationship between decision maker and strategist, and the many differences between the tactical and operational levels of war vice the truly strategic one.

Those who are looking for a manual of strategy will be disappointed. My assessments of strategy are meant to be heuristic rather than definitive. Still, this is as much a work for the practicing strategist as it is for the student of strategy, for while I endeavor to show that the principles of strategy and war are remarkably robust in the coming ages of space and information power, there are fresh adaptations of them that must be taken into account. The new sciences of chaos and complexity are relied upon to drive home the notion that strategy is about change and adaptation. The strategist must concentrate less on determining specific actions to be taken and far more on manipulating the structure within which all actions are determined.

2

THE END OF VICTORY

The first notion the military strategist must discard is victory, for strategy is not about winning. The pure strategist understands that war is but one aspect of social and political competition, an ongoing interaction that has no finality. This is not to say that victory has no place in strategy. The outcomes of battles and campaigns are critical variables within the strategist's plan, but victory is a concept that has no meaning there; it belongs wholly within the realm of tactics. To the tactical and operational planner, wars are indeed won and lost, and the difference is clear. Success is measurable; failure is obvious.

The differences between strategy and tactics are many, but the meaningful ones are located in the focus of effort and the relationship of the planner to boundaries. Both strategist and tactician are necessary to the prosecution of war; each conducts one dimension of the military way. Tactical thinking is concerned with individual actions and decisions; strategic thinking with aggregate *inter*actions and conditions. Tactical planning takes into account the numerous boundaries that restrict action; strategic planning attempts to manipulate the boundaries that enable action. From the tactical perspective, war is bound by real and artificial restrictions of time and space. Social, historical, geographical, and technological characteristics further provide the context of conflict, offering a structure for actions taken. To be sure, in any socio-political dispute in which a beginning and an end can be discerned, and a culmination of events is desired, victory and defeat are the standards of success.

The closer one gets to the battlefield, the more meaningful—and obvious—the measure of victory becomes. Accordingly, as the conceptual scope widens from battle to campaign, from campaign to war, and from war to policy, the more troublesome it is even to determine a beginning, much less an end, to events. In the grandest scope of history, the best we can state is that the beginning is still open to debate, and the end has not yet come. For the strategist, to whom the tactical and operational outcomes of battles, campaigns, and wars are but moments in the unfolding landscape of politics and history, the impact of military action extends well beyond (and before) the causes and outcomes of wars. This larger focus is appropriate for the strategist, who seeks instead of *culmination* a favorable *continuation* of events. The distinction is vital. Battles and wars may end, but interaction between individuals and states goes on, and 'one can no more achieve final victory than one can "win" history.'[1]

In this broadest and most encompassing view, strategy represents the link between policy and military action. It connects the conduct of war with the intent of politics. It is subtler than the tactical and operational arts of directly matching means to ends, however. It shapes and guides military means in anticipation of an array of possible coming events. In the process, strategy changes the context within which those events will happen. Thus strategy, in its simplest form, is *a plan for attaining continuing advantage*. For the goal of strategy is not to culminate events, to establish finality in the discourse between states, but to influence states' discourse in such a way that it will go forward on favorable terms. For continue it will.

Victory in perspective

From a strategic viewpoint, it is a simple thing to discredit Douglas MacArthur's oft-quoted dictum that 'there is no substitute for victory.'[2] All one needs to do is insert the word Pyrrhic before victory.[3] To be fair, MacArthur was explaining that a great deal of inefficiency, incompetence, or even insubordination could be forgiven in the wake of tactical success, and to that extent, he is probably right—though with the example just given, such an outlook could be strategically disastrous. According to the old saw, it is easier to beg forgiveness after the fact than to get permission beforehand. It is also possible to see in MacArthur's quote a justification for the use of *any means possible* in the achievement of ends, or more malevolently, since the means that were used brought about the desired end, they will be excused. Such a view careens ominously towards corruption.

Either way, the quote reinforces the belief that victory is always desirable and defeat is always to be shunned. In a single instance or case, be it fight, game, or any other kind of competition, the statement rings true. But it is stifling as well. Where the probability that future conflicts will occur is high, victory is just one of several acceptable results. Defeat in this instance, at this time, may even be the optimal outcome. This is a principle known to every game player that ever tried to hustle another by faking incompetence early on. To be sure, stringing together anticipated outcomes is the essence of applied strategy. A strategy that anticipates only victories is unrealistic, however, and will ultimately fail. The outcome of a single engagement is but a piece of the overall campaign. The success of campaigns is measured in war progress and the continuing impact on diplomatic, socio-cultural, economic, and information realms.

Even supposing the goal of strategy *could* be victory, paradox must inevitably ensue. The purpose of strategy would have to be to bring events to a suitable and desired conclusion—to end or finish things. If victory is the means to that end, then a conundrum ensues. Victory cannot be both means and end in the same context. If, however, the purpose of strategy is to enhance the position of the state, then victory is but one means available to the strategist.

6

When investigating the primary means of strategy, that is, predominantly tactical outcomes both past and anticipated, within the context of campaigns and wars, we see that they must be limited in practice. The purpose of tactical decision-making is to *culminate* events, to end them so that the war plan can be updated and modified in support of the political aim. In order even to conceive of culmination, of winning, an end condition or set of criteria must be met. Achievement of those criteria is how we know that a win has occurred. Because there is a tactical end to be achieved, demarcated by measurable criteria, it must be bound first in temporal terms. The end must be achieved within a margin of time in order to have the planned effect, or to properly coalesce with other tactical actions. Since the event is bounded in time, then it is also bounded by technology, forces available, weather, and the like. Moreover, it is conditioned by social and cultural norms and values, and restricted by political dictates (e.g. Geneva Convention requirements). These conditions can be constraining or enabling, but because there are always such limitations on interaction, the tactical contest is defined by its conditions and boundaries. Many of these controls are implicit, but in modern war, especially the American form with its many self-limitations, it is also quite explicitly contained by boundaries. The master tactician understands these boundaries and makes choices with those limits in mind. The strategist, however, conceives of what might happen if those limits were changed, if the boundaries were altered. If the strategist is successful in dictating the terms of the fight, then the probability of a desired outcome in any given combat is raised considerably.

When the probability of success by one side is extremely high and thus obvious to all sides, the actual forcing of an outcome may become unnecessary. Whether it be through the tactician's masterful maneuver within the bounds of the contest or through the clever manipulation of those boundaries by the strategist, the opposing decision maker will come to a point where there appears to be no other acceptable option than to concede to inevitability. Surrendering without a fight will be the most rational decision. This is the pinnacle of tactical success, and its measure is not in casualties or property loss, but in the acceptance of defeat by the opponent. Without that acceptance, a form of cooperation if you will, victory has not occurred. Richard Hart Sinnreich, commenting on the apparently hollow declaration of victory by the United States in its second war with Iraq, wrote: 'In that stubborn resistance lies a fundamental truth that seems too often to have eluded American political leaders since World War II: *It's not the winner who typically decides when victory in a war has been achieved. It's the loser.*'[4] Sinnreich affirms the statement with an anecdote that captured the essence of his argument. The late Vermont senator George Aiken proposed in October of 1966 'that the United States simply declare victory in Vietnam and withdraw. "The credibility of such a unilateral declaration," he insisted with peculiar logic, "can only be successfully challenged by the Viet Cong and the North Vietnamese."'[5] In democratic politics the rule is well known. It is not when the candidate with the most votes proclaims victory that the election is over. It is when the opposing candidate calls to congratulate the winner, and in so doing agrees to stop contesting the election, that contest is truly over.[6]

7

It is a curious thing that cooperation between opponents is such a fundamental part of war. The boundaries of tactical engagements, to include the criteria for victory, are in a fashion agreed upon by all sides. There is a mutual understanding, for example, that a battle will take place at a certain location and time. Even when surprised, the opponent must offer resistance if a battle is to occur. Territory is defended by choice, attacked as an option. Artificial boundaries, such as state borders, are acknowledged and not violated. Civilians may or may not be legitimate targets. It quickly becomes obvious that there must be some agreement to fight under the extant conditions, or battle does not occur. The surrendering side may be butchered upon laying down its arms, but victory occurred the moment the opponent *agreed* to stop. Murder occurs after that.

Indeed, massacre is rarely perceived of as a victory, because either the dead never stopped fighting or they never started. The latter case is obvious. The former includes examples such as the 300 Spartans at Thermopylae and the Defenders of the Alamo. Despite the tactical victories of the Persians and Mexicans in these cases, the glorious strategic defenses spurred heroic efforts in later battles that helped turn the tide of war. Today, the names of these battles give honor to the tactical losers, as perspicacity allows us to see the events as components in the ultimate demise of the prematurely declared victors. Even the infamous Custer massacre was but a symbolic victory for Sitting Bull, a last act of defiance that could not be parlayed into strategic or political success.

Battlefield victory is surely a powerful means to political goals, but even here we must be cautious. The fortunes of war may always work against the best-laid plans. Sun Tzu advises that '… attaining one hundred victories in one hundred battles is not the pinnacle of excellence. Subjugating the enemy's army without fighting is the true pinnacle of success.'[7] Hence the sage tactician may seek victory without battle as the highest proof of skill, but the pure strategist must also be prepared to seek battle without victory.[8] In a situation with a finite conclusion and an absolute set of rules, combatants and players may agree to participate even where there is no chance of victory. It may be important to simply make gains relative to the current position. Tactically, a loss will be accepted if it buys time for a counterstrike or other action, or if it is a feint or ruse intended to force the opponent's attention away from the main avenue of attack. Strategically, it may be to achieve a relative standing in a larger community. A strong showing against a superior opponent demonstrates resolve. It may also provide bargaining power in subsequent negotiations. In all cases, however, to knowingly agree to fight when the probable outcome is defeat is strategic by definition. It occurs as part of a larger plan to attain future or continuing advantages. To fight when victory is highly probable may well be strategic, but it is not necessarily so.

Tactical victory is *absolutely* determined by the submission of the defeated, but it can also be *proclaimed* based on achievement of conditional and relative goals. To inflict measurable losses on the enemy in a given engagement is a component of an attrition strategy, for example, even where the opponent's losses are demonstrably less than one's own. This was the intent of the North Vietnamese in their war with the United States. Victory may also be judged relative to the capacity of the opponent to re-supply or act. The presence of fielded forces may deter the opponent from challenging superiority in a specific territory or for a specified time. In this case, the measurable criteria of victory are difficult if not impossible to assess, and this is one of the classic problems of a deterrence strategy. The absence of a challenge alone does not prove that the fielded force (or threat of retaliation) was the reason or cause of the lack of combat.

Hence we see that victory exists in the grammar and logic of battle, but not so patently of war, and most certainly not in the realm of strategy. This is because, unlike the tactical decision maker, the strategist is not strictly bound by the exigency of the conflict—by its goals or satisfying criteria. For the tactician, war is fought in a certain place and time. What is desired is a culmination of events, or a so-called end-state, a point where no further meaningful actions can take place. For the tactician, such a point is not only desirable—it is inevitable. It comes when no additional forces can be removed or put into play, no room to maneuver is left, no outcome possible but one. No action taken will prevent a victory or stave off a defeat. The tactician has cut off all meaningful options. Should the strategist ever be placed in such a position, however, one of two things has most assuredly happened: either tactical logic has pervaded strategy and made of it something that is against its nature, or the strategist is incompetent. Every action of the master strategist should be intended to increase options, not eliminate them. For there is always another alternative waiting to be found.

But the lure of victory is strong. Even though the most implausible outcome is an end-state, that is, complete fulfillment of all objectives with a stable and positive environment in place, the strategist will continuously have to struggle against succumbing to its charms. Not so for the tactician. Victory can make the master tactician revered. A series of flawless campaigns can invoke legends. To the strategist, however, victory is but a moment in time, a point of reference in a continuously changing web of history. It is never an end. It is ever a new beginning. Not only does the tactician's victory—or defeat—change the situation for the next round of tactics, it creates possibilities for manipulating the boundaries of tactical engagement.

An analogy can be found in the effects of a labor dispute, which has elevated to an active strike by workers. The strike must have a goal. In this case, let us say it is higher wages for union members. The strike is therefore a tactical action, and from a tactical perspective, the strike organizers are attempting to place management into a position where it has no choice but to submit to labor's demands, or risk losing the company. If labor can maneuver management into believing that the strike will not be broken, and the longer the strike goes on the surer the business will go under, then the rational move on the part of management is to surrender quickly, to accede to the demands of labor before additional damage is done. But the strike must also be a part of labor's larger strategic vision. If the strikers get management to meet all their demands, they must face the possibility that it could force production costs to go up—to the point that the company is no longer competitive. At worst, the company could go under and the workers would lose their jobs. A victorious strike such as this would be a disaster.

Strategically, an accommodation needs to be reached; an accord in which the future of the company is robust and solvent and that shapes future negotiations in a way that limits the probability of injurious strikes. Labor and management must be willing to negotiate for a mutually beneficial outcome. If one side or the other perceives that it has lost this negotiation, even if the current strike is called off, it will spend far too much effort preparing for the next conflict to recoup losses. Ideally, there is a wage acceptable to the workers *and* to management. Such a wage would induce higher productivity and thereby overcome the competitive production cost loss. If this wage had been obvious to all sides, then the strike would not have been called. But it was not obvious, and the strategic leaders cannot go back. The strike is in progress and the mere fact of it has changed the event horizon. Old options have been closed off, and new ones opened.

Moreover, both labor and management must realize that if the mutually beneficial relationship of jobs and profits is to continue, there will be future contract negotiations. The next contract will not be the last one. To be completely intractable at this point would be disadvantageous. Management and labor will work side by side in the post-strike environment, negotiate future contracts, and deal with the unforeseen outcomes of those new contracts. It is easy to see how leaders should endeavor to find more options to advance their side's position, but the truly strategic leader will seek to find options for both labor and management. Rather than back management into a corner, forcing it to accept a no-win solution (the tactical ideal), strategists will find an option that allows the other side to meet demands while retaining at least the appearance of a settlement.

One could conclude that the difference between strategy and decision-making, or tactics, is merely one of long-term versus short-term planning, but this is not the case. The master tactician may have extraordinarily long time horizons. This does not change the basic premise or logic. An objective is a culmination regardless of its anticipated point in the future. It can be recognized as such by the fact that time runs out (or compresses) as the objective nears, fewer choices are available, and the focus of effort is sharpened to its attainment. When the objective is obtained, a new conflict may start, but the old one is over. It can be studied, reminisced over, or forgotten, but it is no longer germane to the task at hand. It is over, and a new goal will be established.

It may seem intuitive that the strategist *must* have an end in mind, a goal to be achieved, at least to conceptually organize and make sense of the series of actions that are to be taken. Not so, and herein is another critical difference between tactician and strategist. Tacticians personify decisions made. The plan is owned by them, they are a part of it, responsible for the outcome, positive or negative. The results of these difficult decisions affect them directly and personally. Tacticians *must* act to bring events to conclusion, so as to extricate themselves from the conflict. When the war is over, they go home. When tacticians die, their battles end. Their goals were victory and, regardless of the outcome of the current battle or war, there will be no more for them. But military strategists act on behalf of an abstract concept—the state. They are the reification of the shared image. They plan on behalf of the state or military force and the actions they take continue to shape decisions long after they are removed from authority. The plan embeds itself into the fabric of the state, and the structure it creates becomes the responsibility of everyone in it. The strategist can never finish the business of strategy, and understands that there is no permanence in victory—or defeat. The real winner is the side that has established the framework for the next war (a decidedly realist strategic position) or the conditions for a lasting peace (an idealist outlook).

Since the goal of the tactician is victory, that is, fulfillment of the minimum criteria established by higher command, every decision and act is made to achieve it. Master tacticians recognize that sacrifices and retreats may be necessary to optimize the route to victory, but no tactician consciously seeks defeat. A strategist very well might. Any action or decision that does not further the ultimate goal of victory is outside the realm of the tactician, and properly belongs to strategy.

Theories and definitions

A plan is not strategy, though strategy without a plan is absurd. To have a plan is to have made a decision or decisions regarding the means available to achieve a specified result (a tactical plan) or condition (a strategic plan), and the manner in which those means shall be employed. To be a planner is to understand the process by which means are applied to achieve goals or conditions, and to understand that a plan must be able to anticipate the unforeseen through designed adaptability to changing conditions (a plan that does not anticipate change is simply not strategic). To have a strategy is to have a plan that sets into motion a series of actions or events that lead the state toward a desired condition or policy. To be a strategist is to understand how the parameters of action determine the means and ends chosen in conflict, and to manipulate the processes that transform them. To be a strategist is to know that the strategy needs a plan, but that the plan is not the strategy.

It is difficult to find two eminent works of military strategy that define strategy in the same way, much less look for consensus in its definition. There are a few themes that tend to hold constant in the better texts, and none is more profound in its presentation of them than that of Prussian military philosopher Karl von Clausewitz. Though only the first chapter of Clausewitz's magisterial *On War* was properly finished upon his death, it remains the most insightful investigation of war and strategy yet published. Certainly no single text has had more impact on the Western way of war than his, and none has been more misused. Strategists have since picked through his notes and letters in addition to his extraordinary book to cull snippets that justify virtually any position on the relationship between war and politics. And this is as it should be, for his is a brilliant work that evokes deep passion from readers, regardless of the translation. After Clausewitz, no serious student of military studies could deny the primacy of the politico-military relationship, and military studies has been forever placed front and center in the always contentious political arena.

Clausewitz's contention was that the *theoretical* realm of the mind in war is encompassed by the term strategy, defined as the '*use of engagements for the object of war*,' and differentiated from tactics, which are the '*use of armed forces in the engagement*.'[9] So far, so good; but theory is merely the departure point for Clausewitz's investigation, not the fruit of it. Theory is always necessary when beginning a search for meaning or truth, as there can be no sense made of the world without it. It is the filter through which our mind perceives the world; through which it organizes thought. In his preeminent work, Clausewitz would move seamlessly from the deduction of first principles in theory to the application and testing of those principles in the historical record. Where he was searching for a general and useful theory of war, I attempt the same for strategy.

The widely recognized concept of strategy, in its broadest sense, is the process of matching means to ends. In this most common perception, the idea of strategy is applicable across a wide range of activities; indeed, to almost any pursuit a person undertakes that involves choosing, from the simplest to the most complex. The most straightforward of these are strategies for competition against nature, where the opponent is uncaring of our actions and attitudes towards it. The building of dikes and levees, for example, is part of the application of a strategy to mitigate the effects of flooding. The routine evaluation made when opting whether or not to take my umbrella to work today involves a similar process of decision-making. I do not wish to get wet, and so a plan is devised to prevent it. If the levees hold, or my clothing remains dry, one proclaims the strategy successful.

This is the tactical way of looking at actions mated to ends. It requires that a desired end be established so that efficient or appropriate means can be applied in pursuit of it. It must also be measurable, so that a practical assessment of success can be made. But what if the dikes fail? What if I get wet despite the presence of my umbrella? The tactic was clearly unsuccessful, but did the strategy fail? Should I now toss out my umbrella and never use one again? Of course not. Was the *process* of building dikes useful despite their being overcome by this particular flood? Of course it was. In the latter case, society benefited in uncounted ways through cooperation, community struggle, experience in organization on a large scale, and so on. Good strategy leads to a strong probability of recurring or continuing advantage. Note here that strategy is qualitatively—not quantitatively—judged. It is better or worse, *relative to another strategy*. It is not perfect or perfected, as a tactic could be. At the very least, in our examples, we now know the extent of flooding that will overwhelm the old dikes, and can make corrections in the next ones. One contrary event does not provide enough impetus to abandon dike-making or umbrella-taking, nor do a multitude of conforming events ensure that such activities will always remain beneficial.

We need theory to cope with a world that is so unfathomably intricate. The world is so complex largely because it is an open system. No matter how detailed is the effort to account for all possible events, there is at least one more we could not have accounted for. Indeed, the more we try to account for all the variables necessary to perfect a strategy, the more tangled the process becomes and the less utility the strategy will have. It becomes bloated beyond benefit. When other agents are involved, an actor or actors who can be swayed or moved by my actions, as in a game or a race, then my decision-making process is more complex, approximate, and sensitive to change. It becomes harder, and more specific to (fewer) known events. To assist in making models that incorporate the most data and events, countless tracts are written on decision-making for business, economics, social relations, and, of course, war. Most address the pluses and minuses of applying specific means in certain situations, and most have some tactical utility. Still, and despite the innate desire to discover a handbook of solutions or a checklist for action, making strategy is not the same as decision-making. It entails a different way of looking at the world, and the differences have profound meaning.

The issue is more than semantics, but even were it so, it could not be more important, and would still be worthy of a book on the subject. Semantics is the study of words and meanings, especially with regard to changes over time. It is the scientific study of the relationships between signs and symbols and their significance to disparate interpreters. No issue, then, ought to be more vital for the strategist, who deals daily with perceptions and symbols, than semantics.[10] In this case, the precise placement of strategy into a policy-making context prevents that policy from being overcome by the logic of matching means to ends so necessary in planning, allowing strategy to guide and shape planning rather than be captured by it. Were it not so, the situation would be akin to that of a child who is presented with a hammer. Suddenly, a world made of nails is revealed, and they all need pounding. In other words, differentiating the *purpose* of strategy and tactics prevents the *requirements* of the means or ends from taking over the strategic process. Clausewitz knew well of this tendency, and remarked on it so eloquently: War's 'grammar, indeed, may be its own, but not its logic.'[11] Throughout this work, I will show that the grammar of war can overwhelm the logic of policy if strategy and tactical decision-making are not clearly separated.

A full examination of the levels of policy, war, strategy, and operational and tactical decision-making follows shortly. For now, it is useful simply to differentiate strategic and tactical logic. Consistent with Clausewitz, decision-making *within* the context of war and preparation for war is tactical. Decision-making *about* the context of war and preparation for war is strategic. Tactical decision-making seeks finality; it has specific goals and definable ends. It seeks victory. Strategic decision-making seeks continuity; it is concerned with purpose and processes. Tactical decision-making is contained by boundaries—physical, socio-political, and temporal. There is a start and a finish. Strategic decision-making is unfettered by such as these, and seeks instead to manipulate them. Strategy is confined only by the event horizon of possibilities, a horizon which expands anew with every action. A potentially unlimited panorama of choices may be revealed with the next moment. There is no beginning or end for the strategist; there is only more, or less.

Actions *in* war or in preparation for war are the proper domain of the tactician. Indeed, they are comprehensible only in the context of the recognized boundaries of that conflict and with respect to the events that occur there. These are concrete and dependent elements, bound by time, place, and technology. Decisions and actions are meaningful relative to the specific conflict or situation. For example, a decision to commit forces to a second front is understood in the context of the war, force distributions, readiness, etc. The decision to employ violence is not, or should not be. To go to war because the probability of tactical victory is high is likely a poor strategy, just as the decision to go to war despite a likelihood of battlefield victory is a poor tactical decision—though it may well be a very sound element of strategy. Hence, actions *for or about* war or the preparation for war are the domain of the strategist. The strategist makes sense of the world in terms of abstract causal relationships and aggregate perceptions. Decisions and actions are *absolute* and *independent* of the boundaries of time, place, or technology. It is from the *relative* and *dependent* that battle plans and doctrinal tactics are derived. It is from the absolute that the laws and principles of war apply.

This distinction is too often missed. When strategy as planning is elevated to the level of war, definitions are made that barely rise above the tactical. Only the scope of decision-making is changed. Typical is Zeev Maoz: 'Strategy is the art of using military force to accomplish political ends.'[12] There is no modification in the basic definition of strategy as matching means to ends; only the distinctions that strategy is an art and is limited to the use of military forces separate it from the more banal examples. While typical, this definition is not complete. It does not separate strategy conceptually from the miasma of war. It pours and mixes strategy into war, as cream is stirred into a cup of coffee, and it becomes coincident with it. Like the cream, strategy is thereafter irreclaimable. It becomes the war; it cannot be stirred out. To make the definition encompassing, and therefore distinguish strategy from war and battle, it is incumbent on the theorist to make it more parsimonious, not more generous.[13]

Here I argue that strategy and tactics are theoretically opposite concepts that wax and wane relative to one another, but are always together and can be understood fully only in their relationship with the other. They are powerless alone, ever entwined in reality; yet they remain conceptually separate throughout the conflict. Tactics has its place, on the field of competition or battle space, and there it is supreme. Strategy, too, has a realm of its own, at the point where military force and policy converge. Here the strategist must link the logic of tactics and war with the intent of policy. That link will be identified later as operational art. Despite the clear separation, it should be apparent that a strategy that ignores—or is ignorant of—tactics is as useless as a tactic that defies or confounds strategy.

Clausewitz, strategy, and the better state of peace

The purpose of military strategy is to link military means with political aims in pursuit of a continuing advantage. It does so through the mediums of applied and potential violence. 'Essentially war is fighting,' and the tactical purpose of fighting is to achieve a specific objective that ultimately *must include ending the fight*.[14] When all sides have agreed that the fight is over, the condition is called peace, or concord. A treaty will determine the new status quo, and bargaining power will derive in part from the various results of battles in the war. War is waged, then, in order to conclude fighting on better terms than it began. Thus, the strategic purpose of war is to *attain a better condition of peace*.[15]

If war is about politics and the governing of land and people, as Clausewitz insisted, then like politics, *strategy is a state of being*, and not a series of events. To be sure, military and political campaigns are waged in the furtherance of achieving power. Winning a battle, however, does not end strategy, just as winning an election does not end politics.[16] Both simply add to the characteristics that describe the military and political contexts. The comparison goes further. The purpose of the *political campaign* is to win a position of political authority or to affect the outcome of a political decision. But the purpose of *politics* is to exert continuing influence— to govern, or to rule. The first is but one means to the latter. Hence, politics exists both in the mind and in the actions of political actors. As a function of politics, the purposes of war and campaigns are clear. These are the military means to power.

Military and political campaigns in this way share the same logic of purpose, which is to achieve a position of authority or influence in subsequent decisions. A political campaign is waged to gain a position of influence in policy-making. Military campaigns are waged to gain leverage at the peace table: 'we must always consider that with the conclusion of peace the purpose of war has been achieved and its business is at an end.'[17] Also like politics, the purpose of strategy is to *continue* to exert influence. 'Not every war leads to a final decision and settlement,' says Clausewitz, but even where it appears to culminate there can be lingering effects that are only addressable through political discourse.[18]

In one of his most memorable lines, Clausewitz states that,

> no one starts a war—or rather, no one in his senses ought to do so—
> without first being clear in his mind what he intends to achieve by that
> war and how he intends to conduct it. The former is political purpose;
> the latter its operational objective. This is the governing principle which
> will set its course, prescribe the scale of means and effort which is
> required, and makes its influence felt down to the smallest detail.[19]

Since 'battle is the one and only means that warfare can employ,' we glean from this statement that there is an operational level of war, and that it links the tactical and strategic levels. The operational objective, too, is a component of strategy and strategic purpose.[20]

The first parsing of the kind or type of war to be fought is a matter of scale and of theory. War can be waged in 'its absolute form or one of the variant forms that it actually takes ... [for absolute war] there is only one result that counts: *final victory*.'[21] But in real war, the kind that is actually fought, the goal should be limited,

15

and related directly to the political objective. Overreaching in war is the costliest strategic mistake. 'Conquering Moscow and half of Russia in 1812 was of no avail to Bonaparte unless it brought him the peace he had in view.'[22] It did not, as became plainly evident, and the Russian Campaign was the proximate inauguration of Napoleon's demise.

Clausewitz scours history to find a true case of total war, where absolute victory would indeed be the proper aim, and finds none. Not only are limited wars the only kind that are fought, he notes that

> a review of actual cases shows a whole category of wars in which the very idea of defeating the enemy is unreal; those in which the enemy is essentially the stronger power [and] if war were what pure theory postulates, a war between states of markedly unequal strength would be absurd, and so impossible.[23]

States may even choose to go to war with strategic aims that rule out the possibility of tactical victory. These are for operations that are intended to achieve 'success without defeating the enemy's forces,' including 'operations that have *direct political repercussions*, designed [to] disrupt the opposing alliance, or to paralyze it, [to gain] new allies, favorably effect the political scene, etc.'[24] Clausewitz cannot be more clear on the subject of strategic purpose when he states, 'the analysis [of the kind of war to be fought] must extend to the *ultimate objective*, which is to bring about peace.'[25]

Case upon case is brought to bear as Clausewitz draws on history to aid in the persuasiveness of his argument. His icon, Frederick the Great, is praised for his genius:

> What is really admirable is the King's wisdom: pursuing a major objective with limited resources, he did not try to undertake anything beyond his strength, but always *just enough* to get him what he wanted ... His object was to bring Silesia into the safe harbour of a fully guaranteed peace.[26]

Napoleon's campaigns are also cited many times, although both praised and condemned. In a counter to Frederick's judicious use of force, Clausewitz cites Napoleon's daring March 1797 attack on Austria. The 'object was to force a decision on the Austrians before the arrival of their reinforcements.'[27] Napoleon was a Major General at the time, flush from successes in Northern Italy, and the broader view of state politics was obscured by his own desire for personal gain. The French Directory, according to Clausewitz, could appreciate that his advance through the Alps was an extremely risky gambit. The Directory knew that some 30,000 French reinforcements were preparing to join Napoleon's 43,000 in Italy, but would not arrive for another six weeks. Napoleon's advance was successful, to a point. Austrian losses were heavy, but by the end of the month the Army of Italy had extended too far, and 'the little Corporal' was forced to end his campaign well short of Vienna, his sought-after measure of victory.[28] In the end Napoleon succeeded in his personal ambitions, but 'would the Austrians have thought it worth the sacrifices they entailed—the continuation of the war—when that price could have been avoided by concluding a peace on not too unfavorable terms?'[29]

The problem, according to Clausewitz, was that the Austrians were blinded to the limits of France's weak *strategic* position by Napoleon's *tactical* success in the Alps. With his army stretched thin, revolts in Northern Italy forced Napoleon to offer a truce (which he did not honor), and, blind to the strategic situation, Austria agreed to harsh terms on April 16. Napoleon, without the consent of the Directorate, received Belgium and Holland, the west bank of the Rhine, the Ionian islands, and official recognition of the Cisalpine Republic, Napoleon's personally created vassal state in the Po River Valley.[30] Here we see the practical value of theory and reflection. Had the Austrians taken the time to analyze their position realistically, and let go the tactical notion of victory, they may have come out far better.

True strategy, informed by theory, and 'dealing as it does with ends which bear directly on the restoration of peace,' is the key to securing a continuing advantage.[31] The Austrians would learn from Napoleon's errors, as would Prussia. From 1805 to 1809, when both nations adopted the more modest aim of driving the French back across the Rhine, 'it would have been foolish if they had not begun by carefully reviewing the whole chain of events that success or failure would be likely to bring in consequence of the initial step, and which would lead to peace.'[32] By understanding the true purpose of war, the campaigns of their armies could be better integrated into a comprehensive national strategy.

Finally, if war is an extension of politics (or *politik* in Clausewitz's original) by other means, then war clearly falls under the dominion of political authority and policy. If war *is* politics, and here one could argue that the coincident logic of war and politics makes it so, then a synergistic relationship between the political authority and military leadership should exist. Here is the nexus of one of the great debates over Clausewitz's meaning. Is the military wholly subordinate to the political authority or, in time of war, should the military have free rein? Clausewitz advocates that the military leadership should provide advice and counsel to the political leadership to the best of its ability, but that the political leadership can interject itself into any aspect of war-making that it desires, even though it may be imprudent for them to do so.[33] The more limited the war, argues Clausewitz, the more the political interference. As the stakes rise, however, the political leader is less likely to interfere with the tactical and operational decisions of military professionals. The last words shall be Clausewitz's:

> ... *war is only a branch of political activity; that it is in no sense autonomous* ... the only source of war is politics—the intercourse of governments and peoples; but it is apt to be assumed that war suspends that intercourse and replaces it by a wholly different condition, ruled by no law but its own ... war in itself does not suspend political intercourse or change it into something entirely different ... war cannot be divorced from political life.[34]

3

THE ELEMENTS OF STRATEGY

The strategist must therefore define an aim for the entire operational side of the war that will be in accordance with its purpose.

Carl von Clausewitz, *On War*[1]

J.C. Wylie observed that 'there are probably more kinds of strategy, and more definitions of it, than there are varieties and definitions of economics or politics.'[2] It is no doubt presumptuous to attempt another one, more so an authoritative and encompassing definition of strategy. But without doing so, I am at an impasse. No one definition of the term is alone useful as an embarkation point for my investigation. It would be arrogant to abandon the wisdom of the past, however, and so my modest definition of strategy, *a plan for continuing advantage,* is drawn from insights offered by grand masters of strategy.

Once again, I turn first to Clausewitz, whose magisterial *On War* set the standard for all works of military theory that follow. In it, Clausewitz defines strategy simply and clearly as 'the use of engagements for the object of war.'[3] This concise and extraordinary statement is drawn from his fuller theory of war, discussed in detail further on. Here I use it to highlight the sources that influenced my own definition, and to comment briefly on the crucial inputs. Note that the means manipulated by the strategist are tactical *engagements,* not tactics. The strategist has no business micro-managing the tactical commander, who is master of the situation at hand. The strategist will assign desired outcomes, or objectives for the engagement, and will assign limitations or restrictions on the achievement of them. To be successful, these will generally be negative in the sense that the tactician will be prevented from taking certain actions as opposed to positive limitations in which the tactician must take a specified action, though the latter is not precluded.

To the extent that the assigned objectives are met, the desired tactical outcome is victory, but it is not the only possible or viable result. Defeat and stalemate will also occur. Failure to achieve tactical victory should not be the criterion that scuttles strategy any more than achieving it should lead to pronouncements of strategic success. Mao Tse-Tung, an avid reader of Clausewitz, agreed. He asserted that strategic success is not determined by tactical victory alone. Defeat, too, can support the overall success of the political objective if the politico-military situation is holistically grasped.[4] The worst situation is strategic paralysis caused by the fear of defeat.[5] The strategist makes a plan that shapes campaigns and determines individual engagements, but in a way that allows the 'plan to be adjusted to the modifications that are continuously required.'[6] Since the ends are not the same for strategists as they are for tacticians—although they are linked by policy and operations—the strategist must further intervene appropriately to subordinate tactical outcomes to the broader objective of the war, itself established by the political objective.

A contemporary and rival of Clausewitz, Baron Antoine de Jomini, Napoleon's Chief of Staff and very successful writer on military affairs, gives the pithiest definition. 'Strategy,' he states bluntly, 'is the art of making war upon a map.'[7] Out of context, one could look at this line as a throwaway, but it becomes quite profound upon inspection. With it comes the recognition of strategy as a *plan in the abstract.* The map and its attendant miniatures representing fielded units is a mental order removed from reality. The admiration Jomini had for Napoleon, who spent his evenings in war council, moving pieces from place to place, anticipating the moves of the enemy, is evident. The plans for the next day's battles were yet another order of abstraction, as the mind of the military genius played out before his subordinates in a tour de force upon the construct of a two-dimensional stage. Jomini paid homage to his emperor by separating the elements of planning and action with this clear statement: 'Strategy [below the level of grand strategy or policy] decides *where* to act ... tactics decides the manner of execution.'[8]

Although the planning process for Jomini was clearly abstract and theoretical, his *Art of War* was full of practical advice on the conduct of war and battle. Contemporaries considered it far more useful than Clausewitz's cerebral *On War,* and military commanders routinely carried Jomini's work on campaigns. Even with the central foray into abstraction and categorization, the focus on creating a functional manual of arms added to the widespread belief that the application of means to ends—despite Jomini's admonishments to the contrary—was the most important part of the process of strategic planning.

In a more radical commentary, Helmuth von Moltke (the Elder), a disciple of Clausewitz and architect of the stunning Prussian Campaign in the War of 1870, called strategy 'a system of *ad hoc* expediencies; it is more than knowledge, it is the application of knowledge to practical life, the development of an original idea in accordance with continually changing circumstances.'[9] Von Moltke has expressed the significant divide between knowledge and know-how, and then instantly reconciles the two. There is much here to admire. Strategic genius at the abstract and theoretical level that is not mated to practical reality is spurious and distracting. In the same breath, however, von Moltke reinforces the notion that experience can be gained through study, as well as action. There is room for both the theorist and the veteran here, and the two must find grounds on which to merge their strengths. The interplay of theory and reality forces the requirement for an adaptive strategy, one that sets its sight anew at each juncture. Strategy 'uses the success of each battle and builds on it. The demands of strategy fall silent in the face of a tactical victory; *strategy adapts to the new situation.* Strategy controls the means required by tactics *in order to be ready at the right time in the right place.*'[10] The emphases in this statement are mine.

Moltke is often admonished for his advocacy of maximum military control of armed force *in* war, that is, with the absolute minimum of political interference, and I must concur with the assessment—though I think it is a harsh and unsophisticated reading. A minimum of political interference does not rule out political interference (or more charitably, guidance and direction), nor does it infer that politics should never interfere. Moltke argued that 'in no case must the military leader allow his operations to be influenced by politics *alone;* quite the contrary, he must keep his eye on the military success,' because 'it is of no concern to [that leader] how politics can subsequently use his victories or defeats; it is up to politics to exploit them.'[11] Moltke's clear separation of the ends of policy and the ends of battle, drawn from Clausewitz but carefully refined, will be a central focus of the present work. Whereas politics can and does intercede in the military commander's area of expertise, sometimes regrettably, the military commander in the field must accept it and stay focused on the tactical objective; victory. And while the separation is clear, the link is also exposed: 'it is strategy which gives to tactics the means to strike and the likelihood to win through the leadership of armies and their concentration on the battlefield.'[12] Strategy is thus eloquently described as the realm where political concerns and military means interact.

By the middle of the twentieth century, when military success became widely recognized as contingent upon a variety of economic (techno-industrial) and social (population base, nationalistic fervor) factors, the differentiation of strategy and tactics had become systematically muddled. Prominent British historian B.H. Liddell Hart defined strategy as 'the art of *distributing and applying* military means to fulfill the ends of policy.'[13] Although means and ends can never be truly separated, as the one always influences the other, Liddell Hart did attempt to conceptually separate them by stating when 'the application of the military instrument merges into actual fighting,' it is called tactics.[14] He then asserts that tactics is the application of military force on a 'lower plane,' whereas military strategy falls under the sway of 'grand strategy,' or 'policy in execution.'[15] It is a tortured logic that weaves through his prodigious texts. Depending on the situation or intent, contemporaries would divine between tactics and strategy on some arbitrary criteria of scope, scale, space, or function. In the next section I will spend significant time developing a differentiation of the levels of strategy, operations, and tactics based on *purpose*. The advantage of doing so is that division can be made on grounds that are consistent, and from the division both meaning and utility can be discerned. It is a categorization made with intent to explain, not as an organizational expedient.

Liddell Hart was a notoriously casual writer, rarely using references, and this adds to the confusion in reading his work. It appears that he intentionally misconstrues Clausewitz, ascribing notions so stunningly unfounded that it is difficult (for me) to follow the reasoning behind much of his own argument. But his was a gifted military mind, and his advocacy of the indirect approach to strategy continues to resonate with planners.[16] In a particularly insightful point, drawing on Sun-Tzu for inspiration, Liddell Hart claims the strategist's '*true aim is not so much to seek battle as to seek a strategic situation so advantageous that if it does not of itself produce the decision, its continuation by a battle is sure to achieve this.*'[17] Although Liddell Hart neatly captures one facet of proper strategy in this sentence, it is difficult to find a great appreciation of it in his work. It is advantage, in all its manifestations, not conclusion that the strategist seeks. Liddell Hart's incorporation of Sun-Tsu is further vital to the overall development of post-War strategy in the West. Appreciation of the works of Asian strategic theorists, to include Kaotilya, Mao Tse-Tung, and Ho Chi Minh, is still unfolding.

Colin Gray, the most influential contemporary strategist in the Clausewitzian mode, writes: 'Strategy is the *bridge* that relates military power to political purpose.'[18] While it is Gray's emphasis on the linkage between power and policy that most influences the present work, his modification of Clausewitz's simple definition to emphasize manifestations of military power that are not direct is his most notable contribution here. 'By strategy,' Gray continues, 'I mean *the use that is made of force and the threat of force for the ends of policy.*'[19] The use that is made of force is more inclusive than an emphasis on combat, and underscores the growing roles that deterrence (an explicit threat) and latent military force in noncombatant operations (the implicit threat of force) have taken on in the modern era. Moreover, Gray's definition properly blurs the traditional boundaries of grand strategy through tactics, as it encompasses requirements and limitations of people, society, culture, politics, and ethics before dealing with the issues of preparation for war and war proper. Even if one *could* concentrate solely at the level of military means in support of policy objectives, Gray insists, it would be at least frustrating to do so effectively without an appreciation of popular and political constraints on the use of force by the state. It is just this type of isolated thinking that leads military leaders to lament the political interference of politicians and strategists.

On the logic of using threats or the potential use of force as the means to a policy objective, Thomas Schelling averred that in deterrence situations, 'strategy … is not concerned with the efficient application of force, but with the exploitation of *potential* force.'[20] It is concerned not only with enemies but also with allies. It is concerned not just with the potential rewards of war (the division of spoils), but the possibility that war could leave both sides in a worse position than they would have been without the conflict. This is the view that initially leads to a focus on strategy as a *continuation* of favorable circumstances, that is, a dynamic condition as opposed to some finite end or end-state.

Having isolated the concepts of others fundamental to my own definition, it should prove illuminating to provide an example of what I consider to be a sound strategy. The innovative policy of Athenian demagogue Pericles in the Second Peloponnesian War meets the obligation.[21] Pericles, the acclaimed leader of

Athens in Thucydides' magnificent account, put forward a plan that maximized the advantages of its naval dominance and full treasury. He argued that Athenians could retire behind the great walls of their city and simply wait out the attempts of Sparta and its allies to lay siege. While Sparta engaged in expensive annual campaigns to encircle Athens and destroy its crops, the Athenians would remain safely and comfortably ensconced behind their formidable defenses while their preeminent navy protected the vital trade routes that supplied them. Athens could give the appearance of holding out indefinitely, with no ill effects save challenges to its honor, and no diminution of its expansive empire. Adding to the discomfiture of the Spartans, while on patrol its navy could harass Sparta with hit-and-run raids on its vulnerable coasts, increasing the cost to Sparta of continuing the war, fomenting dissent among the enslaved peoples of the Peloponnesus (the *helots*), and increasing confidence in Athenian leadership. By husbanding its strength in what Clausewitz would recognize as strategic defense (the stronger form of war), Athens could anticipate the inevitable weakening of Sparta and be fully prepared for a counterstrike.

The strategy was not perfect, in retrospect, but as I have already argued, no strategy can be. It does highlight the essentials of strategic thinking, however, making it a most useful example. With this plan, Pericles established the boundaries within which the war would be conducted: political, military, and economic. He set the engagement rules for punishing counter-attacks along Sparta's vulnerable flank, and then let his admirals and generals practice their finely honed martial skills in search of tactical victory. He understood that the next war would be with Persia, and the current one was but a prelude. He further anticipated change and surprise, and so established a plan that was eminently responsive to tactical and strategic developments. Critically, the plan did not mandate specific force structures or battles. As such, it did not rely on the winning of any specific battle or the achievement of any particular condition for its success. In other words, it did not specify means to ends. This is precisely because Pericles' strategy *had no end in view.* It would continue on, subject to review and modification as the context of the war inevitably changed. It was not a strategy of the status quo, as might seem a reasonable interpretation on first glance. It anticipated that the Spartans would weaken while Athens tended to its maritime empire, first conserving and then increasing its strength.

The most important point of Pericles' strategy was that it did not have a satisfying end-state or condition. The end of the war was desirable, of course, with an admission of Spartan defeat—or at least an acceptance of Athenian terms—but the conquest of Sparta was understood as an *un*desirable outcome of the strategy. This was because Pericles recognized that the gravest threat to Athens' continuing prosperity was not Sparta or any combination of Greek states; it was the Persian Empire and its massive, if currently dormant, military power. Persia had twice attempted to conquer the Greek peninsula, under emperors Xerxes and Darius, and was expected to try again. A strategy that bankrupted Athens or that emasculated Sparta could provide Persia the opportunity it awaited, for either eventuality would weaken the pan-Hellenic coalition necessary to thwart Persian plans. Hence the policy of Pericles was a sound plan for attaining and maintaining a continuing advantage, to be modified and updated as the situation inevitably changed. It was pure strategy.

And the situation did change: disastrously. Plague struck Athens and at least a quarter of its population died in the first year of the war, eventually to include Pericles. Without an effective rhetorical champion to articulate its virtues, Pericles' attrition strategy came under attack. It did not seem to be a winning strategy, said its opponents. Where were the victories to prove its merit? Where was the body-count that proved success? Democracies tend to have low tolerance for policies that do not show swift gains, and tangible results were not intended in Pericles' clever design. With the galvanizing influence of the great orator silenced, rivals for political leadership played to anxieties within the population for personal gain. Some claimed that the gods favored Sparta over Athens, in part because of Pericles' cowardly (or at least, non-heroic) defensive plan, and the policy lost backing. But it was not overthrown. As should happen with any well-conceived and working strategy, it remained substantially in place, awaiting another, better strategy to replace it.

Through a stroke of incredible luck, the Athenians were able to gain a major tactical victory over the Spartans at Pylos, enough so that Sparta offered surrender in the hope that the conditions for peace would be less disastrous than continuing the war. Giddy with its relatively minor and non-heroic battlefield victory over Sparta, though still at war with numerous other cities, Athens abandoned Pericles' defensive strategy and embraced a new plan of conquest. The allure of tactical success swept aside sound strategy, and a horrible period of brutal imperial expansion ensued. Sparta, unable to come to amenable terms, reluctantly reentered the war. Aware that the balance in the Aegean was shifting, Persia intervened, doling out just enough money and arms to keep the Spartan alliance from crumbling, but not so much as to allow it to be a serious threat in the aftermath of the war. Athens' fresh bout of imperialism led to overextension, and ended calamitously with a misfortunate campaign in Sicily. More than a third of Athenian military power was wiped out, sealing the fate of Athens. The Second Peloponnesian War ended with both the Spartans and the Athenians exhausted, and Hellenic leadership and culture subordinated first to Persian hegemony, and then to Philip's Macedonian phalanx. Athens never again had a substantial empire, and Sparta faded ignobly into history.

The Clausewitzian method

When Clausewitz unassailably made the case that war is an extension of politics carried on by other (violent) means, military power was precisely the violent means of which he wrote. Clausewitz did not rule out other forms of power, including what we would recognize today as diplomatic, economic, and informational power within the milieu of war. But within the military sphere, Clausewitz wrote only concerning land power. He never applied his theory to the seas—Prussia had no significant naval capacity or ambition—and quite obviously not to air (or space) operations. For Clausewitz, military power and land power were coexistent. Though he comes tantalizingly close in his discussion of campaigns, he never provided a direct operational link between the logic of strategy and the logic of tactics. As circumstance and technology broaden the applicability of his war theory, it is up to us to do so for him. In the process, it is vital to briefly summarize his central argument so that any adaptation of it can be validated.

Clausewitz began *On War* with a precise causal statement: 'War is thus an act of force to compel our enemy to do our will.'[22] It is essential to note that Clausewitz presented this as an opening statement of theoretical conjecture, and definitely not as the result of his thorough analysis. He then carefully separated the means from the object, to grasp precisely its true significance:

> Force [is] the *means* of war; to impose our will on the enemy is its *object*.
> To secure that object we must render the enemy powerless; and that, in theory, is the true aim of warfare. That aim takes the place of the object, discarding it as something not actually part of war itself.'[23]

This statement is so powerful, so compelling, that we may find ourselves quite satisfied that Clausewitz has affirmed the reality of war. But Clausewitz is still in the theoretical realm only, and while he has isolated in a few passages the value of theory to practical strategy, he remains fully aware that what is rational in the model world may prove completely inappropriate to the real world of action.

Clausewitz chose deduction as his method. He worked from first principles, found out by the useful technique of abstraction. It is obvious that all of the myriad variables that impact even simple social behavior—and war is far from simple—cannot be eliminated for practical study. Therefore, theorists often turn to thought experiments for insight. A model or imagined world is created in which only the variables or influences under study are considered. This ideal or idealized world is free of the distractions and messiness of reality, and so the emergence of laws, regularities, and patterns is enhanced. From these are derived chains of causality. But, these causal relationships are not real, they are ideals. They exist in the imagined world only and 'must never be confused with the varied, complex, and subtle individual events of reality.'[24] With the assistance of just a few of these causal chains, however, great insight is possible. ' ... the staggering power of scientific abstraction [is that it allows the theorist] to move beyond the surface of nature toward her interior relationships.'[25] These relationships manifest themselves as order, structure, and patterns discernible to the investigator, from which laws, principles, and axioms are derived. But these constructs are not real. They are abstractions from the real and have no substance. We can treat them as real in our model but cannot transfer them to the real world. 'To argue ... that the second law of thermodynamics causes the running down of a clock or the rusting of an automobile seems to be as muddled as to suppose that a baseball commentary actually determines the state of the game.'[26] What we determine in the model are not causes but relationships, and as we shall see this insight has powerful ramifications for strategy in the next century.

The application of pure theory allows the student of war to go to extremes, Clausewitz tells us, at least in our model world. This useful mental exercise helps isolate important variables, but it *must* lead to logical absurdities when applied to the real world of war. In theory, if force or violence is the means of imposing our will, then for maximum or perfect resolution we must be prepared for and be able to use maximum force, for

> there is no logical limit to the application of that force. [In] the field of abstract thought, the inquiring mind can never rest until it reaches the extreme, [here] a clash of forces freely operating and obedient to no law but their own.[27]

Because of the dual nature of war and strategy (both sides are attempting to win this great 'collision of two living forces'), violence escalation is *inevitable* in theory.[28] What is more, the force available is expressed as '*the total means at his disposal* and *the strength of his will.*'[29] In this situation, assuming equivalent means, war between nations 'is nothing more than a duel on a larger scale.'[30] One side must be killed, or made unable to continue. Thus, 'to overcome the enemy, or disarm him—call it what you will—must always be the aim of warfare.'[31]

Clausewitz finds this mental exercise powerfully heuristic, but insists that the application of the theoretical aim must allow for 'modifications in practice.'[32] Because he could find no historical evidence of total, unrestrained combat in war (it must always be mitigated in some manner or level), he guides us through the transition from theory to applicability. 'Warfare thus eludes the strict theoretical requirement [of extremes, and] it becomes a matter of judgment what degree of effort should be made, and this can only be based on the phenomena of the real world and the *laws of probability.*'[33] Judgment must rule instinct. The head must dictate restraints on the emotions and body lest they be carried away to extremes and place the state in a precarious position for destruction: 'If it is all a calculation of probabilities based on given individuals and conditions, the *political object,* which was the *original motive,* must become the central factor in the equation.'[34]

Theory has allowed Clausewitz to isolate the true nature of war, a nature obfuscated in the real world by the mass of data making demands on the mind in real time. 'The political object—the original motive for the war—will thus determine both the military objective to be reached and the amount of [and, it is asserted here, the *type* of military] effort it requires. The political object cannot, however, *in itself* provide the standards of measurement.'[35]

> When whole communities go to war—whole peoples, and especially civilized peoples—the reason always lies in some political situation, and

the occasion is always due to some political object. War, therefore, is an act of policy. Were it a complete, untrammeled, absolute manifestation of violence (as the pure concept would require), war would of its own independent will usurp the place of policy the moment it had been brought into being; it would then drive policy out of office and rule by the laws of its own nature.[36]

It is only here, after his foundational theoretical work, that Clausewitz unveils the perfected statement of his theory of war, and the basis of his lasting relevance: 'war is not merely an act of policy, but a true political instrument, a continuation of political intercourse, carried out with other means.'[37]

Now we see that the purpose of limited war, the only kind conceivable in reality, is not to render the opponent powerless, but to achieve a more advantageous peace, a condition of continuing influence and benefit. 'The original *means* of strategy is victory—*that is tactical success*; its ends, in the final analysis, are those objects which lead directly to peace.'[38] This clear statement highlights another problem of the dual nature of war. The political object is the goal, yet war is but one tool of statecraft, and a very dangerous one for the state. With the framework exposed, Clausewitz then provided guidance and advice in how to use *limited* military power to achieve *unlimited* political objectives leading to peace.

Differentiating grand strategy, military strategy, operations, and tactics

The purpose of strategy, to put oneself in a position of continuing advantage, is the same regardless of the endeavor or the opponent (to include an uncaring nature). In the military realm, strategy has traditionally been divided into parts and related to levels of war, usually based on the highest level of appropriate decision maker's span of control, or geographic scope. These are the highest political authority in the state (also the commander-in-chief, responsible for *grand strategy*), the highest military authority (in the modern era, the General Staff or joint staff, for *military strategy*), the highest service authority (or service chief, for *operations* or campaigns carried out in a specific medium or theater), and the highest battlefield authority (*tactics*). In addition, there is arguably a level of strategy that has been called *grand tactics,* which includes the training, equipping, and organization of forces for battle, and one we could call grand operations or *operational strategy,* including the elements of technology and equipment acquisition, recruiting, and logistics for extended campaigns.

Grand strategy is the process by which *all* the means available to the state are considered in pursuit of a continuing political influence. These means are myriad, to be sure, and are routinely aggregated into categories for analysis. A typical scheme would include diplomatic, information, military, and economic power, at least. All must be considered as potential means available to the grand strategist, who develops an integrated plan in support of a continuing national influence. In many cases, military means will be selected to advance a political aim. The military strategist then undertakes to use the means at his or her dis-posal—nominally land, sea, and air, but also space and information forces—to design and then advocate a plan that gains a continuing military advantage within limits set by, and subordinate to, the intents of policy. It cannot be over-stated that the military strategist must be aware of the political objectives and accepting of any policy limitations in planning and coordinating with parallel and subordinate strategists, for if sight of them is lost then the absurdities of a war—with its own logic—are sure to occur.

When strategy is bracketed for military means or for war planning, feedback up the chain to civilian command must of course be maintained. The graphic at Figure 3.1 shows the preponderance of interaction going down the chain from grand strategy to strategy, however, for only the grand strategist, or civilian gov-ernment, can be fully aware of the complexity and interaction of all its resources. The military adviser must not be reticent about reporting concerns or relevant information back up the chain, nor in coordinating with the efforts of counterpart strategists. Likewise, the military strategist requires information and advice from subordinate operational strategists, those for land, sea, air and space power—but can tolerate no direction or command from them. It is here we begin to see the theoretical break from strategy to tactics. The extent of force structure capabilities and readiness must be accurately transmitted, as well as concerns over the proba-bilities of success, but once having provided advice and counsel, the subordinate commander must actively and fully implement the instructions of the higher authority. To do any less would confound the logic of the military strategy and plan, and once again would form an entry point for the logic of the (military) means to usurp that of the (political) strategy.

The military strategist formulates a coordinated war plan, developing policy and instructions that conform to the overall and specific political directives. The purpose of the military strategist is clear: to link military means to the political aims of the state. In the modern era, the military strategist's concerns are global. Within the overall military strategy, there is room for a set of subordinate strate-gies to emerge. Each of these must be compatible with and supportive of the military strategy, yet *unique* relative to the other parallel and subordinate strate-gies. Without this uniqueness, there would be no reason to separate them. I will call this subordinate level operational strategy, to distinguish it from the more tac-tically oriented operations planning process, and to set the stage for an argument that it is the operational level that connects the tactical logic of victory with the grand strategic logic of the continuing power of the state.

Uniqueness exerts a powerful influence on the separation of levels and func-tions, and gets us to the crux of the issue implicit in the effort to develop a subordinate theory of seapower, or airpower, or space power. Is space power qual-itatively different from other forms of state and military power, for example, or are all concepts of military operations simply manifestations of an overall theory of war? This may be *the* critical question regarding operational planning and structure. If the latter is the case, and all manifestations of military power are

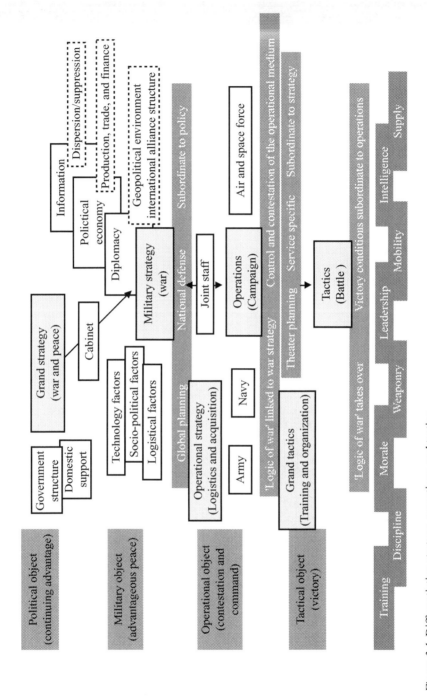

Figure 3.1 Differentiating strategy, operations, and tactics

understood to have the same purpose, that is, to support the policies and aims of the state, then no operational level of war is needed. It would not even be useful, as it would simply be an unnecessary redundancy. The link between political and military purpose would be direct, and a fully encompassing theory of war simply parsed to the scale of combat envisioned. In this case, every campaign is theater (or geographically) differentiated by terrain and force structure, a Pacific plan versus an Atlantic one, for example. Strategies, doctrines, and tactics are essentially interchangeable. The way of fighting is the same, and an experienced land power strategist should be able to function effectively as a sea power strategist— once familiarized with the different equipment and geographical conditions of the theater. Moreover, every soldier, sailor, and airman can and should be directed by the military planners to act in accordance with the state's political aspirations, and use their equipment accordingly. The logic of politics should reach down to the lowest levels of military force.

But that depth of purpose could prove disastrous. The logic of battle would be directly confronted with the logic of strategy. Should fielded forces abandon the tactical end of victory in exchange for a state-level purpose of maintaining a continuing advantage? Of course not. It is rarely to the continuing advantage of the individual combatant or combat unit to put itself in harm's way, regardless of the advantage accruing to the larger force for it having done so. Such an action is completed irrationally, bolstered by the martial virtues of obedience and honor. The logic of politics should not operate in the battle space; tactical victory should always be the paramount end. Victory should be defined by military planners through objectives and rules of engagement, and the combatants should strive to meet those objectives with all the means at their disposal. A delaying action might have as its objective the holding of a larger force for several hours, for example. Achievement of this delay is victory, even if the opponent takes no losses and eventually seizes the territory in question. Within the parameters of acceptable loss of life and equipment dictated by the higher authority, it is clearly a win. Sufficient delay will increase the success of another engagement, in another place and time. That specific knowledge is not needed by those who undertook the delay action, and the success or failure of the latter engagement should be immaterial to them. They have done their duty. Their end is achieved, their logic and their grammar hold fast, for battlefield victory is the means to achieving campaign objectives, which in turn are the means of complying with political policy. It is up to the military planner, not the junior officer, to determine if the cost was worth the end, if the victory was glorious or Pyrrhic.

Accordingly, there must be an intermediate step between the grammar and logic of battle and that of politics. Military strategy links political logic to war (the logic *of* war), but no link from there to military tactics (the logic *in* war) is discernible without some operational level of transition. As with all strategies, operational strategy seeks to achieve a continuing influence or advantage. Operational strategists prepare a plan for the forces within their control, but the operational strategist has a purpose different from that of the grand or military strategist and the tactician. That purpose is *to command the medium* in which his or her forces are to operate. When command is not achievable, then the operational strategist must endeavor to contest the medium, so as not to give unencumbered use of it to the enemy. Only when command is achieved (or at a minimum contested), broadly or limited in scope, can the effects of military power be employed there in the service of the political and military aims.

While feedback is critical in the prior two levels of strategy (discussed in detail later on), direction and command always come from the top down. The operational strategists, however, are in a more balanced and dynamic relationship with the tactical commanders and forces at their control. Force availability, technological enhancement, prior battlefield results, and a myriad of theater and location factors may directly influence control of the medium for a specific time and place. Since the logic of war does operate at the tactical level, control of forces can and should be decentralized to effectively meet mission goals or ends. It is a long respected platitude that the commander on the scene is the best judge of tactical orders, and nothing in the logic so far disputes that ideal. Tactical victory, according to Clausewitz, is the military means by which policy is enacted. Stringing together tactical victories is a plan of operations or campaign, and so it is at the operational level that the logic of war begins to intrude on the political objective. By maintaining a pure clarity of *operational purpose*, to control or contest the appropriate medium (which is not the same as the political or overall military aim), the operational strategist tangibly links the political intent to the military means.

To sum, the purpose of military strategy is to link military means to the political aim. The purpose of operational strategy is to contest or gain command of the medium of battle (land, sea, air, space, or information), which allows the tactical and political aims to remain at odds logically but to converge practically. Military power is but one of the means by which the political object is pursued. Land, sea, air and space, and information power are sub-domains of military power.

A theory of operational strategy

Any theory of military operations that aspires to invigorate strategic thought must identify the attribute of *military power* that makes it *unique*.[39] Without such clear demarcation, operational strategy must be subsumed whole into a broader theory of military power or war. It becomes merely another bureaucratic level of organization in the military hierarchy, necessary as the scale of war increases. It is an efficiency economizer. Theater control in combined arms operations is handed to the services on relatively arbitrary differentiation; for army, navy, and air forces at least.

Here I argue that the services can and do have distinct operational realms, and are deserving of individual and separable theories of war, but not because of differences in technology or combat platform. The discriminator, which establishes the parallel or comparison groups for unique operational strategies, is the *form* of military power. These are at least sea, land, and airpower, with space and information power rounding out the operational realms. For the next several pages, I will use airpower as my primary example, with elucidation from land and seapower theory.

When the problem of differentiation, or uniqueness, for military operations is taken on, analysts have tended to begin with descriptive demarcations based on the primary place of *operation* (air, water, or ground) or the primary *platform* involved (plane, boat, or foot/wheel). Such categorization schemes, while intuitively appealing and readily accomplished, have been the central misconception leading to a lack of enduring utility and value in contemporary operational theory. Moreover, they have caused a great deal of practical confusion in issues of command and control. Is an airplane operated over the water an element of seapower or airpower? Is a soldier occupying a port properly seapower or ground power? The differences may be immaterial, insist those who associate military power by place or platform, since all have the same purpose—to influence adversary decision makers.[40] Assignment and control of forces to different services, and to different commands within those services, is again a matter of administrative convenience, despite continuing inter-service rivalry and significant wartime control issues. I assert, quite to the contrary, that the purpose of airpower is not the same as for other forms of military power, nor does seapower have the same purpose as land power. If purpose were the same for all, then no theoretical differentiation would be needed, or useful. All would conform to a general theory of war, and operational differentiation would be arbitrary.

Purely descriptive differentiations are all too often extraneous, and tend to obscure the goal of the original analysis. When we categorize forms of military power by their most obvious external characteristics, we find nothing meaningful about the *quality* of military power. This can lead to the perspective that any military means is acceptable if it satisfies the conditions of victory. The only analysis that must be undertaken is a cost-utility one: which service will achieve the desired effect most efficiently (or effectively). We know intuitively that this is not the case. An F-22 stealth air strike has a *qualitative* difference when it engages its target, as opposed to, say, a cavalry brigade. Both may kill or destroy the target, and the cavalry brigade is no doubt less expensive, but the *manner* in which one wages war always makes a political statement. In the United States' Operation Allied Force in Kosovo, for example, the decision not to put ground troops at risk was roundly criticized by political and military commentators who claimed that it rendered the massive air campaign impotent. It was not until the US began to threaten the use of ground forces, they argued, that Milosevic capitulated.[41]

Description and categorization are powerful tools for analysis, but they do not substitute for it. They can provide the basis for analysis, however. Aristotle introduced this method some 2,500 years ago. In his search for what made meaningful differences in politics, he selected all the governing forms extant in city-states of the Hellenic world for comparison, of which there appeared more than 200. He categorized them by what was to him their most obvious external characteristic, the size of the ruling group (which he subdivided into one, several, or many). This told him nothing meaningful about the *quality* of government, however, so he looked deeper. He noted that Greeks looked favorably upon monarchies (rule by one), aristocracies (few), and democracies (many); but regarded autarchy (one), oligarchy (few), and mob rule (many) as bad. Aristotle deduced that the shared characteristic of the first group that was absent or different from the shared characteristic of the second could be the meaningful variable he sought. He ultimately determined this shared characteristic to be *purpose*; in other words, for whom did the government speak? Whom did it serve?

When purpose was identified as the essential point of differentiation, Aristotle quickly found that *good* government is that which serves the polis (or state). Bad government serves itself. Regardless of the purely descriptive characteristics of population size or density, geographic location, or structural form the government may take, in all cases of good governance those who rule are constrained by law. In states where the rulers, no matter the number, act in their own self-interests, they do so because they have the *capacity* to act unrestrained. They are unlimited in power and action, and therefore they rule by whim. While it is possible that *some* good persons will always act for the good of the state, and restrain themselves from acting out of selfishness, it is impossible to assure that *all* will do so. Hence, for Aristotle, the prescription for good and stable government is to establish good laws—those that limit the power of the state to act arbitrarily.[42] His was a structural argument.

Eventually, Aristotle would argue that 'a full explanation of anything should include its purpose, or *telos, its final cause.'[43] In most comparative analyses of socio-political structures, *purpose* is found to have an important bearing on the most fundamental analytic questions we can ask. In the current instance, we are searching for *meaningful* differentiations in operational strategy. If all forms of military power have the same purpose (as suggested above, to influence decision makers or to maximize violence in a particular place at a particular time), then a qualitative differentiation of what platform or medium is most effective or efficient in a particular context is theoretically pointless. No differentiation based on the political, cultural, psychological, or other contributions of the various forms of power is necessary. Forms of military power are conceptually no different from tools in a box. The weapon chosen is the one that does the job most efficiently. If the most efficient tool is not available, use the next best. If several tools are available that will service the target effectively, then efficiency-value is the only factor to consider in employment. Such a view is perhaps useful at the tactical level, where victory is the only measure of success, but it is insidious at the strategic, for it places no obligation on military planners to perceive the overall military or political end. Planners are assigned a goal (usually quantifiable), given limitations, and directed to achieve it. In this case, operational differentiation is simply an organizational economizer, an arbitrary differentiation based on a preferred hierarchical concept of war making.

If instead, air, sea, and land power have different purposes within an overarching politico-military means (which is war or the threat of war), and these differences are consequential, then knowledge of them is fundamental to sound strategy. In order to isolate such variables, I must make some basic assumptions. First, if air, sea, and land power demarcate sub-functions of military power, then they must share a set of similar characteristics that can be bundled and set aside for analysis. Second, they are all manifestations of violent or potentially violent force employed by the state for the overarching purpose of carrying out political policies. The use of these forces, therefore, makes a political statement. Third, there are political ramifications of using military power even for non-military purposes, such as the distribution of humanitarian aid. The fact that military forces are employed carries a latent capacity for violence with it. This will affect the political aim.

With these assumptions, we begin to isolate the true purpose of air (and sea and land) power and place it into perspective. The purpose of military power writ large is to provide *an option* for the political decision maker to achieve the political ends of the state. Sub-forms of military power must conform to this higher purpose. Moreover, military power is the *means* of conducting war; it is not the object of it. It is not the target of it. It is not the medium of it. It is also not the platform of war. War or threats of war (potential or latent violence) are policy instruments that the diplomat needs readily available to properly conduct the affairs of state. In theory, then, the manner in which military power supports the political aim is through maximizing—or more precisely, being prepared to maximize—violence at the direction of the state.[44]

We are still in the realm of theory, as any preparation less than the maximum capacity and potential of the state leads to Clausewitzian 'absurdities.'[45] No state can put every bit of its economic, psychological, and political potential into the preparation for carrying out war, but anything less constrains the ability of statespersons to fully carry out the duties of their posts. With the possible exception of a Cold-War scale nuclear holocaust as a hypothetical, there seems to be no plausible scenario for the maximum application of force in war, and certainly there are no empirical examples to draw on. The use of force in war has never been *absolute*—and short of global annihilation, likely never will be. Therefore, modifications of the theory are needed in practice. Tossing out the practical possibility of absolutes, what is desirable is the capacity of the military to provide *measured violence* at the direction of the state.

When land power and military power are synonymous, as they appear to have been for Clausewitz, no functional differentiation between land and military *power* is needed. Prussia, at the time, had no credible naval power and did not seek it, preoccupied as it was with territorial defense. A scale or temporal distinction can be usefully made, however, should war extend beyond a short series of battles, into a set of campaigns. This is for convenience or efficiency, and is not a functional separation based on the form of power. It is an economizing device for command and control.

If the purpose of military power is to be prepared to provide violence, and if necessary, to provide *measured* violence, in support of the political aim, then the *components* of military power must also serve that purpose. Using medium or platform differences to discriminate and group the military services surely has an economizing value for command, control, and execution, but it innately recognizes a functional differentiation between the *types* of military power. Air forces should be prepared to project violence from and into the air; armies on the ground; and navies from and into the water. Each must further prepare to deny a potential enemy the capacity to freely project violence into or from those areas as the need arises. As such, even in times of peace, military power ensures that the latent or potential violence of military power adds to the security of the state.[46] Note again that their purpose is not to project violence, but to be prepared to do so, or in perfect terms, *to be able to do so*. This is the critical discriminator. In order to maximize the projection of violence to or from the medium in support of the political aim, defined as the *exploitation* of the medium, the capacity to operate in the medium must be present a priori. In other words, command or contestation of the air, sea, or land is *required*. The *purpose* of airpower, then, is *to command the air*. The *function* of airpower is to be able to maximize violence at the direction of the political authority, but this is not unique. It is common to all forms of military power.

Command of the air is a situation in which violence can be projected through the medium by friendly forces while denying that capacity to others. Free movement or projection in this case means essentially unhindered by enemy military power.[47] Limitations based on technology, weather, political will, etc. are not included. For some states, functionally useful command of the air may simply be denying the enemy the ability to operate there, especially if the capacities of the denying state to operate *in* the air are limited. This is principally true for small states, or states that cannot match the air forces of their enemies. A robust ground- or sea-based air defense system may give that state the freedom of movement it needs to ensure its defense and protect its territory from bombing, interdiction, and other such exploitation by airpower. This bridges the gap between control and contestation of the air. The latter occurs when there is an added cost to air operations due to enemy activity.

Traditionally, discrimination between the military services is based on functional differentiation, or some characteristic of the primary medium of operation, not on purpose, and it is likely that this distinction has become a severely limiting factor in joint or combined force strategy-making today. But, this is a problem easily resolved. A conceptual shift, while potentially quite useful, will not require a significant change in current training and application. The Army trains and equips itself to win battles on land and to extend violence into the realms of sea and air that infringe on its capacity to do so. It operates in all of the mediums of combat, though primarily on land. And this is as it should be. The Army has a stake in ensuring that no sea-borne invasion can threaten territory, and thus sees a need for coastal defense. It also prefers to have the skies above it void of enemy forces, and therefore develops air defense rockets and artillery (flak) to clear the air above it. Because of its desire to exploit the advantages of the air medium in support of its terrestrial goals, the Army uses mostly rotary winged aircraft (air cavalry) to rapidly move troops and equipment, and for close air support (CAS) of combat operations. The Navy trains and equips itself to win battles at sea (though increasingly to influence battles deep inland). It likewise has a keen interest in affecting the fringe and other areas that interfere with this function, and so it maintains the Marines for invading and occupying coastal areas for ports and beachheads, and in operating aircraft (naval air) that destroy threatening aircraft and ships at sea. Air Forces must prepare for battles in the air, and be able to destroy weapons that threaten the free movement of aircraft be they on the ground or at sea. The first mission of combat aircraft in modern war is to cripple the enemy's ground-based radar, the key element of its air defense system. The Air Force must also maintain land bases for its aircraft, and the security forces necessary to protect those bases. Thus, there is already a great deal of overlap in the services that does not conform to any reasonable definition or separation by medium or platform.

As is clear from the preceding paragraph, airpower and air forces are not synonymous, as are not navies and seapower, nor armies and land power. The separate services today tend to represent bureaucratic differentiations based on expediencies of training, budgeting, equipment, and the skills needed to successfully engage the enemy in anticipated combats. If we focus on the medium or platform, we tend to see the services and the military powers as interchangeable. Whoever can get to the battle will do so. This not only causes significant rivalry where capabilities overlap, it becomes easy to confuse the purpose of the medium-differentiated military power with the mission of the service that usually applies it.

But if the true purpose of operational military power is *to be able to project measured violence at the discretion of the policy maker*, then the *actual* projection of that violence is an *effect* of the purpose. Further, and this is a generally strategic vice tactical effect, holding command of the air means that power may not have to be projected from it to achieve the political aims. The opponent may elect not to bring a challenge there. Command of the medium is in itself valuable. Indeed, deterrence may be the most common outcome or effect of having command of the air or any other medium. The state does not need to project violence there if the opponent or potential enemies of the state do not believe they can successfully contest it. Opponents may find other means of engaging the state, but these undoubtedly will be ones that avoid contact with the dominated medium.

This logic is the causal foundation of asymmetric warfare, of course. The problem with such a view is that it suggests power is inefficient if it induces others to find new ways to engage the state. Missile defenses, for example, are routinely cited. If the defense is made, and is effective, the likely enemy will simply engage in another manner and in an area in which the state is still vulnerable. To which I reply, good. The threat of missile attack is now over. In the strategic view, one does not decide between a defense against this threat *or* that one. It should be how much of this and how much of that. What are the benefits of a defense here and not there?

Thus if the state has command of the air, an opposing state may not risk or wish to risk its own forces to challenge it. The operational *purpose* of airpower has thus been achieved, even if the tactical function of the air forces (which is, among other things, to destroy enemy aircraft) has not. This is an inestimable strategic distinction. The services, using tactical logic, seek to achieve results: engagement and destruction of the enemy. If tactical function is not filtered through to military strategy by the operational purpose, which is to achieve command of the medium, the logic of tactical victory can overwhelm the logic of operational and strategic ends. What we end up with is body-count mentality and war, examples of which are provided below. In Clausewitzian parlance, the grammar of war becomes its logic.

Military power seeks to support a political objective, which is linked to it through strategy. The actual use of violence may not be necessary or even desirable to that purpose. It may be contradictory. In the Cold War, both the United States and Soviet Union constructed enormous nuclear arsenals with the perceived capacity to maximize the application of violence. The *military function* of these arsenals was destructive power, but the *political purpose* behind the development of these weapons was to *never use them*. Not ever; at least, that was the political intent. Military power had to conform. But, in order to maximize efficiency the services must maintain their own purposes, conforming to the dictums of applied violence. In this case, the capacity to deliver nuclear weapons on target using a variety of sophisticated platforms was vital to the overall credibility of the strategy of power-balancing. It had to be more than possible to be effective, in crises it had to be likely. Missileers were screened for reliability. Platforms were stubbornly tested. Weapons were maintained on high alert. And because of all that paradoxical effort, the strategic purpose of the weaponry (never to be used) was achieved. The tactical purpose of these weapons was thankfully never demonstrated; to have actually delivered a nuclear holocaust would not have supported the strategic policies of either side.

Body-count wars

I suggested above that the cross-purposes of tactical ends and military power could lead to strategic inefficiencies where tactical logic supplants operational and strategic purpose. The exemplar is a war in which body-count mentality shapes operational assessment. How such a thing happens is masterfully portrayed by James Salter in his novel of the Korean War.[48] Salter portrays the Air Force tactical mission as one of destroying MiGs. Honor and glory went to the pilots that achieved ace status of five kills, and unit commanders might even pad their reports to add kills to the weekly tally and increase the esteem of their units. Despite the fact that the Chinese aircraft opposing them had some technological advantages over the American planes (a higher operating altitude was one), training and discipline gave the Americans a decided edge in air-to-air combat. Therefore, the Chinese would challenge American command of the air and engage only when they had a large numerical advantage. The perverse consequence was that the Americans would send out smaller patrol forces in order to entice the Chinese to leave their protected havens and engage. And fully consistent with the tactical objectives of destroying MiGs, when patrols got small and dispersed enough, the Chinese obliged. While this allowed the Americans to increase their kill totals, it also gave the Chinese the opportunity to increase theirs. In other words, American pilots and aircraft were deliberately sacrificed to the tactical purpose in order to increase the number of enemy aircraft destroyed. This is clearly counter to the operational logic and purpose of gaining the advantages of having command of the air. The US both operationally and strategically would have been far better served by simply keeping the Chinese on the ground through larger routine patrols. Of course, this would have infringed on the tactical purpose—victory in battle. The strategic advantage of deterrence through command of the air was thus structurally at odds with the tactical assessment mechanism of engaging and destroying the enemy.

A non-literary example is readily found in the debacle (from the American perspective) of the Vietnam War. As a by-product of the Cold War, the complete ramifications are still being felt, but at the time, the most obvious political objective for both sides was the unification of Vietnam, though only as a sympathetic ally. When it was apparent that acceding to free elections would result in a communist state under the leadership of Ho Chi Minh, military means were initiated to coerce the Soviet-allied North into joining the US-allied South under American terms.[49] Quickly, as so often happens when the passions of battle obfuscate the original intent, the political objective was lost as the goal of military *victory* became paramount, a goal that in limited war is so elusive. As Clausewitz has shown, when war is made to do something contrary to its nature, its grammar is incorrectly substituted for logic. It becomes perverse.

With victory or destruction of the enemy forces in Vietnam as the overriding criteria, operational and strategic military planners began to pursue victory in tactical terms. Battlefield success was the only measurement that mattered, and the result was predictable. Historians can show that the United States won every significant engagement of this extended conflict, handily, including deflection of the North's vaunted Tet Offensive of 1968. To prove that the Americans were winning, body counts became all important, and routinely the Americans could show kill ratios of ten and even a hundred to one. Daily tallies were reported at the conclusion of every television newscast. The American public was assured that the war was going well; how could it be otherwise with such glorious combat results? By 1973, the war was lost.

We see that the means used to measure success can alter the manner in which the conflict occurs: measurement and observation *changes* the phenomena under study.[50] In this case, using body counts as a measure of success altered not just the manner in which the war was prosecuted; it obscured the true meaning of such a grisly attrition on the opponent's side. If we assume for a moment that the body-count tallies were even remotely accurate, the tactical view that the war was going well should have been seen as patently false. After decades of conflict, a guerrilla enemy that was able to disperse into the countryside and was notoriously hard to find was now standing its ground.[51] Despite the high rate of casualties, opposition to US actions increased. The escalating resolve and capacity of the North to resist should have been obvious as the body counts increased.

More than thirty years later, strategic errors of this nature are still evident. Lessons have been given, but they have not been learned. The body-count mentality thus highlights the dangers of misidentifying military purpose, and returns us to a discussion of clearly defining the operational purpose of military power; gaining command or contestation of the medium. The practical problems in advocating such a position today are many, but two are prominent. First, the US does not desire universal or imperial control of the entire world—at least not territorially. But, as the US has global commitments, global command of the air and sea serves its interests, yet is a sensitive subject to broach. Therefore, *de facto* global command has been achieved without *de jure* justification. Under the cover of such silence, theory has been late to catch up. Second, and drawn from the first, is that the United States has had command of the air and sea mediums (and increasingly the ground) for so long that many strategists simply assume it as a condition of war. Accordingly, they focus their attention on the effects of command rather than its place in maintaining the overall power of the state. The US Army has been able to operate in an environment of total air command since the middle of the Korean War, and so perhaps it is natural that it has come to see close or tactical air support as the *critical purpose* of the Air Force. Even some notable air strategists will argue that the purpose of airpower is to affect targets or events on the ground.[52] To be sure, the ground perspective effect of perpetual command of the air has been sustained freedom of army operations in the relative absence of enemy air strikes. But CAS or air bombardment, once 'nice to have' benefits, are now misperceived as the highest purpose of airpower.

For the sake of the argument, if the purpose of airpower truly is CAS, then whenever the USAF is not bombing enemy forces it is not performing its mission. Anything else would be a wasted capacity and an inefficient expense. Hence, the body-count mentality prevails. This would lead to strategic paradox, obviously, unless the political aim of the state was to fight wars—not prevent them. CAS, precision long-range bombing, deep intelligence collection, and rapid deployment of goods and personnel (including humanitarian aid and civilian search and rescue operations) are just a few of the operational *manifestations* of airpower, available only once command of the air is achieved.

Command of the battle space

The investigation so far shows that the *purpose* of airpower strategy is to gain or deny command of the air. Command of the air allows the state to project violence from and to it in support of strategic objectives. This is a condition of continuing advantage, the *goal* of the airpower strategist. Without it, the application of force *from* the air is unreliable, if not impossible, as is defense from such attack. The means by which command of the air is gained are many, and spread across the various services, though the Air Force has a perfectly reasonable case for claiming oversight and management of it. Paraphrasing Clausewitz, airpower has its own inherent syntax, but it does not dictate its own employment. To be precise, gaining command of the air has value in itself, but it will eventually be wasted if the owner of that control chooses to stand satisfied and do nothing with it. This does not necessarily or solely mean the tactical purpose of applying force (bombing). Central to this definition is that airpower requires both the active *gain* (and/or denial to the enemy) and *exploitation* of command of the air to link strategic purpose and tactical victory. As in the fictionalized account of air operations in the Korean War, even if an overawing air force can keep and hold command of the air, unless maximum exploitation of that medium is undertaken (to include military support for rapid maneuver of troops and personnel and the denial of that capacity to the enemy through interdiction, enhancing the strategic capacity of all military power; and such things as increased commercial movement through the skies, enhancing the economic and informational capacities of the state; or just the capacity to diplomatically influence events through a leveraged bargaining position), command of the air is ineffectual in policy context.

Having command of the air means having the ability to use the third dimension at will and to prevent others from using it when necessary. The Mahanian notion of seapower, buttressed by Julian Corbett's modifications, is the preferred analogy.[53] Mahan argued that no state could lay claim to the title of Great Power if it did not possess the ability to command the sea at least along its shores. Moreover, the state that could control the vast trade routes of the oceans would inevitably be the greatest of terrestrial powers. In essence, command of the sea was the whole point of seapower; with command secured, all manner of positive results would flow. The nation would be more prosperous, more secure, more technologically advanced (as it adapted and manufactured the latest innovations in motor power, munitions, and metallurgy), and more respected—thus less likely to *have* to go to war. It could also significantly reduce its standing army. The state that could command the seas would reap all these benefits, and more. For Mahan, the goal and purpose of seapower were the same; command of the sea.

Julian Corbett argued that Mahan had missed the critical point. The decisive battle for national power would not, and would never be, on the oceans. The decisive battle would always be on land, thus the *strategic purpose* of seapower was to *support* the army.[54] The *object* of seapower was to provide timely movement of troops and material, thus command of the sea was required in *timely* and *local* fashion only.[55] Corbett insisted that the natural state of the sea was uncommanded, and therefore command of the sea was limited in space and time.[56] It could be held locally or generally, and for a limited time only. But that was enough.

Mahan and Corbett could not be more opposed on the value of broad or general command. Mahan could not separate seapower from its roots in production, trade, and shipping, or the 'principle conditions affecting the seapower of nations,' to include geographic position, size and extent of territory, population, character of citizenry, and the character of government to include its national institutions.[57] The role of Navies was to control the major sea lanes, and to do so by sinking the enemy's fleet.'[58] While his insistence on the engagement was ultimately his undoing relative to Corbett, he was correct on the ultimate impact of what would become Corbett's primary logic. For if its purpose 'is to assure one or more positions ashore, the navy becomes simply a branch of the army for a particular occasion, and subordinates its action accordingly.'[59]

Corbett was adamant in his view that seapower and land power needed no separate or unique overarching theories, as both were simply components of a broader theory of war. Throughout, Corbett argued that the purpose of seapower is to support the land engagement; for it is on land that man lives. In making the case, Corbett implies that seapower will always be subordinate to—or in support of—land power. Hence, seapower has no *raison d'être* of its own in the Mahanian sense. But this part of his argument is specious. People breathe air and drink water. They eat the fruits of the land, the sun, and the sea. Their vital commerce travels across the roads, the sea-lanes, and the skyways. Today, human beings live and work in all three environments (and are permanently occupying space), and all are necessary to their welfare. No element of military power should be permanently subordinate to, or in perpetual support to another, based on this simplistic jingoism. Yet this overall view, that it is events on the ground that are affected by military power, still holds great sway, though not for Corbett's logic.

Command of the medium is not an operational end in itself (as Mahan might have argued for command of the sea). It is the purpose of air strategy but not its *satisfying objective*. To be sure, the state or nation that gains command of the air and can hold it will see positive political, economic, and military results by that fact alone, with no amplifying applications needed. Just as Mahan insisted that command of the sea was necessary for great power status—for it enhanced trade, national security, technological and industrial advantage, and popular support for the state—so too can one make the case for command of the air (and space) in the twenty-first century. But operationally, Mahan was too dogmatic. His principle recommendation in war was to seek out and destroy the enemy fleet. His own magisterial theories should have prevented him from coming up with such a conclusion, by recognizing that if the enemy is unable to affect command of the sea (by staying bottled up in port, for example) then it is effectively disarmed. But in a more sophisticated reading of Mahan and Corbett, unless command of the sea is *actively* exploited, it has no value or meaning. Where Corbett errs is to argue that exploitation of seapower primarily means influencing land conflict. While there is no doubt that such an outcome is desirable, and in Corbett's era seminal, it misses the Mahanian point that command of the sea, in and of itself, allows advantageous land battle outcomes. Prominently, in World War I, Britain had absolutely no fear of a massive land battle on its own territory, command of the sea assured it, likewise for the United States after about 1850—though today America ensures that it will not fight a war on its own soil with the combined benefits of sea and air command.

4

WAR AND STRATEGY, GAMES AND DECISIONS

Decision-making is the essence of planning, and strategy is a plan. As such, it is applicable across a vast array of human activities. But not all plans are strategic. Most are purely functional, and comprise an acceptable application of means to ends. At this level of simplicity, the plan is little more than a decision or a set of rules for making decisions in specific issue areas. But increasing the number of decisions or decision points, even in a series of connected decisions, cannot properly be called strategy. Nor is the *process* of decision-making strategy. Strategy is far more comprehensive than that. Nonetheless, wise decision-making is a key element in designing and employing strategy, and so it is vital to strategic theory.

Decision-making takes place *within* the scope of strategy. An unknowable number of decisions and actions can be accomplished within the boundaries of a single strategy, but no competent strategy can be bound within a decision. Decisions should be informed by and complement the strategy, but they cannot encompass it. Though it may be possible to infer a strategy from an examination of decisions that are consistent with it, the decisions do not and cannot define it. The strategy may very well be dependent on the capabilities and actions of the decision makers, but it is always more than the sum of these. Accordingly, strategy tends to be placed on a higher plane than tactics or decision-making. This is not to say that strategy is more important or more valuable than tactics, it is simply more encompassing.

Decision-making presumes choice. Decision is the act of making *meaningful* choices where uncertainty exists.[1] The decision is meaningful because alternatives are available, and the outcome is at least partially dependent on the selection made. Where the outcome is certain, or cannot be altered by my efforts, then no decision is needed. Events will unfold as they must, and the agent is powerless to affect them. Whether or not I take my umbrella to work—or wash my car—has absolutely no bearing on the probability of rain occurring. I may feel better, or worse, for having done so, as I assess my effort to have been wasted or well spent. But no action I take individually regarding umbrellas or car washes will make a meteorological difference. If my purpose is to stay dry, however, a decision to bring an umbrella when storm clouds are looming may very well have value. I have anticipated the future and acted to mitigate the likely result. I have exercised a measure of influence over that future. I have changed the outcome that *would* have occurred by my action and have thus expended a degree of influence, or more properly, power. Therefore, making decisions, the act of selecting and rejecting among alternatives that have *un*certain outcomes, is the exercise of *power*. Without choice, there is no power. There is only obedience.

And what is meant by power? A discussion on the relationship between power and the concept of feedback occurs later in this work. For now, standard definitions suffice. These hold that power is the capacity that A has to get B to do something B would rather not do, or to continue doing something B would prefer to stop doing, or to not begin doing something B would prefer to start. It is a utilitarian definition that has merit, but it leaves something to be desired in practical application. For example, if A attempts to get B to do something, but B does not do it (or does the opposite), has A expended any power? How much? Is power used up, like money in a bank that draws no interest, or is it like a muscle that atrophies without use? What if B was intending to do the thing that A wanted anyway? Perhaps A wanted B to buy his old car, and so told him if he did not purchase it, he would burn down his house. B had already decided to purchase the car, and so the threat did not *cause* B to buy the car. But how would A know the cause of the car purchase was anything other than the threat, and use that knowledge to advantage in the future? If the threat was meaningless (unless it so enraged B that he decided not to buy the car, just to defy A), or had no effect, it may still be relied upon in the future as a means to increasing sales. Such overdetermined causes are a staple of international relations—or may be so. Was the relatively peaceful outcome of the Cold War due to the mutual threat of assured destruction by nuclear weapons, or in spite of it?[2] More questions arise than can possibly be answered in this study; nonetheless power is always associated with the *capacity to choose*. When one can make a choice, one has power. When one has no choice, he or she is powerless, and succumbs to fatalism.

Indeed, it is precisely the functions of choice and choosing that help separate the tactician from the strategist. Tacticians attempt to limit the options of opponents while increasing their own. Increasing one's options is the result of deeper understanding of the limits and enablers at hand. The boundaries of the battle or campaign limit the span of choices available only to the novice. To the master tactician, the more the boundaries appear to limit choice, the more options become available. The rules become enabling. To be sure, perceived limits and restraints are the source of surprise. When one side believes a thing cannot or will not be done, it is vulnerable to a master tactician who finds a way to do so.[3] Knowledge of the opponent's perceptions of the boundaries of war increases the options available. When one can find no means to overcome the boundaries of battle, the conflict is lost. Military genius is conferred upon the tactician who can limit the opponent's options. Victory or defeat comes when one side perceives that the only option left is surrender, the renouncement of the capacity to choose for oneself and the transference of it to the other. This outcome occurs only because structure and context create the corners into which the opponent can be backed.

Strategists seek to increase available options by *manipulating* structure and context, and in this way dictate the terms of conflict. One of the most captivating discussions of manipulating rules and boundaries to further the end of politics is in William Riker's thought-provoking conception of *heresthetics*.[4] Riker produces more than a dozen examples of a master strategist's manipulation of perceptions, agendas, rules, and procedures to assure the strategist's desired results would ensue. The strategist does not seek a specific outcome or decision; instead the process of decision-making is altered to increase the likelihood that a desired decision will be made. In most cases, the strategist provides *additional* choices for the opponent, inducing the other side to make a decision that was not previously apparent, but now seems necessary. By increasing the choices of others, strategists increase their own power.

The amount of power available—whether military or any other kind—to attain the aims of strategy is more properly understood as the availability of, and the capacity to make, choices. A strategy that allows for no choosing is certitude, a mechanism. There is no choice, and there is no power. The strategist who devises such a restrictive plan is inevitably captured by it, and loses even the responsibility of having created it. The exemplar in this regard is one of the more popular explanations of the cause of World War I. Contemporary general staffs perceived the need to follow rail-based mobilization plans precisely, or risk being overwhelmed by an opponent who could more efficiently do so. If the railroad timetables were not executed perfectly, or were held off too long, the state may as well concede defeat at the outset.[5] Once the decision was made to begin mobilization, the plans of war could not be interrupted. The story may be apocryphal, but the lesson learned is valuable. A strategy that binds the state to specific actions and allows for no modification is a very poor one, and emphasizes the need for *continuing* assessment and decision-making.

In discussions of war, I am not generally concerned here with the making of numerous trifling or routine decisions: what to wear, what to eat, which way to drive to work, and the like. For such trivial and repetitive decisions as these, we tend to fall into patterned behavior—habit—as a coping device. We find a behavior that works well enough, and we stick to it. Similarly, many competent decision makers will pre-select a series of choices or a rule-of-thumb to handle minor or indifferent decisions. This is the logic of game strategy described by Nigel Howard's metagame theory.[6] Metagaming involves choosing a super rule, or *metastrategy,* when confronted with a large number of repeated similar decisions. Instead of weighing options at each decision, the decision maker establishes a rule to deal with all problems of a similar kind. When interacting with another, the decision maker simply determines the type of decision that is needed, and selects the pre-established decision-making tool to apply. Metastrategy is 'a kind of strategy for selecting strategy,' according to Stephen Brams.[7] For example, a metastrategy might be that when engaged in an activity that looks like an iterated prisoner's dilemma game (explained below), a tit-for-tat pattern of behavior is employed.

That metastrategies exist is not a particularly stimulating insight. *How* habits or metastrategies (what I will call metadecisions from this point) are formed is quite interesting and useful, however, and the strength of habits once formed is illuminating. Metadecision is beneficial when making large numbers of complex choices. It is a cognitive economizing device. At some point, however, the metadecision maker will sense that the coping device is not working. More bad or losing decisions are being realized than winning ones. And so an assessment will be made of previous decisions to see if a pattern results that will allow the planner to re-center the base point and start a new sequence of metadecision-making. Note that a metadecision maker does not break a habit or change routine to bring about a small or incremental advantage, but only to bring about a *significant* benefit. The return must be considerable, or the effort of change will be suboptimal.

Routine or habitual decision-making is not simply a function of minor or trivial decision processes. We do the same for highly important issues, as well. Metadecisions are developed for critical issues precisely *because* they are so important. Precedent is established so that new decisions in these areas will not be made hastily or off-handedly. Such decision-making preferences are grounded in systems of belief, consensus, and experience, and they affect military strategy in the form of commander's intent, standard operating procedures, and doctrine. Tremendous thought and effort goes into the formation of doctrine, and decision makers abandon it at their peril. Like habits, a small or incremental cost-utility advantage is not enough to overturn or invalidate doctrine, and that is as it should be. The tried and true method requires a significant upgrade to undergo the effort of implementing change. Nor should doctrine be tossed out simply because it is obsolete or inefficient. Until there is a better alternative, a better doctrine, we are stuck with it. It is therefore imperative that thinking military professionals continuously generate decision scenarios, develop options, and evaluate potential outcomes, and in this manner form alternative approaches so that obsolete or senescing doctrine can be *effectively* replaced.

Just as decisions, even in bulk, cannot comprise or define strategy, neither can metadecision-making. Doctrine is created and promulgated at a higher level than the battlefield, but it is still concerned with outcomes there. It is the operational level of war that encompasses and separates metadecisions from the tactical level, and the application of individual decisions. Doctrine assists tactical and operational decision makers into making optimum selections in a given, though generic, circumstance. Especially when the doctrinaire has more resources or is more powerful than the opponent, to go against doctrine is more likely to be inefficient than beneficial. The most advantageous outcome of following doctrine carefully may simply be to ensure that the most consistent decisions will be made, ones on which decision makers higher in the chain can depend. But most often, it is the intent that doctrine will assist the military leader in making the *best* decision, the one that will ensure victory, which is stressed.

To be sure, making the best decision in any given circumstance is a rather simple task, which is not to say it is easy. Merely select the optimal solution among those available. The problem is, of course, that the best or better alternative in a given situation is rarely obvious. It may not even be discernible. For example, one can only choose from among alternatives that are *known* to exist, or that can be generated. An excellent option might be readily at hand, if only my background or experience permitted me to think of it. I may be prohibited from certain courses of action by physical or imposed limitations from a higher authority. Not only is the best decision rarely discernible, it is often impossible to make a selection that is patently better than another. The trouble with seeking a consistent means to the best or just better decision-making is that in most cases where the outcome is uncertain, we quickly discover that it may not be possible to make a better decision. Especially in political contexts, there simply may be no option that stands above the others. There is often not even a relatively good decision available, one that is just a little bit better than the other in the context at hand. In such cases, we must get comfortable with the practice of making a decision that is *good enough*. At worst, we may have to be satisfied with a decision that we can charitably describe as not bad. The search for slightly better decisions may even be a trap of sorts, as one can fall into a vortex of marginal improvements, and avoid making the decision altogether. This happens when a decision or choice that is good enough is held off to await that last bit of information that will make a clear discrimination between alternatives.

And so a more interesting and important question is where do choices come from? How are the choices winnowed and rank-ordered by the decision maker, or more precisely, by those who bring decisions to the attention of the decision maker? Many are simply given; that is to say, a higher authority imposes them in the form of rules or policies. These can be arbitrary and constraining, but understanding and dealing with such choice sets is a fundamental requirement for making *good* decisions. Other options or choices must be generated by the decision makers themselves, or at least manipulated by them. *How choices are generated and presented* to decision makers is usually far more influential and important than simply how best to evaluate a presented array of choices. And this is the role of the strategist, to generate and *interpret* options. They assist in recognizing relevant factors about the decision to be made, how to get preferred (not better) options onto the ultimate decision maker's agenda, suggest interrelationships among alternatives, and identify those variables that induce the structure of the choice array.

Good strategists are aware that decision-making is always subject to bounded influences, more so even than limitations. They grow to accept the notion that the best (or better) options and choices are not always available, and even if they were, individual decisions are not likely to be made based on a reasoned presentation of the argument from all sides. There may not be a proclivity to do so by the decision maker, and there may not be time. How the argument is made, when it is presented, who makes it, to whom the argument is directed—all these are more likely than objective merit to determine which choice is preferred or selected.

Prevailing theories of decision-making properly highlight the decision-making behavior of specific individuals or *agents* (as opposed to 'states,' 'executive authorities,' or 'governments'). The level of analysis assumes that decisions are made by persons *acting on behalf* of the state, the company, the organization, etc. Thus, perceptions become vital to the process of analyzing both decisions made and decisions to be made. Moreover, in the case of war and military affairs, decision makers are understood to exist within the context of a national political system and culture, an international environment, and a geopolitical situation. The decisions they make are likely to be influenced by all these factors, as well as such reasoning as previous decisions made, short- and long-term considerations, domestic and allied political support bases, and the like. The social and behavioral sciences tend to dominate analysis of decision-making under these conditions. And at the core of all of these is an evaluation of how various means were or are selected to achieve specific ends. Success is the goal. Failure is anathema.

The strategist has much to learn from these analyses, but not from the standpoint of individuals who want to know *how* to make their own decisions better. Rather, the interest is in determining the issues most likely to *inform* decisions. From there, the strategist manipulates the *structure* of the decision-making process so that whatever decision is made will add to the stability of a generally positive condition. Individual decisions are not critical in this view, and are often immaterial. Of course, both the decision maker and the strategist are vital to sound military practice, but this is the essential differentiation: decision-making logic is based on winning, on making the decision that will culminate events in the winner's favor. Strategic logic is based on influencing decisions in order to *continue* events, on establishing the conditions for an enduring advantage.

I am primarily concerned here with decision-making in and about the context of war, but many generalized observations are directly applicable. Decision-making theory writ large examines how individuals in social organizations use different methods to arrive at conclusions in situations where uncertainty and limited resources are the norm. What we find is somewhat startling. Even where distinct options are available and readily discernible, what we quickly learn is that these situations rarely involve a choice between good and evil, or right and wrong. If such were the case, decision-making would be easy. Select good over bad, and correct over wrong, every time. But many policy-related decision situations are concentrated on the margins of morality and rationality, with relatively minor gains or losses at stake. Here one is faced with two or more plans to achieve a laudable goal, say, lower crime rates or a more robust economy. Each makes a plausible case. Which will be the most *effective* is the question that matters. If an answer can be found, the decision is once again easy, even if the gains are small. Choose better over good enough and worse over bad. Though it can be incredibly complex and hard to parse, choose the lesser of two evils, or the better of two goods. The only real predicament in choosing the lesser of two evils is the knowledge that one is still choosing evil, a disagreeable activity but a justifiable one. Unfortunately, most military and policy decisions are made where several good alternatives exist, all of which will benefit some people, and hurt others. The decision must be made between two or more options, each of which has the potential for a high positive payoff for some, and a great loss for others. This is the decision maker's dilemma.

The tragedy is that a choice *must* be made, for choosing *not* to choose will have ramifications for which the decision maker must take responsibility, a situation captured in the now venerable story of *Sophie's Choice*, which I paraphrase here.[8] Imagine a situation in which a World War II-era Polish mother, Sophie, who, along with her two small children is being relocated by train to a Nazi concentration camp. Sophie stops to ask the commandant a question. The commandant, a vicious sociopath, decides to take offense, and tells Sophie that she must board the train directly but can take only one of her children with her. The other will be executed on the spot. Sophie insists that she cannot choose between them, and the commandant replies that if Sophie refuses to choose he will execute *both* children. She tries to rationally assess each child's potential for survival, and on this basis ultimately picks one. The other is shot on the spot. Here is the essence of tragedy.

Any option Sophie selected from those presented would destroy at least one child. There may be no rational means with which to make such a choice. All options appear to be created by the arbitrary whim of a sociopath. Here, by the definition of strategy so far revealed, Sophie is acting as a tactician and the commandant as the strategist. For it is the latter that has manipulated the boundaries of decision-making and perversely increased the number of options, the selection of any of which advances his agenda. It matters not at all to him which child is chosen, or that neither is, for the political aim of *his* strategy is degradation and terror of an entire social group. He forces Sophie into a decision that, whatever the outcome, shatters the psyche of the decision maker and isolates the remainder of the population, who now fear doing anything that might be seen as rebellious. Discipline in the group is maintained at the expense of one family. Lamentable as the case is, it shows that strategic thinking is not limited to laudable ends, and more importantly, engaging in a strategic competition trying to maximize tactical means is a losing gambit.

The combat commander (tactician) is often in a similar position, at least theoretically. Because there are only a set number of alternatives within the structure of the battlefield, and the option of not choosing is disastrous, the commander can be—and often is—placed into a no-win decision situation. To hold back and conserve the unit for a later battle, or to charge and hope for a victory that will turn the tide of war is an example of such a dilemma; neither is certain and both are equally justifiable. The commander can attempt to enlarge the set of options, but time is precious. The longer the battle rages, the more constricted the array of options becomes, and the more certain the outcome. In fact, this is precisely the situation in which the master tactician or strategist attempts to place an opponent. The tactician narrows options so that the opponent is in a decision-making conundrum, and uses the moment of indecision to maneuver and strike decisively.

What could Sophie have done? How would strategic thinking have extricated her from the horrifying dilemma? It is a tough analysis, and much is based on hindsight. It may not have been possible to do better, as Sophie could not extricate herself from the situation and think abstractly about the condition she hoped to achieve. What we now know is that Sophie could not function socially after this. Riddled with guilt, she lapsed into a drunken abyss. The decision ruined her life, not the choice. If she *could* have realized the intent of the Nazi commandant, she might have come up with another option. To hold her children near her and say no. To choose death for all three of them, an option that was not offered to her. In this way, she would have defied the commandant's brutality, retained her dignity, and refused to allow her conundrum to be fodder for totalitarian fear control. She would also be dead.

The anecdote is a powerful one, though fictional, but it highlights some of the difficulties in thinking strategically from a tactical perspective. Perhaps a more salient example is the disputed case of Winston Churchill's decision to allow Germany to bomb Coventry unmolested during the pivotal Battle of Britain.[9] In late summer of 1940, Britain stood alone against the gathering might of the German military. The Luftwaffe outnumbered the Royal Air Force in effective aircraft by more than two to one. Although Britain had developed basic early-warning radar and deployed a Royal Observer Corps—civilians watching the skies, equipped with binoculars and radios—to monitor incoming sorties, the short time between detection and bombing meant that even if an over flight was identified, only luck would allow sufficient aircraft to scramble and intercept. The choices seemed perilous. Either a large force could be deployed around targets of highest value, leaving much of the country unprotected, or interceptor aircraft would have to be spread dangerously thin to guard all possible air approaches to the isles. That Britain could survive the coming assault appeared unlikely.

Unknown to the outside world, however, British intelligence had cracked the vaunted Enigma cipher, and was secretly reading Germany's most sensitive military transmissions. With an undersized and outgunned force, the British were able to intercept efficiently the bulk of incoming bombers because they knew in advance where the Germans were going. Before the Luftwaffe left base, RAF interceptors were en route to intercept at the most vulnerable point in the planned route. To protect Ultra, codename for the super secret intelligence operation that deciphered the encrypted German communications, the British engaged in a massive counter-intelligence effort designed to assure the Germans that their codes were secure. They posted spotters along the coast where they knew bombers would pass, so that the invaders would think they had the rotten luck of being spotted at the earliest point en route, allowing maximum coordination and response of the outnumbered interceptors. They also established phantom air units and sent radio traffic back and forth to fool the Germans into believing the RAF had a much larger air fleet than was the case. All of this was to protect the Ultra secret, for the Germans had to believe the British were not only stronger in number, but that they had a run of nasty luck to account for the uncanny ability of the British to intercept the majority of their bombers.

And this is the critical point; if the British were to intercept *every* bomber that tried to penetrate England, the Germans might have realized that their codes had been compromised, and would likely have turned to another method of securing their sensitive military communications. The intelligence source so vital to the survival of Britain would have been lost. Therefore, which missions to intercept, and which to allow through to their targets, was decided by the highest political authority.

On November 14, 1940, British intelligence intercepted an air order directing a bomber fleet to Coventry, a beautiful and historic city with a significant arms production capacity. More than 500 planes were to take part, the largest raid so far attempted. Curiously, the German radio transmission did not encrypt the word Coventry.[10] A debate ensued, one side arguing that the use of the word Coventry in the open was an error typical of Enigma operators; on the other side were those who thought it might have been done intentionally to see if the British were indeed reading the transmission. Here was Churchill's dilemma. If the RAF intercepted the attack, it could cause the Germans to question the security of Enigma. If, on the other hand, the bomber fleet got through unmolested, then there would also be little reason to suspect the code had been compromised. Failure to defend Coventry could be seen as substantial proof that Enigma had *not* been broken.

Churchill's predicament was plain. Allow Coventry to be bombed, risking its inestimable historic treasures and the incalculable value of the loss of human life sure to occur, or protect Coventry and risk loss of the most decisive intelligence breakthrough of the war. Churchill chose the latter, and the loss was staggering. There were over 1,400 casualties, including 554 dead. Among the many cultural losses was the beautiful Cathedral of St Michael. But, after the Coventry bombing, Enigma's security was not questioned. The Allies continued to receive critical intelligence throughout the war.

Was Churchill right to choose as he did? Did he opt for the greatest good for the greatest number, a terrible and grisly calculation? We can never know what might have happened had he decided to do otherwise, but we can speculate. Either way, it was a tragic and horrible choice that emphasizes the awful responsibilities of power, and the grave range of options that must so often be confronted by great leaders.

The capacity to choose when such dilemmas present themselves, and to never look back, is a type of political corruption. Whether a person is born with the capacity to make Sophie's Choice, or acquires it from positions of power is difficult to determine, but it is precisely this insidious malevolence of which Lord Acton wrote: 'Power tends to corrupt and absolute power corrupts absolutely.'[11] In our zeal to condemn power and politics, we too often take this epigraphic encapsulation at face value, and associate corruption with immorality. But it is not immorality of which Acton writes—at least on the part of great leaders—but amorality, the ability to choose between two evils when a better option is not readily apparent. It is perhaps unfortunate that most people fail to include the very next line of Acton's famous quote: '*Great men are almost always bad men*, even when they exercise influence and not authority: still more when you superadd the tendency or the *certainty* of corruption by authority.'[12] Acton was aiming his moral judgment at historians, those who chose to excuse the actions of great leaders because of the magnitude of their accomplishments or the munificence of their offices; not against those corrupted. In particular, he argued against the tendency to forgive 'Pope and King' merely because of their extra-legal status. Moral and historical responsibility, he insisted, must be assigned to those who lead and who make decisions of life and death.

The corruption of which Acton wrote was equivocal, a natural byproduct of leading *well*. The moral corruption of men like Churchill is evident in their capacity to make amoral choices based on an ability to see the greater good and separate it from the individual misfortune. We can presume that Acton would have argued that Churchill was indeed a great man, but should not get a pass from historians on decisions that affected so many people negatively. Even though the bulk of his decisions seem to have worked out, and despite his place at the center of the defense of democratic freedom, the horror and vileness of those decisions should be preserved in stark objectivity. Acton's was not a blanket condemnation, as it is so often misinterpreted, for corruption is the eventual fate of *all* who gain power. They will unavoidably find themselves in situations where they must face—and make—morally ambiguous choices. Corruption is not a trait to be excused, but it may have to be accepted. The point is that Churchill made uncounted morally ambiguous choices (such as the one described above) that proved his corruption, and *it was this very corruption that made him a great leader.* A moral man may not have been able to allow Coventry to be bombed. A valiant attempt to save every life would be more palatable to an uncorrupted leader, perhaps one who believed that fighting the good fight, regardless of the outcome, was the true mark of honor. But it could have lost the war.

How could a person who had not been corrupted continue to send others on missions that would most certainly lead to their deaths or the death of others, regardless of the greater good that *might* result? A person who does not become corrupted cannot continue quickly and assuredly to make such decisions, and certainly could not keep from dwelling on the implications. Continuous second-guessing leads to wavering and *in*decision, and in time-constrained situations is disastrous. Of course, not all who decide with confidence and who never look back on the moral failings of their decisions are destined to be great men and women; indeed, the preponderance is delusional. But the leader who becomes paralyzed into inaction because of the implications thereof—that is, a leader who has *not* become corrupted enough to make decisions on behalf of others—will *fail* to lead. That person will not be regarded as great in retrospect. Quandary and ambivalence are the variables that pervade policy decisions. Great leaders and great strategists accept the mantel of corruption, make decisions, and move on.

Following Acton, this should not suggest that great leaders get a moral pass. It is the responsibility of historians and analysts to evaluate the moral and calculable impact of decisions made, precisely because the makers of those decisions have lost the perspicacity to do so in their corruption. This is what Acton was asking of his colleagues, brutal honesty in review. But it may very well be that corruptness and greatness arc inseparable.

Games and decisions

In the theory so far presented, tactical and strategic thought have been described as dynamic, interactive components of an overall structure of war. The tactical master takes account of the world as it is. The more completely the current situation can be established, the more accurately the tactician can plan for a certain future. When planning or preparing for war, it is common to project or 'game' scenarios and solutions in advance. War gaming is a phenomenon (and an industry) in its own right, and a useful one at that. The argument made here is that war gaming assists in highlighting the dynamic logic of operational and tactical functions *if* one views the game designer as the strategist and the game player as the tactician. In the final analysis, the strategist must in addition consider the long and extraordinary set of events that brought the decision maker to this place in time.

Thomas Schelling argued that game theory has an inherent prejudice stemming from nomenclature. The term *game*, he noted, 'has frivolous connotations' that imply 'light hearted entertainment and fun.'[13] More problematic, the term *theory* is prematurely assumed. While there is much classical theory in the debate of strategies and the interpretations of goals and pay-offs, Schelling asserted that manipulating the payoff structure of the games, the *foundation* of game analysis, is 'hardly theory.'[14] While Schelling's observations are always keen, in this case the more often criticized game is a perfectly appropriate appellation describing the mechanics of this analytic method. I agree, however, that the latter term theory is at least somewhat misleading. Game analysis is better, as it focuses attention on decision-making. Nonetheless, game theory it is, and game theorists are those who study mathematical games.

Schelling appears to be commingling the concepts of game and play when he maligns the image the former name conveys. Play, as an independent verb, can be understood as the proper term for unstructured amusement, the frivolous social interaction of children. Game is a much more specific term, and cannot be separated from a definition of its *structure*. Play can also be recognized as the activity or conduct of participants *within* a game. It is not synonymous with game; it is a component of it. Games must include, by definition, 'at least one constitutive rule, a piece of enabling legislation that makes possible precise directions, objectives, and even modes of play.'[15] Game is therefore distinguished from play by the presence of rules, restraints, or enablers affecting behavior, which dictate the conduct of the game. To play can simply mean to frolic. To play a game, however, means to act within the parameters of that game, and, presumably, to attempt to *win* that game. A game in which the players ignore the rules, or no longer attempt to win, is no longer functional, and is quickly abandoned. Game play behavior parallels a tactical operation in these respects, and war gaming can be extremely useful in tactical and operational planning and training.

When game theorists establish their analytical models, they are elaborately establishing the rules of a game in which they wish their subjects to indulge. Beginning with *assumptions of rational behavior,* these rules establish the limits of game play, and more importantly, the goals toward which participants will strive. These goals are usually defined within the boundaries of a *payoff matrix,* a rank-ordering of potential rewards and punishments based on all possible combinations of interactive player *moves.* Although the game theorist is nominally attempting to describe goals that are *reflections of existing behavior,* the payoff matrix instantly becomes a *shaper of future behavior.* These goals determine the approach or line of attack a player will develop, and *a change in goals or payoffs creates a change in tactics.* Goals have another valuable aspect in that they allow the game designer to discern the goal-relative position of each of the involved players, that is, to measure their progress. This enables the game theorist (and the players) to identify game leaders and, ultimately, game winners.

Obviously, these assumptions and payoffs, arbitrarily discerned and defined by the game designer, are what transform the theoretic model into a game. Players will attempt to maximize or optimize their positions within the limits of the rules. Those rules will restrict the potential options each player has, but will also suggest avenues of optimization that would not have been obvious before. In this manner, rules give rise to optimal plans or best move sequences for achieving the game goal in the shortest possible time or with the most economical expenditure of resources. The game analysis of dominant or most effective moves in these artificial situations is little more than a projection or observation of outcomes predetermined by the rule dependent structure of the game.

If (and *only* if) the additional assumption is made that the rules and goals of the game *accurately reflect* the constraints, enablers, and payoffs of the real world, can behavior observed within the parameters of the model be directly transformed into applicable public policy or useful political theory. This is a potentially disastrous assumption, of course, and mature game theorists are reluctant to speculate on the wider applicability of their models. Nonetheless, it is done routinely, and policy has both benefited and been harmed by its rampant application. It would be a stretch to claim that any war game yet conceived is an accurate reflection of a battle or campaign to come, although numerous historical simulations are remarkably true to their subjects. What we can say is that games and game theory have proven remarkably heuristic in developing tactical and strategic thought. Moreover, since actions taken *in* war follow the same logic as game play, valuable lessons can be assimilated by tacticians who sharpen their skills in simulations with clear instructions for and definitions of victory. Equally evident is that the role of the strategist, who makes decisions *about* war, can glean a great deal of valuable insight from the game designer.

The parallels are clear. Game, from charades to chess, soccer to patty-cake, is a specific and artificially contrived notion of highly structured and competitive activity. Hence, no game can be understood, much less participated in, without rules. Rules both legitimize and constitute the game. Without them, game play is merely turmoil. Games are, therefore, the observable manifestation of the rules that enable them. Any associative play will be shaped by adherence to them. Genius in play comes from the clever manipulation of possibilities allowed by the rules. With this brief description, we see that an analysis of games is *first and foremost an analysis of the rules of the game*, not, as many participants who become enamored with the game would have us believe, the precise analysis of structure and configuration that appears once the game is set in motion. Without knowledge and understanding of the intent of the rules, the game itself is meaningless.

This is the essential truth that game theorists can unfortunately set aside when applying the fruits of their analysis—the determination of optimum strategies in game situations—to real-world situations. The problem is exacerbated due to a readily admitted reliance on the ability to accurately describe the situation in which players find themselves for the explanatory power of the many game theories. By meticulously detailing the environment, players, and players' motives in a given situation, game theorists contend that meaningful projections of past and future behavior can be analytically derived. The recklessness of this argument is made plain by considering the circumstance of a photograph taken from above a game of chess in progress. Despite the fact that the current situation of the game is perfectly described in this one view, and all of the rules are known, it is simply not possible to provide an adequate account of the whole of the game based on this information alone. While an analysis of the optimum *next* move is quite possible, to project what *will* happen from this information is also perilous. To do so would be to *confuse a happenstance of configuration with true structure*.[16] The extent that games can be understood or defined, or their properties reduced to an adequate formula, is a function of understanding the rules of the game and not its temporary or sequential configurations. Thus, the practical value of game analysis is best understood as a *tool* for decision-making at the tactical level; determining the best next move. Unlike tactics, however, strategy is never about the next move.

These temporary configurations are, in fact, the *object* of the game player, which is to bring about a certain state of affairs, using only means permitted by the rules.[17] It is odd that some game theorists could forget that rules constitute and define the game, since it is an incumbent requirement of the game designer to establish them, and go on to argue that the game somehow defines the rules. It is true, of course, that players who find themselves in a situation bound by rules will tend to develop optimum playing patterns, and that these will dominate, but it is completely in error to assume these subsequent dominant patterns are primal causes for later behavior. They are in fact *dependent* variables. The *independent* variable is the original assumption of the model builder or rule of the game designer. Iterative play can establish *habits* of behavior, even norms that tend to obscure careful cost–benefit analyses at every move, but these repetitive actions are not *causes* for behavior, they are simply optimizing meta-tactics.

Iterative play does appear to help define, distribute, and even establish rules, norms, and behaviors that were not evident at the onset of the game, and this is a fascinating form of emergent behavior. Nonetheless, the emergent behavior, as Steven Wolfram is beginning to demonstrate, is an output of the rules that structure the relations of the players, and it may be possible to structure rules in a system to ensure a desired type or category of emergent behavior occurs.[18] It is certainly not causal, however. To argue that the rules of game play can *cause* a certain behavior is akin to arguing that over time, a traffic light changing to red causes a driver to stop a car, or that the rules of sheet music cause a pianist to play a certain tune. While the traffic laws may *explain* certain human behavior, and the notes on sheet music *allow* the musician to recreate a specific melody, they do not cause anything.

The exemplar in this regard is Robert Axelrod's much lauded work regarding the evolution of cooperation.[19] Theorists have long sought a rigorous scientific explanation for the emergence of social cooperation from a natural state of anarchy, or as Axelrod puts it, '[in] situations where each individual has an incentive to be selfish, how can cooperation develop?'[20] Thomas Hobbes, he claims, asserted that stable or lasting cooperation could only develop with a strong central authority to *enforce* cooperation. But, Axelrod argues, cooperation *does* arise in situations of anarchy—where there is no central authority—and cites two examples: the international arena and the United States Senate. His definition of anarchy is that all 'players' have nominally equal influence and power, and that no central authority (such as a king or hegemon) is present.[21] Axelrod further insists these two examples are sufficient to disprove Hobbes's contention, and therefore it is just a matter of properly applying game theory to the context of anarchy to divine the conditions that allow cooperation to spontaneously emerge: 'The Cooperation Theory presented [here] is based upon an investigation of individuals who pursue their own self-interest *without the aid of a central authority to force them to cooperate with each other.*'[22]

Of course, Hobbes never claimed that cooperation was impossible in anarchy, that awful condition when man is without government, just that it would always be precarious. It is the whole point of Book I in his extraordinary *Leviathan*. Still, it is easy enough to accept Axelrod's definition of anarchy and his assertion that cooperative behavior emerges from the self-interested interactions of individual agents. Where his otherwise brilliant argument is faulted is in the insistence that a careful description of the situation of anarchy will in itself explain the emergence of cooperative behavior, and that force or constitutive requirements are not needed. Unfortunately, because he blurs the roles of rules and assumptions that constitute the state of anarchy with anarchically driven actions, he cannot truly describe causal behavior. What he does quite expertly is illuminate optimal behavior patterns that emerge within continuing rules-based situations.

Axelrod tested his hypotheses by applying a game design he felt adequately described Hobbes's state of anarchy, the Prisoner's Dilemma (PD). The use of PD is quite problematic as a model for anarchy since it presupposes a third player central authority (embodied in the police and court system), but for the sake of argument, this discrepancy will be ignored. Indeed, for most game theorists, PD is an appropriate model of anarchy when the 'acceptance of a non-cooperative strategy' is dominant even 'when a mutually-preferable cooperation strategy [is] available.'[23]

The PD scenario is simple. Two criminals have been arrested on suspicion of committing a crime. They are placed in separate interrogation rooms and questioned simultaneously. The police do not have enough evidence to convict either of them of the crime they were arrested for, but could hold and convict them on lesser charges. Each, in isolation, is offered the same deal. The first is to *defect* from any cooperation agreement with the other prisoner and provide testimony sufficient to convict the other of the original charge. In that case, the prisoner would get off with no jail time while the erstwhile partner would spend a substantial time behind bars. If *neither* provides the evidence to convict the other, that is if both persist in *cooperating* with the other in silence, then both will be convicted of the lesser charges and spend a small amount of time in prison. If, however, *both* defect and turn evidence on the other, they will be convicted of the original charge but will receive a reduced sentence for their assistance.

The payoff matrix describes the structure of the game (see Figure 4.1). There are only two options, cooperate or defect, and one of the two *must* be selected. There are four possible outcomes. Both could cooperate, in which they would each receive a small jail sentence and a reward (R) of three game points (the numbers are for mathematical comparison, and can vary widely). Both could defect, or turn state's evidence, in which case each would receive moderate sentence but would receive a punishment (P) of just one point. The third and fourth possibilities are that one player could cooperate while the other defects. In this case, the defector succumbs to the temptation (T) of no time in prison, and is awarded five points. The cooperator receives the harshest result, called the sucker's payoff (S), and gets no points.

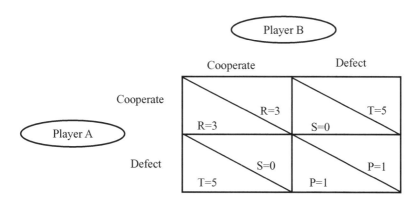

Figure 4.1 Prisoner's dilemma payoff matrix

The question PD appears to answer is what the best choice for either player in this situation would be, *assuming the players want to gain the most points* (win).[24] The point award for T is the best, but it also allows for the possibility of the worst outcome, no points. Nonetheless, since the game has a potential winner, the selection of defect guarantees that the player will not lose (end up with fewer points than the other player). Indeed, every analysis of PD shows defect to be the best move for a self-interested player. The game is so abstract and bounded by artificialities that it is a wonder anyone could suggest that players are by nature competitive defectors, rather than insist that the defection behavior is an output of the structure of this particular game.

Axelrod admits to being annoyed by the dominant strategy of PD, to defect, and wanted cooperation to be the dominant paradigm. One quickly notes that the maximum point total that can be scored by both players is six (if each receives three R points). The worst mutual point total is two (where each player receives one P point). Keeping the pair from choosing a mutually beneficial outcome is the issue of achieving an advantage in relative gains over absolute ones. Winning is the key to understanding PD, Axelrod reasoned, and so he decided to manipulate the structure of the game itself—just as a good strategist should. He did not want to win a specific game of PD. That tactic was already known. He wanted to increase the chances of a different outcome in PD games overall. And so Axelrod decided to try a sequence of PD games, or Iterated PD (IPD). In a simple IPD game, the players make successive decisions with the other player, the length of the game (or number of rounds) varying. The goal is to have the most points at the end of an unknown number of games, a far more strategic outlook than winning individual PDs. In this unending binary conflict, however, the dominant strategy was to defect in every game (always defect or AD). The proof is simple enough. If one player uses the tactic or habit of always defecting, the other player will lose the game by taking a chance on cooperation in *any* round.[25]

Axelrod's next strategic decision was to add players and randomize the interaction decisions among them. He reasoned that what 'makes it possible for cooperation to emerge is the fact that the two players might meet again,' and that, because of this, 'cooperation can get started *even in a world of unconditional defection.*'[26] Now Axelrod had an IPD with multiple players, more accurately describing the condition of anarchy, he believed, than single PD situations. Still, defection proved dominant. Axelrod found that if one player in a two-player game, or a majority of players in an *n*-player game, use a pure defection tactic, the best any other player can hope for is a tie, and only if they too always defect. In a world where all players demonstrate a defection pattern, cooperation can never emerge.[27]

So Axelrod published a challenge to the academic community. He would simulate an IPD game with an unknown number of moves and players. Anyone who wished could submit a program (a pattern of moves) he or she believed could *win* in this situation. Axelrod further assigned a number of inviolable rules or conditions to ensure proper game play: no enforceable treaties or agreements between players; no metagame analysis (accomplished by limiting knowledge of other player's moves); players could not be eliminated nor could they voluntarily withdraw; and the payoff structure could not be altered.

The result of his tournament, Axelrod proclaimed, was that the optimum game plan for IPD is Tit-for-Tat (TT), a cunningly minimal tactic submitted by Anatol Rappaport. TT is simple. Cooperate in round one, and then do whatever your opponent did to you in the previous round. Iterated *reciprocal* behavior based on the other person's play was shown to achieve the highest score more times than any other plan. Thus, Axelrod reasoned, the incentive to cooperate is reinforced in iterative interactions with multiple players. The lessons one should take away from this exercise are somewhat equivocal, but critical to the definition and arguments of pure strategy so far presented.

Clearly if one becomes enmeshed in a situation that appears to have no other option than conflict—and here the US–Soviet Cuban missile crisis of 1963 is routinely cited as the archetype—then a strategist wishing to increase the chances of achieving cooperation should introduce the prospect of future interactions and increase the number of interacting agents. The first is accomplished by reducing the perceived importance of victory in the current round, by stretching out the future. Both sides must recognize that regardless of the outcome of this game, more games will be played—many more. The second is done by creating more options, by increasing knowledge of the variety of tactics available and distributing that knowledge throughout the system.

Not so clear, however, is Axelrod's refutation of the Hobbesian paradigm that stable cooperation emerges from *a mutual contract* in which all agree to a sovereign authority to bind them. Indeed, Axelrod's solution is to redefine the condition of anarchy, or to change the assumptions on which Hobbes's theories are based. Even if we grant Axelrod the point that multiple player IPD describes Hobbesian anarchy faithfully, Rappaport's solution comes astonishingly close to the one that the much-maligned Hobbes recommends. In his many requirements for access to the game, and in Rappaport's requirement that TT players cooperate on the first round (and that they rigorously follow an established set of rules thereafter), Axelrod has arguably introduced Hobbes's Leviathan into the simulation. *Only with these constitutive rules* can cooperation emerge in IPD. We see that without changing the enabling rules of the game, theorists could only project a continuation of the existing configuration (in this case, non-cooperative anarchy). Meaningful and systemic change (to cooperation) was only possible with an understanding of, and a manipulation of, the structure of the game.

TT was able to win the greatest number of IPD games because of an emergent behavior at the systemic level that resulted in the formation of cooperative 'clusters' of successfully cooperating players.[28] The clusters appeared to be forming spontaneously, and without the conscious support of the players themselves. This dynamic interaction of individual agents, determining their actions based on simple rules, created a complex pattern of interactions. This will be the takeoff point for a later argument on the importance of complexity theory in strategy-making today. That endeavor will be to find the constitutive rules that will likely produce a type of system-wide behavior that is advantageous to the strategist.

Context versus structure

It should not be surprising that the proliferation of game theory has been so endemic. Games have an innate quality of self-perpetuation. In order to play a game, one must have knowledge of the rules, or else the activity is random and not a true game. But as the game is played, substantial *understanding* of the nuances of the rules is acquired, and the players become adept at the game. Eventually, the game becomes more exacting, more challenging, and the players become enamored with it and see applications for it that never before existed. Jeffrey Pincus and Edwin Bixenstine questioned the motives for the proliferation of the study of Prisoner's Dilemma games as early as 1977, suggesting it had evolved into a competition of who is most adept at analyzing the game itself rather than a search for application to real-world behavior.[29] Game theorists, having become adept at the techniques of game analysis, find a whole world of applications.

Game theory has a wide range of application and is especially valuable in isolating variables and selecting optimal behavior in carefully refined settings. It can be an outstanding tool for the tactician to find options that are allowed and preferred under the rules. But it should not be mistaken for an overarching theory of behavior, no matter how appealing the notion of a mathematically precise model of prediction is to the social scientist. This is simply because the technique incorrectly defines the happenstance of configuration for structure. Schelling is explicit, game theory is 'abstract and deductive, not the empirical study of how people make decisions but a deductive theory about the conditions that their decisions would have to meet in order to be considered "rational," "consistent," and "noncontradictory."'[30] To be sure, the founders of game theory, Von Neuman and Morganstern, recognized their theory was static, and projected no grandiose uses of the type Brams and Ordeshook portend.[31] It can only be applied to clearly articulated, rational situations, and then is only useful as a guide. In the dynamic of war, where the structure is fluid, goals are not always clearly defined, and actors behave with varying conceptions of rationality, its value is limited to optimizing short-term decision strategies.

The tactician's difficulty in stepping outside of the real world situation to examine the structure that constrains and enables decisions is not a problem that needs to be fixed. It may even be an attribute. The war-fighting tactician is part of the world impacted by tactical decisions, and stepping outside of it, if only for academic perspicacity, may cause more harm than good. It is the tactician's role to manipulate knowledge of the situation and of the rule-structure to limit the opponent's choices, channeling the other's decisions into an inescapable corner where victory will be determined. It is the strategist's role, on the other hand, to increase options, to manipulate structural rules to augment the probability of beneficial actions taking place within and emerging from the structure.

And it may simply be impossible to change the structure in any meaningful way from within. The tactician eschews anything that does not assist in developing an accurate description or picture of the current situation, or claims to have no answers to a specific dilemma. This is because from within the system, it is useful to imagine that actions are *caused* by the situation within which one is found. I went left because my enemy was dug in on my right. I shot the other person because I was just about to be shot. But these are not truly causal factors. They are explanations. My actions are based on underlying norms of proper behavior, expectations of conforming behavior on the part of others, my knowledge of the legal and doctrinal structure at the time, and much more. The distinction, however, is moot on the battlefield. When a tactician fails to gain victory, chroniclers of the event inevitably suggest that a lack of accurate information, a poor understanding of the situation at hand, was to blame. Failure is ascribed to confusion, indecision, rashness, or some other behavior associated with not grasping the *totality* of the situation—Napoleon's *coup d'oeil*.

Increasing the detail of description is the cure for real-world decision-making, it is argued, despite the flaws in such an approach when trying to isolate cause through the useful analytic technique of abstraction. *Coup d'oeil* is in fact the ability to *abstract out* the unnecessary background distractions and details of combat and focus only on the important sweep of tumultuous events in the broader scope of battle or campaign. Games are one of the cleverest ways to 'strip away the messiness of real life and leave an environment governed by just enough rules for something interesting to happen.'[32] They achieve the power of abstraction and highlight causal relationships—but only in the game. This is enough for insight, however, and so games remain incomparably valuable in the realms of decision-making. The transition is inevitably lost in translation, however, and the tacticians and game-players insist on more information, more variables, more detail. The strategist and game designer can be obliging or not. Intense detail can grind both the game and battle to a halt.

Another reason for constructing game models and simulations is that some real activities, especially violent ones like war, cannot (or should not) be enacted simply to test a hypothesis. In these cases, it is useful to try to approximate reality with more complexity, though perfect reflections are by definition impossible. The effect of increasing the variables of the model, however, is to complicate it to a degree where meaningful relationships are difficult to isolate and discern. A more common problem is that the analyst, having created a model believed to reflect reality more perfectly, begins to confuse model-projected behavior with that of the real world. If there is a discrepancy between the two, all that is needed is a minor adjustment, a bit more detail, for the simulation to mimic the subject and foretell the future.

Indeed, accuracy of prediction has long been a standard—if misunderstood— validation of theory. David Easton, citing Karl Popper, commented that 'validity is still determined by the correspondence of the statement to reality.'[33] Despite the existence of notable exceptions (theories which predicted with exquisite accuracy but were nonetheless false—the Ptolemaic system in astronomy, for example), this criterion persists. To be sure, a perfectly reasoned theory that has no utility in reality is especially useless for the tactician. One that predicts well enough is far better than one that may be closer to our conception of reality, but cannot provide real-world answers. Popper, however, also pointed out that reality is *impossible* to see because we are *inside* the system we are evaluating.[34] In such a case, logic must lead to paradox: 'Only by stepping outside the system can one say anything is true or false in a meaningful way. And if you speak only in the language of the system, you are bound by its rules.'[35]

Battle has similar characteristics. The tactician cannot determine from the structure of battle the true purpose of war. The tactician must strive to win, to fulfill the criteria of victory provided by superiors, and to do so ably, enhancing the probability of success with accurate knowledge of the battlefield, the opposing forces, their capabilities, and the like. In other words, the more information the tactician has about the current situation the better. Knowledge of future or planned engagements can surely help in making long-term decisions about this battle, but cannot increase the efficiency of achieving victory in it. Sacrifices can be made today for greater success tomorrow.

There are parallel notions for understanding the value of *past* events in the present decision-making context. The first is not subtle. We study trends of previous actions and decisions of our opponents to more accurately predict their future actions. Whereas anticipated future decision-making needs can cause us to sacrifice efficiency today for advantage tomorrow, for the most part knowledge of the past is intended to increase our decision-making efficiency today. We do not generally accept these as *deterministic* in any way, however. Karl Popper captures the essential nature of this argument by stating flatly that such inductive logic fails the predictive test because 'confidence that the future will be like the past [or the present] is nothing but an undemonstrable faith.'[36]

But what of that trail of events that precedes the situation of the world as it is now? Can I even comprehend causality simply from perfect knowledge of the present? In a game of chess, do I move my queen *because* it is in danger of capture from your rook? Why was the rook moved to threaten the queen? Does that decision have a causal impact on the game? Most assuredly, and because of the abstraction of game play we are able to push the causal chain to its logical limit, and it is here we realize most manifestly that 'the actual context in which the [game takes] place must extend indefinitely.'[37] Just because the enemy has always attacked at dawn does not lead us to believe that the rising of the sun causes the attack. It is a harbinger of it, perhaps, and it would be foolish not to be particularly vigilant at that time. Even the classic reaction of the billiard balls to highlight rules of cause and effect are muddled when we examine the intricate chain of events that pushes one ball into another, and the undeterminable chain of future events it spawns. This is a profound point. Only in theory can a game be completed. Like strategy, the real game is never finished. It is not even finishable.

This second notion is more intriguing. To a certain extent we can divine a measurable, demonstrable advantage for decisions made today by studying the *sequence of decisions* that converged into the situation we now face. This is different than studying past events (writ large) to gain insight. I assert that knowing the whole sweep of decisions that led to the current configuration not only assists the decision maker in predicting the future, but is essential to determining its meaning.

Just as some theorists mistake the extant configuration of a game in progress for causal structure, the particular situation of the real world-in-being is incorrectly viewed as a mirror of causality. If there appear to be contradictions, they are the fault of the observer, for not recognizing this world-in-being with sufficient accuracy. It must be so, they insist. The situation at hand is faultless; it is what it is. It does not matter *how* the enemy came to be here. What matters are the enemy's strength, deployment, condition, and capabilities. Superior decision-making performance, using these assumptions, comes from the best knowledge of what is factual *now*.

But how much credit for the current situation should be given to decisions that were made in the past? How much for those decisions *not* made? We tend to look at history as a series of decisions, good and bad, that create and define it. Yet it remains a sticky point of analysis that history can never be replayed. It is set in deed. The intent of the historian is to find out what really happened, in order to get a more sophisticated understanding of how the present came to be. History is set, in this view, and it would be an enormous waste of time to try to find out what really did not happen.

It cannot be denied, for example, that Germany lost World War II, at least from the tactical perspective put forward here. At the very least, it is pointed out that German officials unconditionally surrendered to Allied forces in 1945. Trying to better understand the current situation by speculating on what it might be like had Germany not lost sounds like an endless exercise in self-indulgent and fruitless speculation. And from a position *inside* the stream of history, it is. But, if we are able to conceptually step away from our position inside that stream, we can ask useful questions as a strategist. What if the Allied victory was a fluke? If World War II could be replayed a hundred times, beginning in 1939, is it possible that the Axis would win more than half the time? I do not know; perhaps I cannot know. But much speculation has been published on decisions made that were *turning points* in history, and on what disastrous events might have happened in their absence. To this view, Umberto Eco has pithily remarked: 'Counterfactual conditions are always true, because the premise is false.'[38] There is something to learn from these stories, but only if we can equate the situation then to the one now.

Since the Axis lost the one time World War II was waged, a detailed enough analysis of the current situation must ultimately show that it could not have won. The past could not have been anything other than it was. To argue something else is to confound the tactical logic, because history has brought us to where we are now. No matter what decisive or turning-point decision we select as the critical one that brought us to where we are today, a prior decision enabling that one can always be found, *reductio ad absurdum*. Since we are here, in this situation, history could not have been different.

Here is highlighted the error in mistaking situational decision-making tools, like prisoner's dilemma patterns of moves, for *strategy*. A strategy that dictates actions to be taken in all cases, that accepts it must choose between options before it, or that projects all options in the future will be like the options today, is not strategy. All such models are structured on the facts of history. They inevitably presume that existing configurations must reflect historical structure, and therefore *history can be ignored for analytic purposes*. The logic is precise, but is only valid if history *had* to play out the way it did, that it *could not have been otherwise*.

This is inconceivable in a world in which decisions are meaningful, in which choice matters. Imagine that only the great events of world history are included for analysis—those widely conceded to be turning points, battles such as Marathon, Trafalgar, and Midway. These have been studied because had they turned out differently, the assumption is that the impact on history would have been significant. In many of these cases, the outcome was judged more miraculous than probable. If this is true, then ignoring alternative history is problematic for current decisions made. For the sake of argument, however, let us say that all meaningful past events had a predominant probability of happening exactly the way they did. After just a tiny fraction of these are charted, the indisputable conclusion of the statistician must be that the possibility all probable events will occur is far less likely than the possibility that some number of low probability events will occur (see Figure 4.2). This simple calculation throws significant doubt on the value of making predictions (though not decisions) based entirely on a detailed description of situations or configurations, no matter how vociferously we argue the situation is historically derived.

If we construct a simplified game tree model, we need just three iterations to make the point. At the first level, only two decisions can be made, Move left (L) or move right (R). The decision maker (agent) has shown a preference for moving left 0.75 percent of the time, and so we predict that the agent will move left now. Let us say that events unfold in the most likely manner, and the agent does indeed move left. Subsequently, at level two, another decision is made. Again, moving left is the preferred decision in any given round, and nothing has shown us that the agent has changed preferences, so we predict a move to the left (to position LL). Again, we are rewarded, the agent does indeed move left. Now, the odds that our agent would make two probable decisions in a row are the multiple of the two individual probabilities, or just over 56 percent ($0.75 \times 0.75 = 0.5625$). It is still the most likely outcome. At level three, given an analysis of the current situation, the odds that L will be selected again are 0.75. By now, however, it should be clear that even though the most likely event in three successive rounds occurred, the chance that outcome LLL (three likely events) would result from a vantage in round one is *un*likely ($0.75 \times 0.75 \times 0.75 = 0.421875$). There is a significantly

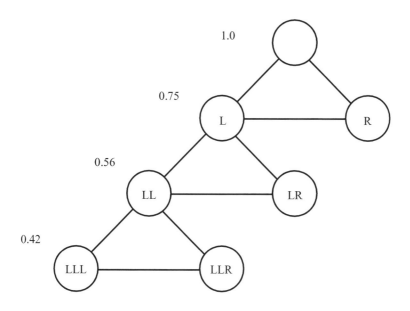

Probability of moving at any level is 1.0
Probability of moving left at any level is 0.75

Figure 4.2 Probability tree

more probable chance that during these three successive decisions, the less likely decision R would have occurred at least once.

The tactician must base the decision ahead on all the information at hand. Indeed, it would be faulty to reason that since the most likely option was chosen twice before, the less likely option will be chosen now. It would simply be a hunch. Even if the agent had moved to the left a dozen times previously, the decision maker should be wary of interpreting the most recent historical pattern to argue that the coming decision is almost assuredly going to be to the right. The logic is drawn from knowledge of random probabilities in binary outcome sets. If a tossed coin has a probability of 0.5 turning up heads, and 0.5 turning up tails, any individual toss of the coin will have the same probability. Even if the coin had been tossed heads the twelve previous iterations, the probability of heads landing on the thirteenth toss would still be 0.5 ... unless, of course, the *sequence* of thirteen tosses was connected.

Let us say a coin had been tossed thirteen times, however, and the results recorded. If you were told that the first twelve tosses had been heads, what would the probability be that the thirteenth toss was also a head? Assuming no untoward modifications of the experiment, that is, the coin is not weighted and the flips were made without prejudice, the likelihood that the thirteenth toss was also a head is minuscule, it will occur only once in ten thousand tries ($0.5^{13} = 0.0001220703125$). I should bet my entire savings on it having been tails. Indeed, the probability that the first twelve tosses were heads is so small that I should probably suspect some sort of malfeasance in the whole process, and may be better served to bet that the thirteenth is fixed as well, regardless of the assurances of the coin tosser that all is fair. The point is that decision-making tools like a game tree always start at a point where *it is presumed the effect of prior decisions made are no longer impacting the current one.*

This is an extraordinary assumption. In the real world, it may be impossible to find a prisoner's dilemma-like situation in which my binary decision is uninfluenced by any other decision than the one made by my opponent. Almost every decision is influenced by the sequence of decisions of which it is a part, and a multitude of decision sequences within the structure that have no direct link to it. In reality, from inside the structure, it is impossible to know where in the sequence of influential decisions the one before me now truly belongs. I will demonstrate with a probability example.

Where in history are we?

At innumerable points in the course of history, an event occurred that by all reason should not have, and if that statement is true then the configuration we find ourselves in today, no matter how well described, is to some extent an anomaly. It is not indicative of a sequence of *probable* outcomes. Thus, it is not credible to regard any single or distinct point in history as a pure reflection of structure. The strategist who relies on historical situations (and not history) for meaningful explanatory power is incorrectly relying on an improbable dependent configuration instead of an independent constitutive structure. This error has unfortunately been long evident in game theory, and in most other decision-making models.[39] If strategists seek real-world predictive capacity or decision support from even the most comprehensive appraisal of the present situation, they will always be frustrated. Stretching the current image into the future will simply reinforce both the likely tendencies and the unlikely events that shaped the present, and so the model will only be able to project a continuation of the current situation. The future will look like the present. Without allowing for modifications as time progresses, the farther out the projection, the more inconsistent with real-world behavior the analysis will become.

The difference between structurally derived strategic awareness and tactically sound decision-making is exemplified in the following coin-toss example. Imagine a situation in which you have entered into a game in which a series of two coin tosses will be made. The entry fee is fifty cents. You will be asked to guess the outcome of the first tossed coin. If you are correct, you will advance to the next round, where you will have the opportunity to predict the outcome of a second tossed coin. If you successfully predict the outcome of the second coin toss, you will win a dollar. The house keeps any remainder. Clearly, the odds are stacked against you. There is a one in four chance that you will be successful ($0.5 \times 0.5 = 0.25$). As you play several itcrations, you will find yourself paying two dollars in entry fees for every dollar you win. The more you play the more you lose.

From inside the game, you cannot do any better. We accept that there is a 0.5 probability of either a head or a tail on every fair toss. It would be reasonable in this case to adopt a metadecision to speed the process of play. You might decide to always choose heads. You may decide to alternate on every throw. You may make purely random selections. There is no pattern mathematically better than any other, and this highlights the value of doctrine and rule-making. To select a rule for decision-making is to acknowledge that the situation has been thoroughly analyzed and no better method is available. The decision maker might argue that one could reevaluate at every toss, but since the analysis of the structure will forever be that it has not changed, the decision will be the same at each juncture: why waste the time? The status quo is projected in perpetuity.

What if the game were presented in a slightly different form, as at Figure 4.3? In this case, you are to predict the outcome of both tosses in advance. The coins are tossed and the results written down. The possible outcomes are four: Two heads (HH), a head then a tail (HT), a tail then a head (TH), or two tails (TT). An assessment of the situation is that any outcome has a 0.25 probability, and so no one selection is better than any other. Only pure luck would let you come away a winner, luck that diminishes to the law of averages the longer you play. This would be a dull game. What if I, as game master, changed the betting procedures? Your first guess is free, but only if you were fortunate enough to correctly predict the first tossed coin are you eligible to bet on the outcome of the second tossed coin. There would be no harm in playing the first round, and since you are bored, you go ahead and make a prediction for the two tossed coins. Now, if you do advance to the second round, I will offer the opportunity to place your bet—with an incentive. You must pay a dollar for the privilege of playing, and if you are right I will pay you two to one. If you are wrong, I get to keep your dollar. The game is more interesting now because you foresee that your chance of winning some cash this night is considerably better. You reckon that there are two possible outcomes and you were fortunate enough to have picked one of the two throws already. You readily agree to bet, reckoning that by the end of the night you will have earned two dollars for every dollar bet.

Somehow, at the end of the night, you find yourself behind. I am winning three dollars for every two I pay out to you. This is better than the original game, but still irksome. The law of averages informs you that over hundreds of tosses it is all but impossible to be wrong three out of four times on successive bets of a fairly tossed coin. You begin to suspect the game is rigged, but you have examined the coin and the tosser is a friend of yours. In order to keep you in the game, I offer you the opportunity to change your pick. Every time you make it to the second round (and, curiously, you always make it to the second round) you can stay with your original pick or switch to the remaining possible outcome from the two already tossed coins.

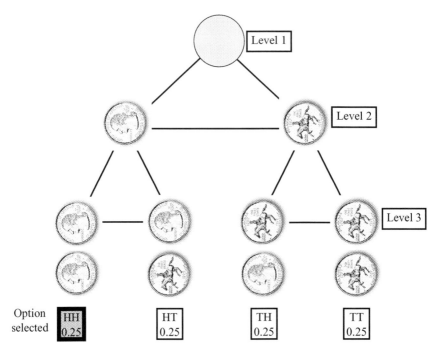

Level 1

Level 2

Level 3

Option
selected

HH	HT	TH	TT
0.25	0.25	0.25	0.25

Figure 4.3 Game one coin-toss tree

At first you are reluctant to change your pick. It was good enough to get you into the second round and your gut instinct is to stay with a good decision. Eventually, however, you begin switching picks as your losses mount. Remarkably, you find that when you do change your pick you win on average three times more often than if you stay! It seems an oddity. Whether or not, and how long it takes you to change your pick will depend on a variety of factors, mostly psychological or cultural, but it should be based on whether you *assess the sequence of throws* or *reassess the second toss* (as in the first game example).

Seen from within the game, it appears the point of prediction for any single round is moot. From a structural or strategic vantage, however, in a sequence of coins tossed modeled on this example, it matters a great deal *when* a prediction for subsequent tosses is made. If it is done anew before each toss, the decision maker has a 0.5 probability of choosing correctly. If however, the decision for *all* tosses is made before the first toss in the sequence, the odds are just 0.25 that the decision maker will choose correctly for two tosses, 0.125 on three, 0.0625 on four, and so on. In this case, any one sequence selected is no more likely to win than any other—so in the game at Figure 4.3, you opt for outcome HH. In the next game I inform you that heads was tossed on the first throw, and as a result you have made it to the second round. Outcomes TH and TT have been eliminated as a result. I then offer you the opportunity to switch your pick from HH to HT.

If you choose to analyze the situation *at present,* you will determine that you are predicting the outcome of a single coin tossed. Whether or not you switch is arbitrary, you reason, since the odds of winning are the same. In other words, you find yourself at a decision juncture where you have the opportunity to predict the outcome of a coin toss that has already been made, but the result of which is not known. There are only two possible outcomes, and so, assuming the toss was fair, you reason that each has a 0.5 chance of being correct. Having been trained that unnecessary wavering is a sign of indecisiveness, you stay with the original selection (HH).

The strategist, however, sees that in this situation switching to outcome HT will be correct considerably more often than staying with HH. This is because the strategist knows that the decision juncture at hand is but one part of the whole construct. In the game tree model at Figure 4.3, there are three levels and seven configurations. From the starting point at level one, the strategist sees (as the previous player did) that there is a one in four chance that any one of the outcomes will occur. By selecting one of the outcomes (HH), a number of bits of very useful information are known. First, there is a 0.25 probability that the first prediction is correct. Second, there is a 0.75 probability that it is incorrect. Third, *at least two of the three outcomes I did not select are also incorrect.*

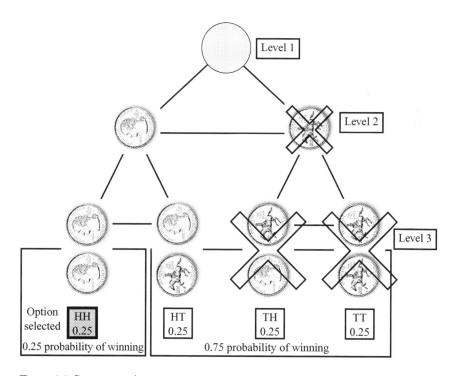

Figure 4.4 Game two coin-toss tree

When the game master tells you that the first toss was heads, and as a result the only two possible outcomes are HH and HT, you have not gained any useful knowledge. The odds that you are correct are still 0.25. The odds that you are wrong are still 0.75. That two of the options you did not select are not winners has only been verified. You already knew that; hence the odds have not changed. If you are offered the opportunity to switch to the remaining outcome you did not select, you should jump at it. In essence, the game master is offering you the opportunity to stay with your original selection, or take all three non-selected outcomes, two of which were obviously not winners. If offered at the beginning of the game, you would not hesitate to switch (three for one, this is a good deal). Nonetheless, from a detailed assessment of everything knowable at level 2, you will insist that the odds *have* changed. It is now just as likely as not, you will assert, that you selected the winner.

You probably stay with your original selection because you think the revealed information is meaningful, that it has the capacity to somehow change the odds in mid game. They were correctly assessed at 0.25 at level 1, but are now determined to be 0.5 at level 2. This could only happen if previous history is disregarded or *if the second coin were to be tossed anew*. Since the two coins had *already been tossed*, how could the odds change from level to level? The truth is, they cannot.

This example, a variation of the Monty Hall or Three Goats problem, has been psychologically tainted by using a series of coin tosses to make the point.[40] We all know that any coin tossed has a 0.5 probability of turning up either heads or tails, regardless of the sequence or string in which it resides. When faced with what appears to be a decision about a single coin toss, we revert to our metadecision. But I played a bit of a trick here. The information I provided you was a misleading way of saying 'at least two of the options you did not select cannot be correct, would you like me to demonstrate?' I would then look at the card on which I had written down the outcome of the two coin tosses and see which two of the three were incorrect, and reveal that information to you. If you had luckily picked the correct outcome, I would randomly reveal two of the three. Instead, I said 'the first toss was indeed a head.' This is a way of giving you the same information. Now you know you are either right, or outcome HT occurred. Had TH been the outcome, I might have presented the information to you as; 'the second toss was indeed a head.' If TT were the winner, I would have said, 'both tosses were the same' (in which case it could not have been HT or TH). In fact, there are only six statements needed to allow the game master to offer the player a choice to switch predictions regardless of the player's pick and the actual outcome. The other three are: the first toss was a tail (not HH or HT); the second toss was a tail (not HH or TH); the tosses were different (not HH or TT).

We see that detailing the condition of configuration at a given point in time (or a certain round of a game) can easily lead to mistaken calculations of dependent probabilities. The longer the participant continues to play each round independent of the previous rounds and ignorant of the enabling rules of the first round, the more misrepresentative of reality the analysis becomes. The game model will continue to predict the status quo, and the real world it attempts to describe will continue to undergo fundamental change.

The game theorist may be compelled to argue that game trees do not deal with predetermined outcomes, rather, they assist in choosing rational decisions in real situations of undetermined futures. To this I would have no argument. But the example of the coin tosses raises the mathematical proof that in a sequence of decisions, and it is difficult to argue that any decision is not related to another in time, knowledge of probabilities and proclivities of the entire sequence would be necessary to make a good decision.

History, truth, and strategy

Bringing history into strategy is vital for sound decision-making, but it is more likely to be misused than applied correctly. The conviction that history is a guide to the future has significant devotion, and at some level is no doubt valid. But which history shall we pursue as our oracle? What events are relevant and mandate change, and which are outliers to be studied and discarded? There are so many lessons to be learned, it seems, so much serendipity. Worse, from the perspective of the truth-seeker, not only is every conflict different, every situation unique, each is *perceived* differently by the historian or decision maker who examines it. This essential quandary is somewhat awkwardly captured in an unwieldy question. How can we be sure that actions taken today will lead to a tomorrow that looks like the past?

Equally cumbersome, but no less germane: how can we be sure that the past of today looked anything like the today of the past? As time moves on, as it becomes more difficult to put our modern thought-processes and morality aside to truly comprehend the actions and decisions of the past, dominant and accepted interpretations of historical truth emerge and change. Not just across time, but also across systems (cultural, social, and economic) and levels (domestic and international), perceptions will differ. Most confounding is the observation that after all this time, history still has not been settled, and it certainly has not been set. And it probably cannot be made so. Add to this conundrum the researcher's tendency for preoccupation with detail, based upon a misguided belief that the closer and more meticulous the look at history the more likely it is to reflect the truth, and the problem is magnified.

Historians delve ever deeper into the archives of history for numerous reasons, most of them related to the desire to know precisely what happened in this or that place at such and such a time. There is a faith that this type of an investigation is invaluable, a faith I share. But there is a perfidious tendency contained within it that allows the imprudent researcher to move from a necessarily biased investigation in search of broader insight or truth to one that seeks truth in the *un*biased investigation, in the arcane trivia of the archive. The first enhances our understanding of the larger structure of context. The latter trivializes history. It sends us down a critical path of decisions and actions that could not have been different than history requires, as each was a necessary output of the actions and decisions that led to it. And so the researcher is compelled to wade through the vast body of potential evidence and search ever more deeply for the critical moment of decision, the precise fulcrum on which the destiny of humanity is leveraged. The slightest error could bring down an empire; the subtlest tactic could change the course of a war. By ascribing failure or success to a single point or event, the belief is maintained that the more that is (or can be) known about the details of the past situation, the more advantage that can be gained for the present. Somewhere in the record is truth and accuracy, simply waiting to be revealed.

Adherence to such causality must surely ensnare the investigator. If history is the irreproducible product of the decisions and actions of individuals, then any and every moment sets that course anew. No decision is more profound than another, no action more salient. Every event traces a cause and effect trail to minute irrelevance. Such a view denies the magnitude of structural factors that limit the individual agent's options, and partially explains why the student of history sees extraordinary implications in the smallest detail. The master historian rightly shuns such emphasis on minutiae, but the logic is seductive. It is reminiscent of the tale of the king who laments the want of a nail.[41] If only the nail held, the shoe would not have been thrown, the horse would not have gone lame, and the king would have made good his escape. This view is oblivious to the king's no doubt onerous policies and the politico-economic context that triggered the revolt, perhaps a more worthy causal argument for the downfall of a kingdom than shoddy blacksmithing.

The key that unlocks the meticulously cataloged chronography of human events is the philosopher's stone of such tedious research. If that moment of profound decision can be found and reproduced in the present, the modern leader might never lose again. Recreating the genius of Alexander or Scipio would be child's play. Anyone with access to that knowledge could use it as a recipe for action. A feint here, a thrust there, and all is well. Perhaps surprisingly, at the tactical and operational levels, I find little in this logic with which to quarrel. In battle, where victory is the paramount goal, the adaptation of a previously successful procedure or technique may prove fruitful, even decisive. Avoiding the clever traps of a previous campaign is absolutely essential for success. In fact, the more deeply military leaders immerse themselves in the study of past campaigns, the better. Genius flows from experience, even the vicarious experience of books and records.

For the strategist, however, a logical flaw appears from this relentless search for a perfected knowledge of the past. Once we fix or set a version of history, that is, accept it as the true and only interpretation of the past, do we not have to conclude that perfect knowledge of the past predestines the future? If actions taken in the past were the only ones that could have occurred, because any deviation would have brought us to a different present, then at any point in the future we could look back and come to the same conclusion. The events between now and then would have been inevitable. Does that make them inevitable now? The notion seems verified by 'the reversibility [quality] of the laws of physics [which] implies that given the state of a physical system at a particular time, it is always possible to work out uniquely both its future and its past.'[42] A conundrum is provoked that has implications beyond any answer to the manifest question.

If past actions taken in similar situations are guides to future success, and the more complete the knowledge of the past the more sure the victory, then the future is cast. As historian Thomas Hughes is fond of saying, with full awareness of its irony: 'We may not be able to predict the future, but we can probably invent it.'[43] Once the perfect solution to battle or war is worked out, from an investigation of the details, then it must be followed. Any deviation would be irrational. This enchanting possibility would no doubt be quite welcome. With the future a foregone event, war need never be fought. The outcome would be obvious to all. If both sides have the same view of the future, based on a precise and parallel view of the past and present, then the victor will be known in advance. The vanquished will immediately sue for peace, and get the best out of this no-win situation.

The logic of the perfect solution is fine for the tactician, who seeks to put the opponent into a position in which defeat is the only foreseeable outcome, thus making surrender the only rational option. In essence, a *prophecy of future reality is shared* by all parties. Ergo, setting the future into inevitability is a desired and useful concept. In strategy-making, however, with its wider view and structural emphasis, the notion is counterproductive. Countless past decisions and actions are like the one faced now, or like enough, according to the historical interpretation. Some may appear perfectly correlated, but the placement of those past events into the current context—*which is a product of the past and as such is shaped by the awareness and interpretation of past analogous events*—is simply not reproducible. The decisions of the past have placed the decisions of today into a new context, no matter how similar or analogous. The horizon of insight is broader, the intellectual view has expanded, and the assortment of possibilities is increased. Prior events have fundamentally changed the situation faced today at the structural level.

What the strategist sees, instead of discernible individual events *making* history, is the aggregate of innumerable events *shaping* history. Structural forces well up from the multitude of (similar and unique) interactions between agents, and these forces are far more deterministic than any single action (or set of actions) of one agent. To shape structural forces in order to bring about an increase in the number of desirable outcomes from the interactions of many agents is the proper ambition of strategy. Therefore, the strategist does not seek certainty in history, but support from it. History is not a subject to be certified, but a *force to be mobilized*.[44] History in its detail is mastered so that the events of the past can be marshaled in support of an argument or policy. The accuracy of interpretation is not questioned or advocated unless to do so would enhance or refute the point made. History is thus picked and picked through to make a plausible case for a set of actions that will shape future conditions. Interpretation is inherently subject to bias and limitation, and the evidence of history can never be absolutely proclaimed. It is not inviolate. The strategist uses that plasticity to advantage.

The process by which the student of history becomes the master of it is reminiscent of the process of growth and development drawn from the new sciences of chaos and complexity that follow in later sections. Historical detail can be collected and cataloged in perpetuity without the researcher becoming enlightened to master status. Only by making connections between the details does the possibility of complex emergence occur. Not only are the connections between historical details necessary to the process, so too are correlations to policy, politics, technology, and more. An understanding of the world of today and the anticipation of tomorrow combine with an understanding of the past into a network of information that brings *wisdom*, and the ability to act. History that is not applied to the decision-making processes of today will not create the rich web of interactions that allows for the possibility that the student of military history will emerge a strategist.

This notion of interaction and emergence occurs despite the understanding that none of what is thought to be known is universal. This is a crucial distinction for both history and strategy; truth and accuracy are only rarely the same. Facts are not truth, and the truth is only partially factual. Truth is a matter of utility; accuracy is not. This is a difficult assertion for the historian to embrace, but in the sciences it is widely accepted. Niehls Bohr is purported to have 'formalized his difference with Einstein by proposing, only half in jest, an Uncertainty Principle of Scientific Knowledge: ... clarity and truth, are complementary. Increasing one automatically decreases the other.'[45]

A theory is considered *true*—or more properly valid—to the extent that it is *useful*. That is, to the extent to which it aligns our expectations of the future and in this way makes our actions *meaningful*. Experience is thus a filtered familiarity. Accuracy in research and experimentation is sought to refine truth, or utility, but greater truth is in no way the result of greater accuracy. Indeed, as we shall see later, greater accuracy quite often obscures the truth. History—the inextricable entwinement of the researcher's own experience and methods and the experiential bias of the record—can never be simply a collection of inviolate facts, some sort of ultimate truth awaiting full catalog. It is always a construct of the mind, forever open to new interpretation. Facts cannot speak for themselves; they are always spoken for.

To the student, history is minutiae to be remembered for exams. To the master historian and to the strategist, it is a never-ending search for meaning and relevance in a sea of churning data and interpretation. With this inevitable realization, the student's initial reaction is to toss books in the air and curse the futility of study, but there is great benefit as well as promise in this view. It may indeed be that there is no such thing as an historical fact, and if this is so, then there is no limit to the manipulation of history in support of the possible. So the strategist makes of history what is needed, a practice long accepted and understood. Ontologically, fact is a derivative of the Latin verb *factum*, which means to do or to make. A fact, then, is a thing or deed made real in the mind. True history is a narrative of such facts. The master historian uses the narrative to make sense of the decisions or actions that occurred, to give them meaning and to transmit truth. It is never a straightforward or unbiased chronicle of events. It cannot be.

So sure is the preceding axiom that one could say with a straight face the more accurate history or theory is, the less true it is. Truth may be little more than a matter of utility; accuracy is not. History that is studied for meaning and not simply accuracy has the same quality. We could say, for example: 'The temperature at 7:00 am on July 15, 1805, was 78 degrees Fahrenheit. The commanding general of the invading force ate three portions of pickled herring for breakfast. His mess included a complete set of the most expensive Delft porcelain. At his disposal were 6,420 troops from three Maritime Provinces.' Such statements might be perfectly accurate, but are not in themselves particularly useful. The following account is better: 'It was hot that morning, and getting hotter. The general delayed setting off until he finished an elegant breakfast, while his troops stood rigidly in formation, waiting to depart.' The latter description gives a sense of the situation, and the reader is prepared for the analysis of the course of battle that will follow. It foreshadows a relatively poor showing, as the general is uncaring of his troops, and his troops, for their parts, are standing ready while the growing heat is sapping their strength. Clearly the first account is more factual, and less biased, but until the historian places those details into meaningful context, it is trivia. It also shows that bias is not an evil to be shunned. The historian cannot provide *all* of the details of that morning, most of which would be inane (the color of a passing peasant's sandals, numbers of cicadas emerging from seventeen-year hibernation, etc.), and so *chooses* to present the ones deemed most compelling. In this way the reader's perceptions are inevitably shaped and the truth of the battle and its repercussions are passed on.

It is impossible not to show bias when presenting the truth, no matter how much the chronicler attempts to avoid it. If true, then bias is immaterial. Knowing the biases, however, helps to comprehend the truth of the chronicle. It may even be impossible to be objective when simply looking for data. This is because the researcher takes a set of assumptions on a journey into the past. The specific era or event is studied because it is assumed there will be some value in it, or at least some interest. The specific archive or set of information is selected because it is thought important, or simply because it is available. Ultimately, the data a researcher chooses to look at and chronicle is selected on preconceived notions that they will be useful in answering a theoretical question, making the search at least somewhat economical. One does not study sword manufacturing in Damascus when searching for the origins of Iroquois civilization—though one cannot rule it out. Such a researcher would be thought daft. In other words, I think I know why such an event occurred, or at least what may have had an impact; now I must go prove it. And this has great utility in the search for the truth. Unbiased research does not mean that the researcher has no idea what will be found. Quite the opposite, the result is presumed to flow from the data selected for study. It is a rare researcher who, at the end of a lifetime of investigation, declares that no value has come of it. Truly unbiased research and chronicling occurs when the researcher keeps an open mind, acknowledges plausible alternatives, and accepts the truth of contrary evidence. Inevitable bias means that as historians we must rewrite history in our own images, we cannot do otherwise. This is why we should acknowledge that history is no more, and no less, than what we make of it. *Historia facta est.*

Clearly, the fruits of such biased and flawed research have been bountiful—when properly understood. George Santayana put forward the adage that those who fail to learn from history are doomed to repeat it. No doubt, this is true, but the negative emphasis is clear. The *mistakes* of history do not have to be repeated. Learning *can* occur. One does not have to experience putting one's bare hand on a hot stove burner to know that it is an unwise activity—although this experience, too, can have unwanted repercussions. The cat that sits on a hot stove burner will not intentionally do so again; nor is it likely to sit on a cold stove burner. I am in no way suggesting the positive corollary, however, that the successes of history can be recast into the future as some form of roadmap. This is especially so the more one fixates on the historical details associated with events and loses sight of the longer view of history. Indeed, Santayana would have been dismayed at such a conclusion. It is the lessons of history that are emphasized, the conclusions that we draw from an examination of it, not history for itself. A thorough comprehension of the timeline of history and the stories that relate to war and politics, gained through study and reflection, provides a powerful advantage for the strategist, but it is not a guide with which to slavishly adhere. Because a specific decision worked then does not mean that it will work now, or ever again. This distinction has spurred a number of anonymous wags to reverse Santayana's adage and declare that those who study history too carefully are doomed to repeat it.

All of this should impart that history, in all its practiced bias and circuitous interpretation, is of incalculable value to the strategist. The strategist who does not have a firm grounding in the events and lessons of the past is doomed to fail, in precisely the manner Santayana predicted. This crucial point was proved with mathematical precision earlier in this chapter. Decisions made based on an understanding of the current situation and context, no matter how detailed, must be flawed, because the situation that presents itself today is in part a product of the decisions of the past. This is because history itself is one of the structures that bind. The future that the strategist desires to shape is as much a product of the events and perception of events that *have already occurred* (history) as it is of any set of decisions or actions that *will be made.*

This is further consistent with the assertion that the strategist, quite unlike the tactician, should not be constrained or limited by a diminishing number of choices. Instead, the strategist rejects the very notion that choices are limited or the future is set. The strategist perpetually creates fresh options, for there is always another way waiting in the imagination. In the present work, the imagination is not heavily taxed. Rather than recreate the methods described above, I merely shift the approach to one that reasons deductively from theory and principles from one that does so inductively from observation and case. Deductions from theory are then tested against Santayana's lessons of history. If the perceptions of the events of history are not consistent with the theory, then the theory has no utility. It cannot be true. History is not pushed aside; it is harnessed. Historical references are selected for their persuasiveness. Wherever needed, historical interpretation will be used to illuminate and support the argument. But, there will be no effort to validate any particular interpretation of the past, nor any future action demanded by it.

5

PRINCIPLES AND RULES

Actors follow rules [because] rules serve as guides for action.
Friedrich Kratochwil, *Rules, Norms, and Decisions*[1]

The tactician examines events within the limitations of context. The strategist examines the contextual limitations of events. The tactician seeks to settle an issue, to close off further examination with an unassailable or perfect explanation. The perfect plan is analogous to the definitive or ideal historical account. Once established, no further inquiry is needed. The question has been answered. The strategist seeks instead to raise issues, to extend examination continuously, to look at events from a new perspective. Tactical thinkers seek a specific set of actions that, given extant conditions, will force opponents to bend to their will. Strategic thinkers seek the constraining conditions that are most likely to allow such a tactical set of actions to work. Tactical thinkers seek to define and describe situations. Decision-making in a real-time tactical mode requires it. The more knowledge of the limits to conflict, the more creatively the tactical genius can deploy, maneuver, and engage forces. Knowing completely what *cannot* be done allows for an investigation of what *can* be done. This is how the tactician exploits a set of rules to the greatest advantage.

Much of the difference is due to disparate frames of reference. Tactical thinkers seek optimal actions for a given set of circumstances. Their principles and rules are relative or dependent on context. They recognize that what works here may not work there, because no real situation can be precisely replicated. Strategists seek principles that are useful in all situations, regardless of the contextual limits. Their principles are absolute and independent, modified by details of context called rules.

Rules

The power of rules is not that they force behavior but that they constrain and shape it. The master decision maker acts within the limits placed by context, force structure, policy, and morality so as to efficiently and effectively match available means to externally mandated ends. That the ends are mandated from without is essential, lest the tactician fall prey to the Clausewitzian illogic of war. Imagine a military force that sought victory without political guidance. Its application of violence would not be random or uncontrolled. It would be a slave to the logic of war. To maximize such a goal it would engage only when it was sure of winning, and whenever it was sure of winning. Rules allow sense to be made of the context of war. Unconstrained violence is not war; it is senseless. It has no political purpose and therefore no meaning. War without purpose is war without strategy, and while brutal, is irrelevant.

Rules are directives. They simplify decision-making by limiting the factors an agent must take into account. They are economizing devices. Rules are therefore not commands; they are not specific to a situation. They relate to a set of decisions or events by specifying the conditions within which they apply. They are also not inviolate. In the real world, rules can be broken. There is no rule that makes obeying rules mandatory. But this does not invalidate their importance. When rules in war are broken, the winner often cannot be clearly established. Peace is less likely to follow, as there is no enforcement mechanism beyond the sanctions of the state. Breaking rules is not the same as changing them, and rules and decision-making procedures must change over time to cope with shifting circumstance. The set of potential rules that comply with a given principle and its norms is vast.

Nonetheless, it is vitally important to the tactician that the rules do not change during the course of battle, for this will add an undesirable element of surprise. A consistent combat environment that is in accordance with the strengths and knowledge of the tactician is highly desired, and nominally expected. Even in the situation where the outmatched agent decides to break the rules in an attempt to gain an advantage of surprise, it is done so on the expectation that the stronger agent will be anticipating compliance. The stronger agent is stronger precisely because of the extant structure of rules and context, and should not desire rule changes. Within the rules and expectations of warfare, an attempt to surprise the other is done because there is a gap in knowledge on the other side, a way of acting within the rules that is unknown to the other. This is an exploitation of the other's weakness, however, and is not true change or surprise. It is tactical mastery asserting itself.

The tactician is comfortable when knowledge of the situation is complete. When all rules are understood and none are violated, the planning process is precise. Changes in the rules or boundaries in mid-campaign are frustrating, and often considered illegitimate. Victory would have occurred, it will be argued, if not for the meddling of the politicians. The military's hands were bound unfairly. While this is an understandable view, it is flawed. The rules in war always change. The strategist is comfortable with the knowledge that rules are constantly in flux, and instead of matching capabilities to ends within given limits, acts to modify the limits. Indeed, should the master tactician's desire for complete predictability and control be achieved, the strategist has no place. When the war plan has been worked to the smallest detail, such that any deviation would be disastrous, strategy is set aside. Change is unacceptable and certainty takes over. This is one of the more accepted interpretations for the cause of Word War I. States had locked themselves into a complicated set of binding rules (in the form of treaties) and subordinated independent decision-making to rail-based mobilization tables.[2]

Expecting and adapting to change is the essence of the strategic thinker's planning. Indeed, *without at least the possibility of change there is no strategy:* to plan for a continuance of the present condition in perpetuity is not strategy; it is either ignorance or foolishness. Logically, it eliminates the role of the strategist. If the future will be like the past, then the boundaries are set and immutable. The more we know about the past the more we can predict the future. Master tacticians need expect no surprises, no meaningful change, and can hone their craft in a study of past battles and in simulations. Only the pressures of combat cannot be fully experienced. But this is the essence of the chess master's dominance. Through study, practice, and knowledge of the rules, everything important is already known.

Of course, rules, conditions, and boundaries always change in the course of war, despite the master tactician's efforts to control or eliminate the impact of change. Unexpected variations in the weather can scuttle the best of plans, as can the sudden appearance of reinforcements not expected for another week. It is a standard military adage that no plan of battle survives contact with the enemy. The tactician cannot plan for the unexpected (by definition), and so prepares for the probable. This may be an unavoidable effect of the regime of military command, an output of design. Military planning requires commanders to obey and carry out orders, and to improvise only within carefully defined boundaries. It is expected that junior officers and NCOs will carry out their duties in the manner in which they have been trained. Anything else would lead to surprise, and while tactical surprise by the enemy is not desirable, surprising behavior by subordinates is egregious. Only when the lower command levels are cut off from superiors or are operating independently are they expected to adapt to conditions freely, to change operating procedures, and then only within the boundaries of pre-established rules.

This is the situation where strategic leadership is most readily identifiable, at the highest levels of command (the general staff and governing command authority), where there is room to challenge even the boundaries of war. The fewer levels above the decision maker, the more latitude to improvise, change, and manipulate the boundaries. Moreover, the strategist discovers artistry in situations of war and crisis, when change and surprise are endemic. To say that great strategists are rare is less accurate than to say they are uncommon.

Principles, regimes, and values in the constitution of action

There has been a great deal of intimation that rules and principles have an intrinsically crucial role for the strategist. The import will be more salient as we move into information warfare applications, but as these notions pervade the exposition of pure strategy, a fuller review is warranted. The master tactician takes rules as given, and works within them to demonstrate genius. To be sure, tactical genius and creativity are not stifled by rules. They are *enabled* by them. A game of chess, for example, would be completely uninteresting, even futile, if there were no rules. Creative genius would have no place to flourish. A game would be won by the person who takes the first move, probably by tossing the chessboard with its pieces off the table. But within the very strict rules of chess, true genius does emerge, as centuries of grand masters demonstrate.

The same is true of the relationship between art and craft. In the beginning of the artist's education, the emphasis is on colors, techniques, composition, and precision. Only when the apprentice has learned basic skills of artistry is it possible to break through traditional boundaries and achieve art. Most students never do, and yet good crafters are in no less demand than the extraordinarily few geniuses that emerge to change the esthetics of art forever, for artisanship is valued in itself—often more so than the work of the artist. A master artisan will always be in demand, creating a vision of perfection that is preferred by society in the manner it has come to expect. There is great value in the perfectly rendered form. A masterfully executed craft is a thing of tremendous beauty. True art is always unexampled, but much that is unexampled is not fit to be hung on a wall. Great art endures, and is copied.

Rules represent the physical, moral, and political means by which the tactician pursues ends. They are limits to absolute behavior, and are constraining to the extent that certain actions cannot be taken, while others must be accomplished. Within those limits, however, means can fulfill goals in an infinite variety of ways, much as the chess master takes the few rules and pieces of the chessboard to create an endless array of possibilities within the game. Moreover, without limits, or constraining rules, there can be no concept of victory. A win is the fulfillment of conditions within the boundaries established. Without rules, a winner cannot be determined or even agreed upon, and a war cannot be ended by mutual understanding or surrender.

The impact of rules and principles on behavior and expectations is summed in the concept of regime. Regimes describe the structure within which the agent operates, and the relationship between regimes and war behavior is fundamental to understanding the role of pure strategy. Regimes are the body of rules and normative values that describe a structure within which agents operate. All social behavior is patterned and ultimately conventionalized. The explicit and implicit usage, customs, conventions, norms, and laws that result lead to expectations of future behavior, and of reprimand for deviations from ongoing practice. Behavior patterns coincide with and generate recognized norms and principles, which in turn justify rules and decision-making procedures. Whether established by repeated interactions over time, coercion, or calculations of self-interest, regimes recognize, legitimize, and reinforce patterned behavior. In this way, a distinction is made between structure (regime) and agent (individuals acting within the constraints of the regime).

Regimes, as they are commonly understood today, are conceptually well established, but were clearly presaged by Clausewitz in his analysis of war. He developed a structure that began with laws (see Figure 5.1), 'a relationship between things and their effects ... a determinant of action ... synonymous with *decree* and *prohibition*.'[3] Laws are the equivalent of policy, and as such reside at the apex of the strategy pyramid. They are followed by principles, which 'represent the spirit and the sense of the law.'[4] They assist the decision maker 'where the diversity of the real world cannot be contained within the rigid form of law.'[5] Principles allow room for judgment, and are of two types: objective principles that are valid for all (resting on a sense of universal truth), and subjective ones that apply only to the specific decision maker. Rules fall within the purview of principles, and become the 'means' of action, the ability to participate within established principles: 'Rules in a game are like this.'[6] Alongside rules, Clausewitz places regulations and directions, 'dealing with a mass of minor, more detailed circumstances, too numerous and too trivial for general laws.'[7] These are *ad hoc*, established by circumstance and contingency, but within the spirit of the laws and principles. Finally is method, or mode of procedure, which is useful in that it leads to routine, repetitive, common action that is 'prescribed by method rather than by general principles or individual regulation.'[8] Such 'methodical procedure should be designed to meet the most probable cases. Routine is not based on definite individual preferences, but rather on the *average probability* of analogous cases.'[9]

The distinctions are part of Clausewitz's intense separation of political and military logic, and preference for civilian control over the military. This is apparent in that no aspect of military operation rises to the level of law. The setting of law (policy) is a function outside the military realm. It is recognized or made by the highest political authority and bounds the actions of the military forces. But the rest are vital to sound command. An example of a 'tactical principle' is that 'firearms should not be used until the enemy is within effective range.'[10] Even this sound truth is tested in individual situations, and must be evaluated as appropriate. Principles and rules, then, fall within the purview of the commander, who interprets and applies them as need arises. Regulations and methods are the structure within which non-commissioned officers (NCOs) conduct training and education. These are passed on from the commander; they 'represent the dominance of principles and rules, carried through to actual application.'[11]

Stephen Krasner, who has done more than any other theorist to develop the notion and explain the relevance of regimes to the academic community, describes regimes as: 'Principles, norms, rules, and decision-making procedures around which actor expectations converge in a given issue area.'[12] The four characteristics are arrayed in a strict top-down hierarchy: 'Principles,' he writes, 'are beliefs of fact, causation, and rectitude. Norms are standards of behavior defined in terms of rights and obligations. Rules are specific prescriptions or proscriptions for action. Decision-making procedures are prevailing practices for making and implementing collective choice.'[13]

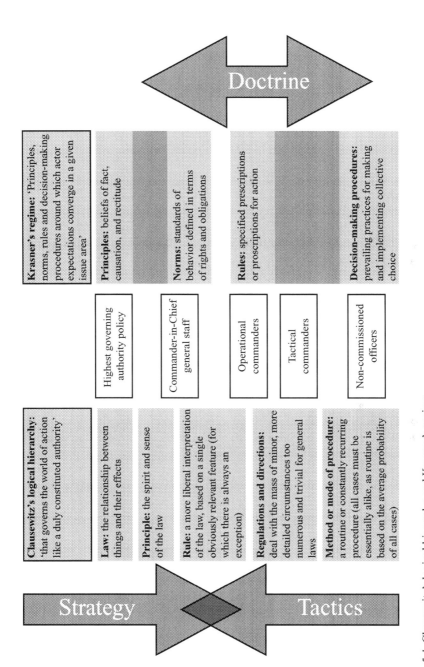

Doctrine

Krasner's regime: 'Principles, norms, rules and decision-making procedures around which actor expectations converge in a given issue area'

Principles: beliefs of fact, causation, and rectitude

Norms: standards of behavior defined in terms of rights and obligations

Rules: specified prescriptions or proscriptions for action

Decision-making procedures: prevailing practices for making and implementing collective choice

Highest governing authority policy

Commander-in-Chief general staff

Operational commanders

Tactical commanders

Non-commissioned officers

Clausewitz's logical hierarchy: 'that governs the world of action like a duly constituted authority'

Law: the relationship between things and their effects

Principle: the spirit and sense of the law

Rule: a more liberal interpretation of the law, based on a single obviously relevant feature (for which there is always an exception)

Regulations and directions: deal with the mass of minor, more detailed circumstances too numerous and trivial for general laws

Method or mode of procedure: a routine or constantly recurring procedure (all cases must be essentially alike, as routine is based on the average probability of all cases)

Strategy **Tactics**

Figure 5.1 Clausewitz's logical hierarchy and Krasner's regime

81

Regimes structure political arrangements. Their purpose is to enhance or facilitate all interactions, but most especially negotiation, bargaining, and —ideally—cooperation. In this definition, regimes can be implicit or explicit, and the issue areas can be specified or limited. Krasner further notes the difference between regimes, which are intended to be lasting structures, and international agreements or treaties, which are often *ad hoc* and conditional on an exclusive set of ongoing behaviors and circumstances. Over time, the latter are overcome by events, and, *rebus sic stantibus,* fall from use. Successful regimes adapt to changing conditions and can conform practice through habituation. Expectations of future actions are predictable and, over time, behavior changes.

Regimes are thus intended to be more than a substitute or expediency for short-term self-interest. They imply a continuing area of agreement and cooperation. Too commonly we mistake regimes for the functioning bodies and bureaucracies associated with them, and lose sight of the regime as a process for cooperation. The World Trade Organization (WTO), for example, is not a regime. It is part of a regime, the embodiment of the rules and decision-making procedures that structure an international system's adherence to principles and norms associated with free trade theory. For those who believe (in principle) that all states can gain from free trade, behavior should be guided by the *norm,* among several others, that tariffs and other trade barriers should be gradually reduced and ultimately eliminated. Within that mandate, the WTO is established to monitor rules adherence, provide a forum for agreement, and an adjudicating body for trade disputes. The WTO is no more than a set of rules and decision-making procedures established by a voluntary association of states working to make real the principles and norms of a liberal world free trade system.

Likewise, the United Nations is not a regime in and of itself. It is the manifestation of a belief (*principle*) that national or individual state sovereignty can best be achieved through collective means (a permanent coalition opposed to aggression), structured within the norms of open negotiation and constant vigilance. *Rules* and *decision-making procedures* (international agreements and the physical presence of the UN as a negotiating, public forum) can be formulated in a variety of ways that comply with the extant principles and norms of a regime, and so changes or modifications in the agreements/institutions do not overturn—though they can seriously weaken—the regime itself. Changes in principles or norms, however, do require acceptance or establishment of a new regime. Should the principle that all states are sovereign be revoked over time or by circumstance, the United Nations as an organization would crumble.

Although it is more difficult to isolate regimes in war, these too are quite evident when one knows where to look. Article One of the UN Treaty affirms the principle of collective security as the basis for world peace. If a large enough coalition can band together and agree to collectively repel an attack against any member, then war should be deterred. This requires the *norms* that participating states are both willing and able to come to the assistance of other members, and the *rules* and *decision-making procedures* that determine, among others, if an attack has occurred, how much each member is obligated to provide in the defense of the attacked state, which nations shall control the coalition forces, and the like.

That the UN security regime has been arguably ineffective in preventing or deterring most wars is blamed mostly on the rules and decision-making procedures that allow any of the five permanent members of the Security Council to veto an effort to act in defense of the victim member. It is interesting to note that despite the dysfunctional attributes of the rules and decision-making procedures of the body, they are still infused with normative significance and support after 50 years in force.

George H. Bush recognized this durability when he attempted to restructure the principles of war in a speech to Congress on March 6, 1991. He declared that a New World Order had emerged in the aftermath of the US-led coalition to restore Kuwaiti sovereignty in Operation Desert Storm. The UN's dysfunction had been aggravated by the occasion of one member state attacking another. Though the rules and decision-making procedures of the UN remained intact, Bush was making the argument that the realist principle of collective security had been replaced by the idealist notion that aggression is wrong in principle. No state should need to be a member of a coalition to enhance its security. Its recognized sovereignty should be enough that all states come to the aid of the attacked state. This is coherent with the democratic polity that accepts passionate dissent and argument in domestic political disputes, but condemns the first to resort to violence in the process.

Regime theory has powerful explanatory capacity, but is often chided in the case of war as being a meaningless overlay, a set of agreements that hold no real sway in crises. Kenneth Waltz, for example, has argued that the only consequential difference between states is in their capabilities, specifically the amount of power each holds relative to the others.[14] This neo-realist view of international politics is a powerful and compelling theory. States will interact at a variety of levels and with an assortment of means, this view holds, but when push comes to shove the *ultima ratio* determining their interactions is the capacity to wield violence. Thucydides' assertion that 'the strong do as they will, and the weak suffer what they must,' is the foundational concept.[15] In this view, the actions of states are easy to discern, at least in retrospect, when better knowledge of power capabilities is determined. States are further said to operate in consistent ways when dealing with others.

This alternative perception is very much a Newtonian physical worldview, where state interactions are likened to those of billiard balls in a game of snooker. Force adjusted by angle equals reaction. Because of the power of such analogies, a later chapter will describe the impact of science and scientific theory on modern strategy. If the logic of quantum theory is a better analogy for strategy than Newtonian concepts, then the *pattern* of interactions will have a much greater explanatory value than a strict capabilities-based nodal analysis. The new sciences may in fact be the key to understanding and harnessing truly emergent behavior at the systemic level of international relations. At this juncture, however, regime theory helps to make sense of those interactions. It is the *network* that determines power relationships, and network behavior is governed by principles and rules.

It is perhaps difficult to see the development of the international network. Its agents (states) are cumbersome, and interactions between them can take place over months and years—even generations. It requires a macro-historic view to discern emergent characteristics of the system from the pattern of behavior over thousands of years.[16] Analysis is difficult to portray in the abstract, and an abstract justification of regime-based behavior over power-based behavior is difficult to make precise. To assist in any investigation of the relationship between agent and structure, however, we can apply insights gained from analyses of the economic market. Both the international system and the free market are described as decentralized decision-making structures, with an associated disbursement of power to the maximum number of agents. The agent in microeconomic analysis is the individual; interactions take place repeatedly and quickly, and clusters of interactions form markets.

The economic free market, according to most economists, spontaneously emerges wherever individuals come into increasingly varied contact. Specialization at the agent level appears when trade advantages are evident. The natural condition of man is therefore *homo economicus*. Political and social scientists should mostly disagree. Not only are the two satisfying conditions of the free market—no one can be prevented from entering the market and no one can dictate the terms of exchange—impossible without a governing authority to ensure compliance, without the cultural and social norms that allow for a common language with which to communicate, a common value system for trade (to include precisely what can be owned), and a common understanding of the rights of individuals against theft, the market *cannot* be established. Moreover, without a money system to move the trade network beyond barter, and a property rights adjudicator (law) with the power to punish those who do not follow the social norms of trade by reneging on contracts made (including thievery), the free market cannot be maintained. In this view, the natural condition of man is *homo politicus*.

We can easily imagine the result of an economic system spontaneously emerging based on the more dishonorable traits of humanity that would still comply with the economist's minimal market requirements of individuals freely entering into agreements that are mutually advantageous. When a robber wields a weapon and demands of another, 'your property, or your life,' the victim has an opportunity to make a rational choice. An economic exchange occurs when the property is handed over. The robber is richer and the victim is alive. Both are arguably better off. But such activity is not likely to establish a market, much less a regime, even where 'the interaction occurs repeatedly and all participants share the same expectations.'[17] This is because the vital requirement of shared norms of proper behavior is not evident, and the economic system that would emerge is anarchy.

Ordered behavior is the result of properly constituted regimes, and whether they inform free market or collective security behavior, they must be based in established principles and norms. These can be created top down, in which the principles are established first and rules are devised to assist in compliance, or from the bottom up, when standards of practice become infused with normative value. Long-standing practices, even when established out of self-interest, quickly lead to shared expectations about what will happen. The shared expectation component then leads to an understanding of what ought happen. Routine behavior becomes infused with moral or normative value. The case of driving on the right side of the road is an example. Rather arbitrarily established (it could have been right or left, depending on local custom) to prevent collisions, agents follow the rule in their own self-interest. It has a practical personal value. Over time, it became a social value. Today, when we see someone driving on the wrong side of the road, our initial reaction is that the person is intoxicated, or otherwise acting irrationally, against the common good. On an open road where visibility is clear for miles, and there are no other travelers in sight, it still *feels wrong* to drive on the left side.

So strong is this tendency that a pattern of behavior initially established by economic coercion or force may ultimately come to be regarded as legitimate, even by those upon whom it has been imposed. Taxes are the most obvious of these, but there are many examples. In the midst of the oil crises of 1973, the US Congress tied federal highway funding to a requirement that states impose a maximum speed limit of 55 mph. Most states complied quickly, but some held out until roads were in such poor shape that residents demanded compliance. State police enforced the new limits, and gradually but significantly, the driving habits of the country changed. In the midst of oil gluts in the late 1980s, pressure mounted to raise the speed limits on the argument that strict conservation was constraining economic growth. The counter-argument, after less than two decades of habituation, was most persuasive on a normative basis. The lower speed limit saved lives, proponents claimed. It had value in itself.

Rules that are arbitrarily constructed will not withstand the interactions of time if they are not associated with normative values and principles. This is simply because '… it is the function of norms to fortify socially optimal solutions against the temptations of individually rational defections.'[18] The logic extends to war, and the notion that deterrence, for example, could work without common understanding is as foolish as the one which insists a free market develops independent of social and political standards:

> Precisely because deterrence is a psychological relationship between the contestants, a common universe of meaning is crucial for its proper functioning. When deterrence fails, [it is] because one actor did not believe the other would retaliate, because he hoped [he] could remain undetected, [etc.] … Note in this context that 'irrational' actors like terrorists cannot be deterred and that therefore a strategy of deterrence crucially depends upon normative understandings.[19]

Regimes are thus best understood as problem-solving or decision-making devices for dealing with political and social issues that recur. That the issues are socio-political is necessary. Wherever one agent is making decisions in the process of achieving goals or aims in the absence of other actors doing the same, there would be no need for a normative component in that actor's calculation. The agent would simply self-maximize. But wherever one actor's pursuit of self-maximization conflicts with another's, there will be conflict or potential conflict of interest. Only in a world without scarcity could multiple agents interact with pure self-maximizing behavior and not inevitably come into disagreement. Such a world does not exist. Some coping devices must be implicitly or explicitly established to determine what is mine and what is yours, or perpetual conflict will result. Regimes in their simplest form are social devices aimed at reducing conflict and/or enhancing cooperation. Regimes facilitate such behavior by pointing agents to acceptable actions. Regimes provide specific guidance to integrate individuals into the network or society in which they function. They do this by providing essential knowledge and mechanisms for reducing uncertainty.

Regimes tend to propagate essential and shared information to all, and in so doing help make 'actions conform to predictable patterns so that contemplated actions can go forward with some hope of achieving a rational relationship between means and ends.'[20] One of the most difficult barriers to negotiation and conciliation is information disparity between parties. This is especially difficult across the socio-political and cultural divides that separate states, but it is readily described in the common experience of purchasing a car. It is obvious that the side that has the most knowledge about the particular vehicle has the most leverage. Mileage, accident history, and the like; all of these affect the car's value. The seller wants to know the maximum amount the buyer is willing (or able) to pay, and the buyer wants to know the minimum the seller is willing to take. If one side even imagines that the other is withholding important information, it makes a mutually beneficial deal very difficult to reach. So what is the solution? Savvy car sellers provide information to buyers. Most reputable dealerships have Blue Books readily available, some will provide third party verification of vehicle history, and many (since the information is readily available on the Internet) will provide the dealer invoice on new cars. All of this is designed to make the buyer feel comfortable that the price paid is reasonable. The dealer needs to make a profit to stay in business, and with perfect openness from both sides, an agreement can be reached that is considered fair. When done in this manner, the dealer can expect to have a repeat customer who tells friends and acquaintances of the positive experience.

This is a far cry from the stereotypical used car salesman who assures the buyer that an automobile was driven only on Sundays by a little old lady going to and from church. The problem of such unbalanced information is that it is most likely to appear when dishonest behavior provides the possibility of gaining a large advantage. So much so that the more advantageous dishonest behavior is, the more likely the attempt to suppress or control accurate information.

Conversely, the more available accurate information is, the less incentive for dishonest behavior. This is an extremely useful insight for operations in war and conflict, and is the basis for the existence of national intelligence agencies and their activities. Where conflict exists or is expected, the maximum effort to gain accurate information about the opponent while hiding accurate information about oneself—or disseminating incorrect information—is a standard practice. The problem is, all conflict is not war, and all wars are not total. The more states attempt to conceal accurate information, the more likely conflict becomes, and in the event of conflict, the less likely it will be to find a suitable or mutually agreeable solution.

Regimes do not cure all ills. Agreements and treaties are not always respected. Some states and individuals will enter into agreements they have no intentions of keeping. Others find loopholes that allow them to abide by the letter of the agreement but not its spirit. By increasing openness and information, however, regimes can assist in identifying agents that persist in manipulating the system for dishonest gain.

Rules, choice, and action

As we shall see in the discussion of chaos and complexity, the behavior of complex adaptive systems can be explained by an individual agent's adherence to simple rules, but the rules that guide the behavior of individual agents do not manifest themselves at higher levels. The extraordinary variation of *emergent* behaviors cannot be predicted in advance, but what is apparent is that the rules guiding behavior at the micro level do not transfer intact to the macro one. As rule behavior becomes layered ever higher, the depth of rule adherence in individual agents is so powerful that from at least Aristotle on, philosophers and scientists have consistently argued that the world itself is but an ideal, a mere representation of the real and not reality itself.

This metaphysical abstraction has meaningful ramifications for the real world. Choice is a profoundly social function. Animals that operate on instinct do so at a subconscious level of stimulus and response; their reactions are hard-wired. Human beings have limited instinctual mandates, and most if not all of these can be overcome or denied in social or political settings. While it takes enormous personal fortitude, a soldier *can* overcome the instinct to cower or run from an artillery barrage. The mechanism that allows such control over instinct is the construction of an abstracted world of ideas and ideals. Since they are not continuously impelled to action by internal stimuli (instinct), human beings must consciously and incessantly make *choices*.[21] Instinct has an influence, to be sure, but only humans are truly *responsible* for their actions.

Socrates argued that the difference between human and animal was the capacity for speech. In this, he meant more than the physical requirement of making a variety of sounds. Many species of birds can be taught to mimic the words of people, for instance, but only people have the capacity to transfer ideas and concepts

87

through *language*. And language is the key to transferring or communicating knowledge *in the absence of direct experience*. Not only does language allow me to transcend the present, that is, to tell stories of the past and to project them into the future, it allows me to *learn* from the experience and wisdom of others. But to do so I must learn and adopt the basic rules of language, rules that cannot be derived from nature.

Language is *emergent behavior*. Its manifestation cannot be predicted from the many interactions of primitive humans, the components of a complex adaptive system of biological interrelationships. When the number of individuals is small, and encounters with strangers are rare, the communication requirements of the group are few. Basic signs and symbols can express anger, satisfaction, hunger, and the like. Indeed, this is common with pack animals. But as the number of individuals increases, and interactions with strangers or outside groups become common, instinctively derived norms and rules of interaction are insufficient for expanded cooperation and development. In order for communication to occur in a meaningful sense, language emerges to accommodate the group's needs. To work efficiently, all language requires the existing norm of a desire to cooperate and to share experiences, and a relatively stable set of linguistic rules.

Language is one of the first and most powerful constrictors *and* enablers of human capacity precisely because of its clearly understood rules of use. The rules of language are more than a level of abstraction above nature, however. They incorporate and reinforce the principles and norms of the group and then propel understanding and belief coincident with them. Abstractions from reality are then introduced: a danger I cannot see, for example, a time that is not now, a place that is not here. The notion of the *other* as a thinking, rational being is enforced. The experience of the other can be shared, because I can see myself in the description the other provides. When the interactions among speakers of this rudimentary language are increased, the abstraction of the world increases. We begin to describe emotions, rather than simply show them, and then to describe shared values: pride, anger, delight, to honor, loyalty, and courage. Concepts now completely removed from instinct have emerged, and then *the word becomes the deed*. We promise, forbid, consent, demand, agree, threaten, apologize, persuade, praise, authorize, and appoint. These 'speech acts' are real only because they are based on shared normative values.[22] In language, we have completed the full abstraction from reality.

We accept the rules of language in order to cooperate more fully with others. We are not forced to obey them, nor are we compelled to use certain syntax. We simply agree to do so, and if the benefits are worth the cost of learning, we accept them. By the time we have reached higher levels of emergent behavior, we tend to forget how arbitrary the rules of language must have been when they were established, and ultimately our relationship with the world becomes not a direct, sensual experience, but a filtered one, a mere description of the world. By then, we find ourselves thinking in words. We make sense of the world in words. We no longer are controlled by our emotions and instincts; we can choose to do otherwise. We have created the possibility of freedom by bounding our intellects in a rule structure.

The arbitrary structure of the unenforceable rules of language has demonstrated its power. It shapes the way we think. We started language to increase cooperation and communicate our values. We end up with language at least partially determining our values, often without our knowledge of it being done. It seems like an extravagant claim, but a simple thought experiment verifies the process. What might our values be if our language was constructed in a manner that had no possessive form?[23] Imagine describing events thus: instead of stating 'I hit my thumb with a hammer,' the correct grammatical construction would be, 'I hit the thumb with a hammer.' Social relations would not be exempt. Instead of asking for 'my mother,' I would call out for 'the mother,' or 'the mother of me.' The last allows for the personal identification needed for the taking on of social obligation and responsibility, for example, 'I did it,' or 'you did it for me.' In this construction, I would be unable to convey the more complex possessive notion 'you took my shirt, give it back,' but could state: 'you are transporting the shirt I was wearing, I would prefer to wear it some more.' In such a world, would I even be able to *conceive* of the notion of ownership? Would property rights, the defining of which Nobel laureate Douglass North argues is the foundational explanation of understanding political history, be nonexistent?[24] Imagine the potential for shaping human behavior simply by manipulating the rules of language.

Rules can be embedded so far down in our understanding of how the world is that we may not even be aware they are shaping our thoughts. In the case of words-as-deeds, we recognize that every instance of such speech acts has a normative component. When I make a promise, I am obliged to keep it. When I utter, 'I do,' in a wedding ceremony, I have taken on the obligation of spouse, and have agreed to the rules and norms that define the association of marriage. Without the underlying *values* associated with these words, they would make no sense. Unlike rules, which are often arbitrary and are stated in absolute terms of 'must do' or 'must not do,' principles and norms are *value-structuring,* and so are stated in terms of 'ought' and 'should.'[25] This form of value-structuring takes place at a minimum of two levels of abstraction above instinct.

Highlighting the cooperative basis of abstraction, Friedrich Kratochwil points out that 'individuals resort to norms when they make a promise, but not when they make a threat ... as opposed to rules which prescribe [or proscribe] certain *actions*, values inform the *attitudes* of actors.'[26] The latter appeals to base instinct and emotions, the former are only possible within the context of emergent properties in communication and language. Promises emphasize the choice capacity of individuals, highlighting the power of the other, whereas threats are most effective when they eliminate meaningful choice. Kratochwil further distinguishes the difference between value-infused and arbitrary language with the terms 'command' and 'commandment.'[27] Commands are situation-specific, and the likelihood of obeisance is based in an understanding of authority mechanisms, which can be normative-based but can be arbitrary (as when one obeys in an attempt to curry favor with the other). Commandments show evidence of rule-like adherence to a value or normative structure, and are applicable to a broad range or class of events. With these examples, the realm of the strategist comes into focus. True strategic power is the capacity to manipulate *shared understanding* of rules, norms, and other boundaries that set the parameters of action.

When we insert rule-based behavior into the context of decision-making, the inherent notion of a rational actor choosing to maximize benefits becomes contradictory. Even where we begin with the assumption that self-interested agents choose and act based on internal preferences, in a world of scarcity and a clear understanding that they will have to interact with other similarly motivated agents in the future, we find ourselves at a loss to explain most observed social interactions. Without an understanding of the rules that assist the actors in anticipating future conditions, and of the principles and norms that establish the context for which they accept those rules, rational actor theory is by itself unsatisfying. Principles, norms, and rules give meaning to choice and actions, for 'it is largely the underlying rule or norm and not the observable overt behavior which gives a customary practice its recognizability and coherence.'[28]

Principle and norm constrained rules guide the behavior of rational actors seeking to maximize goal achievement, but they also allow other actors to make sense of the choices and actions taken. The normative structure that bounds the rules provides not only the general guidance of what ought to be done, but a framework for evaluating the array of options that allow the actor to determine how best a thing is to be done. It further provides the framework for assessment, both before and after the decision or action, that can be shared with others for criticism, justification, and reasoning processes—judgment. The situation must be commonly understood and the mitigating factors interpreted. The deliberation that led to the decision, choice, or action is the basis of assessment, and would not be understandable without the normative structure that shaped it.

Without the structure, our deliberative processing would be overwhelmed by data and information. Agents would act impulsively, react reflexively, and pursue goals with single-minded self-interest. Cooperation would be mandated by the situation and by instinct, much as occurs in the behavior of pack animals. But language, which is a set of rules and operating procedures, allows the mutual and efficient transmission of intent, preference, reasoning, and critique. The capacity to reason within a set of symbols makes it possible to generate options and choose among them in a way that refutes the pure matching of ends and means in rational choice theories, as well as for pure strategists.

The normative structure with its rules of logic and grammar allows extremely complex interactions to occur at the level of abstract thought. This includes the notion of causes that do not empirically precede actions, a situation often deemed invalid by behavioralists, as this requires an explanation that cannot be derived from output alone. In the theoretical statement, 'if x, then y,' x must occur before y. The variables must first be temporally linked before they can be causally linked— a reasonable and convincing argument for how or why x causes b satisfies this condition.

But norms and rules do not function like causes. The explanation that is required is complex, and subject to individual interpretation. Consider the case of causal explanations of death in a murder trial. 'The defense attorney blames jealousy, [whereas] the coroner claims it was the entrance of a knife between the fourth and fifth ribs on the left side' that caused the victim's demise. Either way, 'what we accept as adequate explanation obviously depends on our interests and upon the context and roles that we consider to be germane to our assessment.'[29] Norms and rules set standards that allow actions to be understood in a setting that extends well beyond cause and effect.

If *reasons* can be *causes*, that is, an action is taken because a favorable outcome is projected from it, or an unfavorable one can be avoided, it is generally impossible to determine from observation alone. We might see the leader of one state moving military force away from a disputed territory because of the *expected* reaction of an opposing leader. Perhaps the leader wishes to curry favor with the other, or signal a desire to negotiate. From an external point of observation, if the other responds in like fashion, and removes forces from the disputed region as well, we might argue successfully that the initial action was rational. But if the other took the opportunity to occupy the disputed territory, would we then have to argue that the first move was irrational? From observed actions alone, how would we know the true intent of either actor? Rule-based activity allows for interpretations of actions that go beyond the future intent rationale of the self-interested actor. Kratochwil asserts that

> it would be odd to say that a person who missed his/her train thereby 'refuted' the explanation that he/she intended to catch it ... when we explain an action in terms of an underlying norm, a counterfactual observation will usually not impel us to consider the norm invalid.[30]

An analysis of context based solely on observable facts or data is likely to be misinterpreted, quite badly, by the onlooker. Imagine an outside observer from a distant time or place, with no knowledge of the norms and rules involved, trying to *explain* a wedding ceremony. There is a great deal of standing and sitting, apparently timed to music, ritualized exchanges of persons and gifts, and the pelting with rice of two of the primary participants who narrowly escape by a combustion-powered vehicle. We would have *accurately* described the event but could not possibly have understood it. Now imagine trying to understand the game of football without knowing the rules and norms that guide it.[31] The regular transition that occurs repetitively from relatively ordered behavior to seemingly chaotic violence, and then back to order, would be maddening. Strategy and tactics are equally baffling without knowledge of the normative structure and the rules that constrain behavior within them. The same could be said for a description of a boxing match, a North American Indian counting coup, or respect of Swiss neutrality.

The obvious statement that the norms and rules of war are not, and cannot, be enforced, does not denigrate the capacity of those boundaries to determine behavior. For rules to be useful, they must be agreed to. Though the calculation may be heavily influenced by the threats and actions of others, nothing can make state decision makers abide by the terms of a treaty except their assessment of the value of doing so. A prime example is the Geneva Convention rules regarding treatment of prisoners in war. Are these all calculations of self-interest? The convention is based on 1922 standards of civilized (European) behavior, but has remained largely robust. Still, the undeniable fact is that some states abide by the rules more consistently and humanely than others. If it is in my interest to treat prisoners humanely on the condition that my opponent does so, what is the rationale for abiding by the rules when the opponent does not? In this case, the strategist will do so *especially* when the opponent does not. This will provide the condition of continuing advantage so carefully sought. If the enemy's forces anticipate that they will be treated well if captured, they will be less willing to fight vigorously in a tactically lost situation; they will surrender. If, on the other hand, my forces expect they will be tortured upon capture, they may fight harder even as the tactical situation deteriorates.

Regimes guide and shape behavior because of the normative association between rules and principles. One of the more compelling sets of rules in the military sphere is doctrine. These rules adhere to the principle of achieving military (tactical) victory by standardizing training and operations. The normative basis behind them is the belief that the best summary knowledge of the techniques and standards of military operations are compiled there, based on the experience and wisdom of the best military practitioners and theorists. Without that faith, that belief in the wisdom of doctrine, adherence to it would be based on rote training and discipline, both of which would be suboptimal.

For rules like doctrine to have an *independent* impact on the conduct of war, they must be widely accepted as the codification of the best or state-of-the-art knowledge available. The essence of nuclear deterrence strategy was accepted because the best minds of political and social science applied their collective wisdom to it. Acceptable levels of noncombatant casualties in war were radically altered in the US military after the debut of stealth technology increased the precision and lethality of aerial bombardment. Once it becomes possible, even just in theory, to hit what one aims at, then one becomes morally liable for missing.

In the main, regimes have an independent effect on agent actions because they reduce the transaction cost of making decisions. This is how they enhance cooperation, even cooperation in the deadliest of social activities, war. By establishing acceptable limits, the decision maker reduces the panoply of options to be considered. By choosing doctrinal solutions, the decision maker also limits personal liability in the case that events turn out badly. By establishing acceptable limits, regimes also highlight the act of deviation. This is called transparency. Agents that become known for abiding by the regime are rewarded with reduced costs for future cooperation. Agents can expect another who has a history of abiding by the rules to continue to do so. The dividend is called trust. On the other hand, an agent who has broken the rules will find the cost of cooperation in future endeavors has increased. For this reason, one breaks with doctrine only under the most compelling circumstances. Tactical success may be enough to regain the confidence of peers and commanders (recall MacArthur's unsubstitutable victory), and may even cause a change in doctrine, but failure will engender the harshest response.

For the most part, doctrine creates an economy of scale in decision-making. It reduces uncertainty and increases information flow. It helps in the latter by filtering out and then funneling in relevant information. Regimes, principles, and rules shape and in many ways determine behavior. Within the structure of regimes are allowances for individual initiative and action, and the tactician makes the most of these opportunities. By shaping and manipulating the conditions, however, the true genius of the strategist emerges.

6

CHAOS, COMPLEXITY, AND WAR

The crucial skill was insight, the ability to see connections.
M. Mitchell Waldrop, *Complexity*[1]

The rapidly unfolding tenets of chaos and complexity are only the most recent scientific theories that strategists have attempted to incorporate into their own field. The physical sciences have the oldest lineage in this regard, but the social ones have surely made their mark. Chaos theory tells us that the smallest action can reverberate through a system and produce extraordinary and completely unpredictable results—as in the flap of the butterfly's wing that is the source of a hurricane, or the single change of heart that brings down an empire. Complexity theory accepts the basic logic of chaos theory, which preceded it, but instead of concentrating on chaos as an indeterminable force at the level of individual decisions and actions, complexity theorists instead attempt to understand the fundamental *structure* of chaos.

Traditional linear analysis suggests that output is equivalent to input. This makes prediction possible. Where a small amount of force brings about a certain level of desirable outcome, a larger amount will surely bring more. Chaos theory asserts that where the system rules are non-linear, as is the case with all social systems (of which war is the most violent), the system may display extreme sensitivity or indifference to inputs. This is the metaphor of the straw that broke the camel's back. Input may be consistently added to a system with no discernible or unexpected result until suddenly, a minor addition of input collapses the system. Chaotic behavior is thus inherently unpredictable, and prediction or control of future systems extraordinarily difficult.

Conversely, where the inputs are impossible to equate in advance of the output, the outputs themselves may be predictable. This aggregate assessment does provide the potential for the strategist to, at a minimum, predict the extent to which a system will display chaotic behavior and avoid overly disruptive or dangerous inputs. This is the essence of complexity theory. Systems that display core related activities (and here chaos–random or disordered activity–is separated from complex patterned activity) have the capacity to display a variety of interrelated *patterns*. These patterns can be analyzed and assessed, and projections of future aggregate behavior made. If these complex systems are adaptive they will react at a systemic level to new inputs or stimuli with a new form of behavior not previously seen. This is called emergent behavior and is the focal point of state of the art complexity theory.

> Such a system is distinguished by a set of interrelated parts, each one of which is potentially capable of being an autonomous agent that, through acting autonomously, can impact on the others, and all of which either engage in patterned behavior as they sustain day-to-day routines or break with the routines when new challenges require new responses and new patterns.[2]

It is this interrelationship of the independently acting agents that is the key to understanding the capacity to react to change without implied or formal direction. It is the structure of the system that allows the independent agents to act in the aggregate to positively transform the system.

Science, rationality, and war

The intellectual revolution of the modern era was founded then propelled on the belief that applied science could reveal the inner working of the universe, and through it, humanity could one day be delivered unto paradise. Theory led the way, in astronomy, mathematics, and physics. These in turn were validated with practical application in chemistry, medicine, and engineering. Advances were adopted and adapted for the social sciences, including economics, psychology, and political studies. From there, the logic extended to the problems of interstate relations, and the ideals of both perfected peace and war were promised. For the latter, it was presumed that a pure science of war could be determined and applied, and that in the future, victory would belong to those who most deeply understood its foundation in nature's eternal laws.

Beginning in the Renaissance, with the philosophy of Machiavelli and the new astronomies of Galileo and Copernicus, the notion that *all* existence could be rational, explainable, and infused with clockwork precision became increasingly enticing. God may work in mysterious ways, but it appeared as though the world around us was meticulously preset. Newton's calculations describing the movements of the moon and planets suggested a cosmic precision that could be determined for *every* phenomenon. Even the brutal turmoil of war could be studied scientifically. Machiavelli envisioned such a mechanistic form, and his application of mathematics to military organization suggested that the army itself could be thought of as 'a deliberately created system of interacting parts,' subject to quantification, that was part of a description of the state as 'a mechanical contrivance.'[3] Every effect had a cause, and if all the forces of nature could be identified and measured, the future itself was knowable. The calculus would be straightforward.

The heuristic value of such a view was considerable. Strategists and tacticians looked for a scientific explanation of war, a set of determinist laws and principles that would guarantee victory. J.F.C. Fuller took the notion to its extreme, one of many military theorists to attempt it. Even those who eschewed the possibility of an exact science of war nonetheless sought principles and formulae that would be grounded in science and useful at least as a *guide* in war. From the mid-eighteenth century to the middle of the twentieth, the search for such a guide used physics and the hard sciences as a model. The concepts of mass, vector, and velocity were easily transferred to gunpowder-based doctrine, and ultimately to grand strategy. National military power was calculated in raw numbers of men in arms, cannons, and tonnage of ships. When the theories of physics transitioned from Newtonian to quantum mechanics, military theory was understandably slow to catch on. There seemed little real world strategic utility for these intuitively bizarre micro-cosmic states-of-being. War was still viewed as the violent application of mass and energy in structures of human dimension. The technologies developed from quantum theory, most especially the atomic bomb, showed that the application of these theories would indeed have a profound impact on the future of strategy. With advances in cybernetics and systems theory, based in communication and biological sciences, the war paradigm began to shift. Today, strategists look to breakthroughs in a variety of sciences for insights. Application of nanotechnologies and robotics drive the new look. What strategists and planners will do with these new technologies is not fully understood, but a faith that they will change the face of war is ubiquitous.

At present, the twin notions of chaos and complexity, described first in the scientific literature of physics, are the most pervasive ontological influences in the art of war. The US Military is already grappling with these concepts in the development of its doctrine.[4] At the joint services level, state-of-the-art strategy includes 'network centric warfare' and 'swarming,' which purport to transfer chaos and complexity intact to a theory of war.[5] Colin Gray observes that 'the complex subject of strategy and revolutions in military affairs *necessarily always stands on the edge of chaos,'* and readily acknowledges the 'writings on chaos and complexity theory as one of the propellants' for his most recent analysis.[6]

Classical physics and strategy

Radical changes in established ways of thinking often come from the margins of theory. The recognized experts are often too steeped in established methodologies and the orthodoxy of accepted knowledge to make revolutionary breakthroughs.[7] When Einstein published his first papers on relativity, for example, he was working as a postal clerk in Switzerland. It is also a pattern of scientific change that revolutionaries do not start with an attempt to overturn an established view; they are more likely trying to account for a puzzling bit of data that does not seem to fit. Such was also the case for Einstein, who wanted nothing more than to reconcile a few recently debated anomalies with traditional physics.

Einstein began with the assumption that the laws of physics *must* be the same for everyone, everywhere.[8] This is a reasonable approach, to be sure. If there are immutable laws at work, then they must apply to everyone in all places. The structure of the physical universe could not be different for an observer here as opposed to one there, Einstein reasoned, as appeared to be the case if one accepted the logical ramifications of some of the more radical experiments being conducted at the time on the properties of light. Strategists have tended to assume the same, that there are immutable laws of war, and perhaps correctly so. Problems arise when contextual factors overwhelm the extant theory—or seem to—and are mistaken for principles themselves.

Relativity is a particularly apt idea for an investigation of strategy, for it is a trite analysis that goes without regard for a thinking opponent. To be sure, any concept of *cognitive* relativity—such as Einstein's—requires a notion of the other, someone else's perspective with whom to be relative. More important, for the development of both physics and strategy, it requires the ability to share perspectives despite those different observations. This is essentially the problem Einstein was attempting to overcome with his Special Theory of Relativity. He was searching for a common frame of reference for observers at different locations traveling at different velocities. Thus, his Special Theory is more about what is *not* relative than what is—the capacity for one observer to make observations from one viewpoint usable to an observer in another. This was not new. Galileo had made a similar argument 300 years before when he observed that movement is always relative to movement—or the lack of it—in something else. Without a frame of reference, another observable state of motion (including rest) with which to make a comparison, movement is undetectable. Hence, it is precisely because the laws of movement are the same for all points of view that motion can be equally understood from different points of view. A single set of tools—measuring devices—should suffice for *any* position at any relative motion.

The problem for Einstein was that in repeated tests, the speed of light was constant. Regardless of the motion of the observer, light always moved past at 186,000 miles per second. If both the fixed (constant) speed of light and the relativity principle that the laws of physics are equally valid from different perspectives, then he reasoned the tools we use to measure the speed of light must change with motion. The measuring device will actually get shorter (and more massive) as the observer goes faster. This also explains how a person at a fixed position relative to a moving object can measure it at different lengths according to its speed. 'According to Einstein, it is *motion itself* that causes contraction, and, in addition, time dilation.'[9]

This revolutionary concept is of course widely accepted today, and it has its parallel in strategy and tactics through the notion of *tempo* in war. By compressing the decision-time frame of the opponent, the capacity to assess (measure) and react using standard methods and means is made more difficult. In conceptualizing the immutable properties of physics, Einstein showed that the *appearance* of reality, and the ability to comprehend it accurately, changes from one frame of reference to another. In strategy, appearances hold great sway.

It takes just a small stretch of the imagination to view war in the terms of physics. In the Newtonian view of reality, nature is absolute and exists concretely, unconcerned with the concerns or thoughts of people. Human perceptions regarding nature can be correct or incorrect, but nature itself endures. John Schmitt argues that war in the nineteenth and early twentieth centuries was heavily influenced by the Newtonian worldview. In this period warfare is highly procedural, with methodical approaches to the conduct of military operations; it is doctrinaire and rigidly structured, with checklists and procedures; it has precise command and control, with rigid command and support relationships; and it employs very detailed and highly orchestrated or synchronized plans.[10]

Einstein's theories of relativity did more than challenge the Newtonian view; they ultimately shattered it. He showed 'that no phenomenon—not even the flow of time itself—can be described without reference to the state of motion of the observer.'[11] Einstein brought physics to the edge of 'the abyss subjectivity,' but it would be for Niehls Bohr and the Copenhagen school of quantum physics to propel it into a brave new world where not only the observer becomes an integral component of the study of reality, the selection of measuring device 'partially determines the possible answers to the question at hand.'[12] In the quantum view that followed, nature is indeterminate until the observer fixes its reality. It is therefore a realm of possibilities and probabilities.

Quantum physics and strategy

Chaos theory describes the physicist's attempt to understand and explain the basic nature of reality at the sub-microscopic level, at the level of quantum mechanics. As such, it is appealing to strategists, who have always adapted freely from the sciences, even when they have been convinced that a perfected science of war could never be truly achieved. Clausewitz, more a product of the German Romanticist tradition than the Enlightenment, may have done so intuitively. He could accept the tenets of probability and uncertainty that quantum physics would identify more readily than his Newtonian counterparts in the West.[13] This is not surprising. Some of the outcomes of quantum analysis are so foreign to the Western intuitive sense of reality that they have only been reluctantly applied to date. Those strategists educated into Enlightenment values and holding a faith in scientific positivism (a thing is true only if it can be proven by observation), could not so easily accept that nature, at its core, could be unknowable.

If the world were truly governed by natural laws that could not be violated, then the essence of science was thought to be (and still is, in some quarters) observation and prediction. The more carefully we define our experiments, and the more keenly we measure and chart changes over time, the closer we get to a perfect comprehension of reality. Some of the less obvious strategic connotations of this view are presented in the following chapter, but the most perilous may be the always-present implication that reality is rational, explainable, and perfectible. Implicitly or stated plainly, it must lead to the belief that the universe can be comprehensively understood. It is a cosmic machine in perfect harmony.[14] One has only to know the fundamental laws acting upon the fundamental material particles (atoms) and one could, in theory, predict future events with certitude. This is similar to various attempts to invigorate tactics to make the outcome of battle, and ultimately war, assured. If the individual soldier is trained to clockwork precision, and will perform all tasks flawlessly, then a perfect calculation of battle is conceivable. The dilemma for the Newtonian physicists and Maurician grand tacticians is plain. If the outcome is certain, then the future is predestined. There is no choice, and so there is no power.

The Copenhagen interpretation of quantum physics claimed, among many other dazzling notions, that perfect prediction is not only practically impossible, it is so even in theory. Because the future cannot be known, the new physics predicted probabilities only. This is partly because we can never know precisely the reality in which we exist. We comprehend the universe by interpreting (with our brains) the senses of our bodies and the measurements of our instruments. Thus, it is only possible to know the shadow of reality, much as Plato insisted in his famous allegory of the cave.[15] Some philosophers go so far as to state that all notions of reality are equally valid, as each is merely the individual interpretation of sensory and data input, and so all realities are created. Any reality is possible. The response of the realist, like the Zen master, is to smack the philosopher on the head with a stick. Interpret that reality.

Nonetheless, the model is a powerful one that spawns an incredible array of insights. It stems, innocuously enough, from Einstein's resolution of the centuries-old dispute whether light was composed of particles, and thus mass, or whether it was composed of energy, like a frequency wave. The result of two-slit experiments, repeated and verified innumerable times, showed that light acts as both a particle and a wave. Einstein's solution was simple; it is both. He envisioned a new physical construct called a photon that at times exhibited the characteristics of a particle and at other times those of a wave. The problem was that the characteristics they exhibited depended on the means one used to measure them.

The activity of the photon is *indeterminate* until one decides to measure the activity. This must lead to the notion that a fundamental basis of nature is its inherent unpredictability. Not that we have too little understanding to be able to predict the future with certainty, but that even if all the relevant information were available, it would not be possible to do so. This is the essence of Werner Heisenberg's extraordinary Uncertainty Principle. This indispensable principle of quantum physics states that it is impossible to simultaneously know both the location and the velocity of *any* object. Quantities of position and momentum, when measured in relationships, generate uncertainties. We can know one or the other exactly, but the more precisely we determine one, the vaguer is our knowledge of the other.

The most troubling notion for the Newtonian or linear thinker is not that speed and position were fundamentally unknowable, but that the speed and position of 'an atom does not exist until the question is properly formulated, and the appropriate measurement is performed.'[16] Worse yet, 'Heisenberg's Uncertainty Principle seemed to say that nothing in the universe really happened unless it was watched.'[17] To be precise, and fair, Heisenberg was investigating effects at the subatomic realm, and his description of it implied that it was at its foundation unknowable. Nature is uncertain. The formula Heisenberg devised could be stated, 'the product of incertainties for position and velocity ... was always greater than a very small physical quantity.'[18] Since the quantity was so small, the uncertainty was generally thought insignificant for the world in which we lived. Our calculations can never be perfect, but the variance is small enough not to matter.

Thus, much of the uncertainty of nature comes from our own intrusive attempts to measure it, and conjectures drawn from Heisenberg's principle for information gathering are startling. If the subatomic (micro) realm proves to be a better model for information flow than the macro one, then the limit of what is even *possible* to know is severely constrained. First, the easy part: since we cannot know all things precisely, only approximately, we must become comfortable with knowledge of the world around us stated in probabilities, and not absolutes. We cannot say with certainty that a war will occur, much less precisely when, where, and with whom such an event will transpire. But, with increasing reliability, we should be able to predict the exact likelihood a certain type of war, perhaps in a certain region and with specified foes, will occur within a given time, and prepare accordingly. We simply cannot know the specifics. The phenomenon is highlighted in the process of radioactive decay.[19] In this case, precisely predictable overall behavior (rate of decay) is based on the patterns observed in completely unpredictable individual events. Wars of attrition are fought this way. Predictions of success are based on the numbers of troops that will be killed (versus those of the opponent) in a given situation. Without knowing who will be killed, the total casualty rate can be quite accurately projected. It is a grisly calculus, but at times a useful one.

Now the more difficult notion: our very attempts to determine the likelihood of an event happening alters the probability of that event happening. Not only do we alter the probabilities of reality by observing it, but in the act of observing, we *choose the future* in which we will act. This is clearly counter to the Newtonian view based on universal laws that govern mass and movement. If all the laws and properties of nature could be discovered, and understood completely, then the future would be knowable. It would be predestined. Pre-quantum physics adheres to the belief that nature is fixed, that our measurements of it have no effect on what is or what will be. This real world is external to us, at least to our inquiring minds. It is what it is. Moreover, it is indifferent to us. In this image, the course of human history is akin to an oarless and rudderless boat floating down a river. Its course is buffeted and complex, it goes from right to left and back, but its destination is inevitable and the desires or observations of the people on the boat have no affect on the outcome of its journey.

Quantum mechanics tells us it is impossible to know precisely the future of any phenomenon, only the probabilities that lay ahead. The quantum vision sees humanity as a part of nature, an element in its journey that continuously interacts with and influences it, with or without intent. Any choice that we make changes nature forever, because it fixes the past. Staying with the analogy, the boat on the river has oars and a rudder. It does not float utterly without direction. The people on board look downstream for the best passage through rapids and shoals. The boat is moved in anticipation of the perceived danger, and the course is different than it would have been without the observation. And the river itself has changed, too. Eddies and currents are altered minutely. There will always be the image of what might have happened if we did not steer from right to left, and even though we will never float through that section of the river in the same way again, that image will impact future decisions as much as the physical lay of the stream. The strategist is no different from the quantum physicist in this regard. No one can be truly objective, for everyone is an element *within* the world of war. What one chooses to examine will change the future, because every choice is real, and reality cannot be observed without changing it.

This notion of choosing one's reality is undoubtedly more tenable to the strategist than to the tactician. It would be quite wrong to persuade a naval battle planner that the enemy is both over the horizon and not over it, for example, and that both realities will remain in being until we choose (or are forced) to look for it. This is because the enemy ships are things, or objects, and our experience tells us the thing is there or it is not, regardless of my attention. Whether or not I choose to look does not change the reality of its coming. I cannot avoid being struck by a bullet by closing my eyes.

But strategists do not deal directly with things or objects in planning (that aspect should be left to the tactician); they seek instead a condition or situation of advantage, and manipulate the structure of rules and principles. This world of ideas and possibilities is more compatible with the microphysical world of the quantum physicists than the macro-physical one of Newton, because quantum particles should not be thought of as *things*. They are more correctly understood as a 'tendency to exist' or 'tendencies to happen.'[20] They are events, phases, and fields. The smallest of reality's building blocks may not even have mass.[21] At the base of the universe may lie only strings or harmonics, a code if you will, expressing a single rule. Hence the strengths of these quantum tendencies are expressed as probabilities, or wave functions. The result is that careful study and examination of aggregate characteristics over time, the province of statistical analysis, cannot provide with assurance a prediction of the actions of any one individual agent—but can give an uncannily accurate projection of the future behavior of a group. Political pollsters have long known this phenomenon, and have established methods that work extremely well. They collect data to determine the characteristics of a voter likely to be swayed by a particular argument, or use it to make projections of future elections. They recognize that not all the members of the target group will be equally swayed, nor is the decision of any one voter known with any greater accuracy than personal acquaintance or intuition. But, the outcome of a large number of likely decision makers arriving at a particular group decision, and by what size plurality, can be known with astonishing accuracy.

That a group acts in predictable ways but an individual does not has far-reaching and intuitive consequences for the military planner. It points to the *patterns* inherent in actions as the source of true understanding, and not the actions themselves. Perhaps most disconcerting, the tactician's correct and proper search for perfect knowledge in the conduct of campaigns and battles could prove to be suboptimal as one moves toward the level of strategy. If we follow the logic to conclusion, however, it may prove that the more we attempt to know about one characteristic of the enemy, the less we can know about another, a phenomenon of telescoping mentality. We can peer deeply into the space of a single engagement, but the field of view so narrows that the broader battle is invisible. Telescoping can be issue-specific as well. The more we try to get perfect knowledge about the enemy's intent, for example, the less we may be able to know about the enemy's actions.

This is a serious conundrum. It is desirable, for example, to know which of two individual combatants in a boxing contest will win. It is even possible to make a good deal of money betting on the winner. But, it is not yet possible to accurately predict every action or event in the course of the fight. These can be stated as probabilities only. The outcome of any single engagement is thus unknowable in advance. But the aggregate outcome of thousands of similar actions or events can be known with a high degree of reliability. For instance, the planner cannot know which aircraft will make it to an assigned objective, which ordinance will hit its target, or which of the enemy will be killed, but over time can determine how many aircraft of a certain kind carrying what type of load are needed to achieve the desired effect with near certainty. One of the functions of doctrine is to assist the tactical and operational planner in calculations like this for specific engagements, and it is commonly practiced. It is quite rare to see it done efficiently for entire battles—as components of campaigns or wars—and rarer still for wars as components of grand strategy.

The ability of the battle planner to efficiently predict the aggregate outcome of numerous indeterminable tactical engagements is extremely useful in the effort to maximize the probability of achieving broad tactical goals. For the operational planner to be able to determine the aggregate outcome of numerous battles is equally valuable in campaign planning. For the operational planner to reach down to the level of engagements, however, to increase the probability that specific battles would be judged successful, would skew the probability set for aggregate outcomes of all battles, and so it must be scrupulously avoided. The temptation to reach *multiple* levels down to increase control over variables should be even more shunned. Strategists should thus abandon any attempt to exercise control at the micro-level (the individual soldier, sailor, or airman), entrusting that function to the commander on the scene. Operational strategy or grand tactics raises the aggregate level of success through better training and equipping, and the strategist must support these efforts, but *the strategist should guide military matters so that the tactical outcome of any war, much less any individual battle, is not critical to success* (or continuing advantage). To be sure, a strategist whose plan rests on the outcome of a specific action working in a precise way is not thinking strategically. Such a mindset locks the strategist into predetermined choices, and the capacity to control events is lost.

Quantum physics forever changed the manner in which we understand choices and decisions. In the old physics, choices were understood as either-or. A thing can be done, or it cannot. With the remarkable significance of photon studies, a thing can be both. In the simplest binary construct (on-off, right-wrong, yes-no), there are at least three possible states (for example; on, off, and *both* on *and* off). Classical logic, and not the world of experience, placed these rules of either-or upon us. Greek philosophers demonstrated the fallacy long ago, with two confounding paradoxes.[22] The first was Epimenides' famous Cretan paradox, in which a traveler from Crete states that all Cretans are liars. The paradox can be boiled down to the statement, 'I am lying,' or simply, 'this statement is false.' In a world of either-or logic, where A and B are clearly defined and existence of one cancels the other, the statement is impossible. Nonetheless, it can be made.

To a significant extent, Gödel's Incompleteness Theorem, which states that 'all consistent axiomatic formulations of number theory include undecipherable propositions,' is a mathematical investigation of the Cretan paradox.[23] Gödel demonstrated that for any logical system, statements could be formulated that cannot be proven true or false (they are 'undecidable') from *within* the system, starting with the statement: 'This statement is unprovable.' This is actually the First Incompleteness Theorem. The Second Incompleteness Theorem proved that the statement 'the axioms of arithmetic are consistent' could not be proved by using those same axioms.[24]

Gödel's Theorem concerned self-referencing systems, and holds sway in the logic developed here to separate tactics and strategy. One of the significant steps in scientific analysis is to differentiate when one is making hypotheses and taking measurements from *within* the system being studied, and when one is doing the same from an observational vantage *outside* the system. Such a distinction cannot always be made. At the strategic level, it is possible to step outside the arena of combat and make decisions *about* war. At the tactical level we are by definition *within* the system of war, and must make rational decisions that impact individual lives directly. Tactics is in effect a self-referencing milieu, and can usefully be portrayed in that manner. But, it will cause paradoxes to develop—of necessity—because decisions are made within the system.

Paradox is a fundamental effect of closed systems, and perhaps the most telling evidence of systemic flaws and corrective action. A few of the paradoxes that inhabit the realm of international security studies are caused by bringing the tactical either-or mindset into the strategic realm. These include the classic security dilemma; my security is a threat to you, and your response to add power to increase your own security is not only a spur to me to increase my own, but a verification of my initial efforts. Zeev Moaz identifies several more. The paradox of successful deterrence suggests that deterrence may work too well, and that 'Perfectly reasonable people confronted by an effective deterrent threat may find it logical—in fact, may find it imperative—to defy it.'[25] In addition, the paradox of crisis escalation asserts there are wars that nobody wanted and everybody tried to prevent; the paradox of attrition finds 'Cases where military operations run aground not because of defective planning, but because they are well-planned'–since war fighters want a quick and decisive war, they plan for it, and if their plan doesn't work, they get caught in a long war of attrition that they are neither prepared for nor able to win;[26] the Allies Paradox, or as Moaz puts it, with friends like these, who needs enemies?; and the loser's paradox, a variation of the sunk-cost paradox, in which it takes more time and more casualties to end a war once one recognizes that it is lost than it takes to realize one is going to lose.

In the either-or logic of tactics, a war fighter might see the current battle as the most crucial event on the road to victory, and be perfectly convinced of the truth of the statement. Yet even if the statement were true, there is no way to prove it from within the system of reference—the tactical level of war. More to the point, it is a meaningless assessment at the level of strategy. This is because the strategist instead recognizes the war for what it is; an event or series of events that has become part of the context of what is now the structure of decision-making—a structure that will change with the next event.

Likewise, victory is a self-referencing notion in tactics, evident in the statement, 'this war is winnable if politicians do not interfere.' Since the decision-maker at the tactical level cannot step outside the circumstances of his or her condition, anything that appears to confound the established criteria for victory is absurd. If one could withdraw from the immediacy of one's experience for a moment, the order to withdraw from a well-fortified position (for example) might make perfect sense. From the tactical perspective, doing so will put the unit at risk of heavier casualties—in addition to giving up territory that may have come at a stiff price—than simply staying put. In an overall battle plan, the movement could be part of a ruse to draw the enemy into a losing position elsewhere. But what of the decision by a government to withdraw or remove its forces from combat, despite having won (by the standards of victory) every battle of the war?[27] This can make no sense at all to the tactician, for the standards of victory *in* war do not apply to the strategic level requirement for war to support policy.

A better illustration of self-referential paradox, because it uses gradients within the either-or parameters, is the second of two classical Greek examples: Xeno's use of the rules of logic to prove that an archer can never hit a tree with an arrow. In order for an arrow shot from a bow to hit the tree, he reasoned (tongue firmly planted in cheek), it must first travel half the distance to the tree. In order to travel the remaining distance, the arrow must first travel half of that. No matter how small the remaining distance to the tree, the arrow must first transit half that before it can travel the whole of it. Thus, it will never reach its target.

Xeno's paradox does more than highlight the limitations of either-or logic; it is an excellent example of the *dis*continuity of linear thinking. The real world of experience accepts thought (and movement, in the case of the arrow) as a *fluid* process, and not one of discrete steps. This is because we know that the arrow *does* hit the tree. Our *experience* tells us so. Hence, the world is necessarily perceived in a sliding scale of grays, of possible states as well as confirmed ones. It is not just black or white. This is the lesson the strategist can never reject when musing over the paradox: there is always another alternative. Indeed, there may be an unlimited number of them.

As we have seen, any attempt to understand the essence of nature by a careful study of its extant configuration must be incomplete. 'Nature, therefore, is somewhat like a ballet dancer, the meaning of whose gestures are contained in the *whole movement*.'[28] Imagine taking a photograph of the ballet in mid-performance, and asking someone who had not seen the ballet to explain its meaning. No amount of reductionism could deconstruct the intent or purpose of the position the ballerina was in, much less describe the grace or beauty of the movement (though I suppose it could assist the dancer with her technique). 'While it is possible to analyze the motion of the dancer's body by means of photographs, it is clear that each element [so viewed] has its origin in the entire gesture and any static element is therefore incomplete.'[29] For the strategist, no assessment of the current situation without an understanding of the sweep of battle, the movement of the war, or the intent of policy will be valid.

Fred Alan Wolf argues that more than a potential to misperceive the present is inherent in self-referential systems; it is impossible to make predictions about the future as well. This is simply because 'we can never see ourselves as we are now.'[30] It will seem obvious in hindsight what should have been done in the past, simply because we have stepped outside of our personal experience by looking back on a past that is now knowable only in the abstract. Unfortunately, we cannot do the same for an unfixed future.

The classic illustration is found in the parable of Schrödinger's Cat. Erwin Schrödinger concocted a thought experiment in which a cat was placed in a box with a device that *might* release a poison gas. The trigger for the device is a quantum event. A material with a known rate of decay is placed in the box with a 50 percent probability of emitting an electron. If emitted, the electron triggers the gas, and the cat is killed. The conundrum is that until we open the box, we cannot determine the disposition of the cat. Classical physics tells us to look in the box and see which it is. Quantum physics says the cat is both alive and dead, and one reality actualizes upon observation. The other event possibility collapses upon verification of the first. The cat's fate is not just unknown until we look into the box; it is yet to be.

The transition from possible reality to reality comes at a stiff price. It requires us to accept the notion that something comes from nothing. In Newtonian physics, matter is the basic element. It is a thing. Mass is the finite amount or quantity of matter a thing contains. What Einstein found is that the mass of a thing in motion is greater than the mass of that same thing at rest, to the point that matter moving at the speed of light is infinitely massive. This is because motion is always relative, and so mass will be measured differently by observers at different velocities. Thus, mass is not a finite or intrinsic characteristic of a thing. It is not a thing at all, since it can lose mass as it slows down, and gain it as it speeds up— and *it can do both at the same time* if observed from separate relative velocities. Moreover, if the aggregate matter (mass) of a body can change with velocity, and velocity is a function of energy expenditure—that is, mass in motion absorbs energy when it speeds up (grows larger) and emits it as it slows—then mass itself is a type of energy. This is consistent with the quantum notion that particles smaller than atoms are in their proper description *tendencies to exist*, as we have seen, and not *things* at all.

The terms of this discussion are precise. There is a meaningful difference between possibility, probability, and tendency. A tendency exists 'in and of itself, even if it never [becomes] an event.'[31] It is locked into probability waves, or mathematical catalogs of those tendencies. When we toss a die in a game of chance, we understand the mathematical probability of getting any particular number is one in six. The tendency to roll six is the same regardless of the specific roll. The probability wave, according to Heisenberg, is a *tendency* for an event to occur. Reality may fix an event, but it does not alter the tendency. In this manner, Heisenberg 'introduced something standing in the middle between the idea of an event and the actual event, a strange kind of physical reality in the middle between possibility and reality.'[32]

Let us presume two possibilities, A and B. Let us further stipulate that it is not possible for both to transpire at the same time. They cannot exist together in reality. When one possibility does come about, the probability of the other occurring is zero. In this case, let us say that our interest is in turning a possibility into an actuality. We desire to have A *or* B. So, we make a measurement. Doing so intrudes on probability development, for as soon as we detect one or the other, the realm of alternate possibilities collapses. Until a measure is taken, both A and B *do* exist in a state-of-being external to reality. This is the probability wave. When quantum potentiality is changed from probability to reality, the effect occurs suddenly, and it can be extremely discontinuous.

The Heisenberg uncertainty principle applies for subatomic scale observation, and not necessarily to the macroscopic view of human interaction. The arithmetical perfection of the cosmos is generally more appropriate for the world of our experience. Still, experts from a variety of fields attempted to extrapolate the findings, mostly with strained results. If there is an application for strategy, it may be that the more we focus our attention in one area to make it clear, of necessity the blurrier other areas become. Perhaps information and strategy share this characteristic. Any attempt to determine plans or intent of another (perhaps even of ourselves) *changes* the strategy in an indeterminate manner. The methods we use to discern the other's plan alter the way in which the other plans. So long as I understand this principle, I can use it to my advantage.

The Newtonian worldview was based on the idea of order beneath chaos. What appears to be an unfathomable cacophony of events is in fact the result of a finely balanced universal machine. The search for a science of war was based in the belief that a calculable structure must exist beneath the maelstrom of combat. Some of this was psychological, perhaps, a search for justification where violence ruled so pitilessly. The quantum perspective is that of chaos beneath order, an unknowable swirl of tendencies that in aggregate form made sense. But this is awkward for the strategist, who sees only energy at the bottom-most layer of reality, nothing but a confusing turmoil of probable creation, annihilation, and resurgence. From this miasmic pit, however, formed from a basic structure of rules, comes order. Somehow, principles emerge that define new rules, from which come new, higher forms of structure.

In strategy, as in quantum theory, it is not that one chooses to reject a more detailed analysis of a problem, a Quixotic search for the maximum amount of information possible, but that the search itself will not enhance what is known about the world in general. It is excluded a priori. Of course, people do not live in the world in general, but in the real world. If I say that an attack occurring tomorrow has a 70 percent probability, does the subsequent attack (or lack thereof) change the probability to certitude? Conversely, if I predict an attack will happen tomorrow, regardless of the probability, and it does, did I foresee the future? In retrospect, was the attack inevitable?

The acceptance of a world that is knowable, a linear one in which inputs always equal outputs and strict natural laws govern the behavior of phenomena, will lead us to acceptance of an inevitable future. If one can attain perfect knowledge, then both the past and the future are perfected. But quantum physics is based on the idea that a very limited and bounded amount of knowledge about the world is possible, and that leads to the notion that our reality, including our past and future, is what we make it. As described in Heisenberg's uncertainty theorem, since we must choose which aspect of the phenomenon we wish to inspect, to a limited extent we determine the reality in which we wish to take part. Strategy, in so much as it deals with tendencies rather than things, has a similar conundrum.

In Newtonian physics it is possible to investigate, measure, analyze, and speculate on nature without affecting it. It is what it is. It does not respond to our perception of it. In quantum physics, since the very act of observing changes the phenomenon, we must choose how we wish to shape reality. This is the essence of true or pure strategy. In our making of it, our consideration of it, our projections based on an understanding of it, we change the world in which we live. An opponent's response to our strategy, whether aware of our strategy or not, itself changes strategy, sometimes in ways we cannot predict. The world around us cannot be perfectly known; therefore, the future cannot be assuredly predicted. Our strategy must encompass the realm of possibility and embrace the fuzzy reality of complexity. There can be no laws of strategy or principles that elevate themselves over time to the level of laws. There are only tendencies. When the tendency is very strong, that is, the probability of occurrence is great, it may be elevated to the level of a principle, but no higher.

From chaos to complexity

Michael Waldrop assists in making sense of the vision of chaos beneath order. Think of 'an impressionist painting, whereby the picture is assembled through a riot of flecks of color.'[33] As one moves back, one gains perspective, and the riot becomes a landscape. The same occurs in battle, according to numerous first-hand accounts of combat. What appears as chaos at one level has order and meaning at another. This is what makes the *emergence* of order more than a trivial coincidence. Simple 'patterns can emerge out of uncoordinated local actions' by chance, but to do so by design is a powerful and astonishing thing: 'how does a seed know how to grow into a flower?'[34]

What we see are complex actions. What we do not see are the multitudinous levels of regressively simpler actions that make up the hierarchy of actions that we do experience. Despite the dependence of the higher level actions on the lower level ones, the more complex activities are seldom even aware of the lower level actions. Imagine the brain, which is a complex of neural and synaptic activity. From the billions of interactions and relationships at one level, consciousness and intelligence arrive at another. Yet the consciousness is not so much as aware of the neural activity, without which it could not exist. And no dissection of the brain— at least none that we are yet aware of—could infer consciousness and intelligence from the neural activity. Complexity is thus discovered in the coordination of simple tasks, in decision-making for the aggregate. What is created is a

> society of the mind ... Any agent that seems to do more than one auto-
> matic, repeatable task, that exhibits complexity, must, in fact, consist of
> several interconnected agents ... Intelligence is the complexity that arises
> from the communication and coordination of simple units. Minds are col-
> lections of millions of such agents, each autonomous and mindless.[35]

Complex systems are nonlinear. Such systems are those in which inputs do not necessarily equate to outputs, at least, they are not proportional in any easily discernible manner. Linear systems, in contrast, are ones in which cause and effect are observable and proportional. 'It is an environment where prediction is facilitated by careful planning; success is pursued by detailed monitoring and control; and a premium is placed upon reductionism, rewarding those who excel in reductionist processes.'[36] The association with reductionism is a keen insight—it is the notion that difficult problems can be made more manageable by reducing them into their constituent parts. Nonlinear systems are not so reducible. The parts do not add up to output, quantitatively or qualitatively. Cause and effect are not normally evident. In this view,

> ... there is no true 'fundamental level' in nature but rather each level
> involves its own unique description and is conditioned by the levels around
> it ... whenever one level is chosen as a foundation it will, ultimately, be

found to depend on all other levels for the definition of its concepts and the context of its meanings.'[37]

Because each level is defined and shaped by those above and below it, and by systems outside of it, the true nature of cause and effect cannot be discerned from solely within the system.

It may be in our nature to expect linear relationships. In a linear system, if a little inducement or use of force gets a little of what we desire, then more force will get more of what we want. 'If a little foreign aid slightly increases economic growth, then more aid should produce greater growth.'[38] For military planners, if a small bomb will get a certain amount of damage, a bigger bomb will have bigger damage effects. But in a nonlinear system, we cannot make the same judgment. Sometimes the tiniest amount of additional force will have catastrophic results; other times a great deal of additional force will have no perceptible impact. It may also be that 'a small amount of the variable can do a great deal of work and then the law of diminishing returns sets in, as is often the case for the role of catalysts. In other cases very little impact is felt until a critical mass is assembled. For example, women may thrive in a profession only after there are enough of them so that they do not feel like strangers.'[39]

The ability to describe a system by breaking it down into its constitutive parts, and vice versa, is linear reductionism. Where the whole is less or greater than the sum of its parts, we find nonlinear systems. The two are paralleled in the mathematics of linear and nonlinear equations, from which we derive the names.[40] Linear differential equations, and the systems they describe, are smooth. Hence, they are predictable. Breaking the equations down into their constituent parts helps mathematicians discover relationships and assists in the formulation of other linear equations. The steady drip of a leaky faucet is a fine example. It is regular, monotonous flow. As water pressure increases, the drip increases accordingly. At some point, however, an increase in water pressure causes the drip to become a turbulent flow, completely unconnected to the addition of water pressure and completely unpredictable within the paradigm of linear equations. The change can be sudden and extremely violent, as the steadily increasing pressure applied in the bending of a tree branch culminates in a violent snapping of the limb. In some instances, however, 'these nonlinear effects may not be destructive but can involve novel forms of behavior and the emergence of new forms of structure.'[41]

Reductionism is a powerful tool. No less a scholar than Edward O. Wilson has called it 'the primary and essential activity of science.'[42] Through it, most of the laws of physics were derived and established. In socio-political systems, unlike those of the hard sciences, such approaches are rarely satisfying. While the war may be conceivable as a collection of battles, the important meaning of war is lost when doing so. While valor and honor can be extrapolated from the combats of a few, they cannot explain the policies of the government that are to be advanced by them. The difference, the ability to see the forest for the trees, comes from a disentanglement of 'petty' and 'grand reductionism,' according to Hans Von Bayer.[43] The former is linear reductionism, the belief that things behave the way they do according to the properties of their constituent parts. The latter, says Von Bayer, is 'much more interesting.'[44] It is the notion that all natural and social systems are the way they appear 'because of simple universal laws, to which all other scientific laws may in some way be reduced. In other words, not things ... but laws, the way Galileo's law of falling can be reduced to Newton's universal law of gravity.'[45] Thus, grand reductionism is the belief that each level of complex organization exhibits its own meaning from lower, more fundamental laws of nature. This is still a type of linear thinking, however, and Von Bayer asserts that 'at each level of complex organization, especially at the living cell and above, there are laws and principles that have not yet been derived from more general laws, and may never be.'[46]

Complexity analysis is thus a form of systems analysis, pioneered in biology and now accepted implicitly throughout the sciences. Complexity theorists study complex systems, defined as having a large number of independent components (called agents) that interact with each other in a myriad of rule-based relationships, and which, through those interactions, display emergent behavior at the level of the system.[47] Chaos theorists said that small actions by an agent could cascade through a complex system and cause extremely large and essentially unpredictable outcomes. This is the essence of nonlinear thinking—an understanding that inputs and outputs do not necessarily equate. The whole can indeed be greater than the sum of all parts. But from that knowledge, there is little to gain. The insight of the complexity theorists is that, although the individual actions that cause systemic change cannot be predicted, the pattern of change can be discerned and understood. It is in fact, 'the very richness of these interactions [that] allows the system as a whole to undergo *spontaneous self-organization.*'[48]

The advantage of a self-organizing system is that it is dynamically *adaptive.* The system appears, through the interactions of its subcomponents, to guide or steer the whole to an advantageous position—at its essence, the function of strategy. Complex adaptive systems continuously organize and reorganize the patterns of internal connection in such a way that a form of *learning* can be discerned. Thus, complex adaptive systems have a *neural,* or brain-like, *network* structure. What appears as a mass of simple, repeated events at the micro-level translates to a discernible, logical, and increasingly advantageous behavior at the macro-level. This is a vastly different perspective than chaos theory provides.

Complexity theory recognizes the condition of chaos, but it is just one of three broadly defined states. Chaos occurs in a network where events or interactions fail to create any structure at all; what structure there may be appears completely random. The structure is dynamic, to be sure; it is constantly changing, but there is no evidence of advances in learning (adaptability). No progress is made. No patterns are discerned. On the other side of the realm of possibilities is perfect order. The interactions between agents create a structure that is practically fixed. It does not change, and so it does not progress. It does not adapt.

Pure chaos and perfect order are absolutes. A system can be described as more or less orderly, but once it crosses a certain line, it is chaotic. The line itself is the third general state of being for a complex, adaptive system. It has been described as a balancing or tipping point, but in complexity theory, it is called the *edge of chaos*.[49] It is here where the system is perched precariously in the greatest possible flux without going over to chaos, from which it might never recover. As the region of greatest interconnected activity and experimentation, it is where the greatest potential for emergent behavior is found. Self-organizing systems are the most dynamic and fruitful here. This 'edge of chaos is a constantly shifting battle zone between stagnation and anarchy.'[50]

Anarchy is not chaos, though it can be. Chaos refers to relationships between agents that have no order, no discernible or meaningful pattern. Anarchy can be quite patterned, but it is not ordered. It does not have an external force (government) establishing bounded activities. In a functioning anarchy, boundaries and limits are established solely by the pattern of interactions themselves. Chaos is the complete absence of order and pattern. It is an extension of the Second Law of Thermodynamics, which states that elements in a closed system tend to seek their most probable distribution. That most probable distribution is a state of the greatest molecular *dis*order. Chaos is therefore the final manifestation of entropy, which must always increase in a closed system. The world is not closed, however, though all models are and the universe may be, and so we see continuous and spontaneous creation of order and structure in a seemingly disordered environment. The proponents of chaos theory adapted this observation of nonlinear dynamics to try and understand the root causes of every kind of self-organizing behavior from weather to traffic flows. What seemed clear was that rather than being swallowed up in the mass of relationships over time and distance, small effects could evoke vast changes. In fact, at some level of analysis, every event could be shown to have a minor, routinely unnoticed, ultimate cause. The so-called 'butterfly effect' is the preeminent example.[51] The flap of a butterfly's wings could begin the chain of meteorological events that eventually become a hurricane. The difficulties in this kind of thinking have already been discussed. There is little predictive value in such a view and a reductionism into absurdity is certain. While the flap of a butterfly's wings is obviously not sufficient to generate a hurricane, it is not in the slightest bit necessary for one. It would be foolish to initiate a program of butterfly eradication in order to eliminate hurricanes.

The problem lies in the complexity of the analysis. Newton's calculus imagined a simplified world, in which the three-body problem did not exist. The permutations of so many interactions were simply beyond comprehension. But in today's hyper-computing age of convergent technology in information flows and processing power, the capacity exists to calculate previously impenetrable problems. Studying individual air currents as slight as those formed in a butterfly's wake is extremely hard to do, but it may not be impossible. Yet this innate or unthinking behavior is just the beginning of truly complex situations. Interactions become more difficult when multiple agents are able to make decisions. Traffic and stock market flows, for example, are the result of an extraordinary number of interacting willful decisions. But, these too can be scientifically studied, and extremely useful projections of future conditions are in fact routinely made. What we find is that the interactions of all these agents are not random, nor are they flawlessly and logically ordered. They are complex. They exist somewhere between the poles of order and chaos, and their locations on that unidimensional scale are important.

War is among the most complicated of social endeavors, of course. It is described by the interactions of agents at varying levels of scope and scale. It is extremely complex. Chaos theory allows us to look into the cauldron and determine with some degree of satisfaction why a particular operation failed or succeeded. It does not give us a strong sense of reliability or guidance in planning for the future, however. We can attempt to assure that a specific mistake, forgetting to transcribe feet into meters for example, will not recur. But we cannot state that the same path that led to success in the past will do so in the future. In fact, we *know* that it cannot have identical results, for history, in all its detail, can never be repeated.

It is once again reminiscent of Heraclitus' observation that one could never step into the same river twice. The river's swirling particulars change in minute detail, and the act of stepping into it changes it from what would have been. Everything is different. But this is a trivial point, and our experience rejects such a notion. We still recognize the river in its general form. We still know where it will take us, and the dominant pattern of rapids and shoals endures. We understand its basic nature and what is required to cross it, even if every crossing will be different in the swirl of molecular details. That each entry into the river is different does not obviate the fact that each entry *will be similar enough* in the aggregate that expectations can be established and activities adjusted to meet contingencies. It is complex but not chaotic, this river, and our distinction also provides guidance.

When setting out on a course of action, for example, it helps to have accomplished the general form of activity in the past, to have records and guidance from those who have been on the course before, and to make assumptions about factors likely and unlikely to influence that course en route. So important are these factors that one can say that even when setting out on a new course of action, exploring a river for the first time, perhaps, one who has explored uncharted rivers in the past will be more likely successful in the venture than one who has never navigated the unknown before. That this river will be different from any before is fully accepted. That it will have unexpected and unexpectable differences and challenges is presumed. Such ambiguity is understood intuitively. From the macro view, such newness is not a surprise, but a manageable component of preparation for the journey.

The river analogy continues as we transit from the insights of chaos to the applications of complexity. Chaos theory demonstrated that the world is nonlinear; input and output were not precisely equivalent. Small events could have powerful repercussions. In this manner the whole truly is greater then the sum of its parts. Complexity further confirms the adage. If you have two agents, A and B, you have three relationships: A (alone), B, and the set A and B. With three inter-acting agents, there are seven independent relations (A, B, C, A and B, B and C, C and A, and A, B, and C). Four agents have fifteen relationships; five agents have thirty-one, and so on. This interconnectivity, which grows exponentially with the addition of new agents, proved to be the key to understanding, then undoing, basic chaos theory. In the real world, *everything* is connected. The potential of all known agents' interactions is infinite and unknowable. Chaos theory could not help make the predictions of nonlinear outputs that science sought, especially when the systems under design were made up of independent, thinking agents.

There was simply too much information to be scrutinized. Statistical analysis could assist with defining the processes and structures of complex systems, but after only a few algorithmic abstractions of scale, the universe of relationships became far too copious for existing tools of examination to embrace. The key to breaking the impasse was the observation that a hierarchy of complexity existed. As interacting agents at one level increased in their total numbers, discernible pat-terns of interactions emerged at the level of the whole. This notion of emergence, the movement from low-level rules to higher-level sophistication, proved to be the essence of truly complex interactive behavior.[52] In a 'system composed of many, many "agents" ... whatever its nature, the agents were constantly organizing and reorganizing themselves into larger structures through the clash of mutual accom-modation and mutual rivalry ... Complexity, in other words, was really a science of emergence.'[53]

7

ADAPTATION AND EMERGENCE
IN STRATEGY

All complex adaptive systems display emergent behavior. 'In these systems, agents residing on one scale start producing behavior that lies on the scale above them ... The movement from low-level rules to higher-level sophistication is what we call emergence.'[1] The simplest form of emergent behavior would be 'a system with multiple agents dynamically interacting in multiple ways, following local rules and oblivious to any higher order instructions. But it wouldn't be truly *emergent* until those local interactions resulted in some kind of discernible macrobehavior [or *pattern*].'[2] And it *is* behavior. Emergence in this context is *purposeful*. Behavior becomes manifest at the level of the system, to increase efficiency and options. Without purposeful adaptation, increasing complexity is merely interesting.

By adapting to a dynamic and changing environment, the system displays a rudimentary form of intelligence. Over time and multiple adaptations, the system learns. Its adaptations become macrobehaviors that shape and guide the interactions of agents on levels below it. Those agents do not need to be aware of the macrobehavior, perhaps most are not, but if the agents form complex adaptive systems (for example, people in a cultural or political milieu), they are likely to make reverberating adaptations within the larger system. Patterns emerge not just in actions and behaviors, but over time. The simple process of assessing and reacting to changes in the environment can have this effect. In turn, the effect is cumulative.

The notion was not new to twentieth-century science. Adam Smith perceived it when he argued that the uncounted actions of individuals acting in their own self-interest would, taken together, promote the common good.[3] His venerable 'hidden hand' of commerce was the structural genie that guided selfish behavior at one level to manifest itself as altruistic at another. To be sure, classical economic analysis of free markets has always been an attempt to understand this phenomenon. Some, like Marx, tried to show how individual economic behavior manifested itself as the engine of history. The union of economic concepts and the inquiries of the physical sciences were not merged until the insights of communications theory laid down the principles of systems and networks, and computer engineers provided the tools necessary to begin the proper analysis of complexity and emergence.

Complexity theory is based in the observation that individual agents interacting repeatedly on the basis of simple rules or behavioral guides may self-organize to form a structure that exhibits characteristics or properties that cannot be predicted on knowledge of those interactions alone. When we discuss complexity theories, we are of necessity dealing with systems, and these are easy to discern. A system has a set of interconnected elements or agents such that a change in one element or agent has the potential to change all other elements or agents. By this, I mean that the constituent parts of the system are interconnected.[4] The critical interconnectivity is *feedback*, a notion discussed in detail later on. In addition, the system itself 'exhibits properties and behaviors that are different from those of the parts.'[5] When the system appears to act independently of the agents, which is much different than the system's structure acting to constrain or enable agents, then it is properly called a complex system. This is the critical complex system characteristic for emergent behavior.

Emergence refers to the appearance of a characteristic or function not previously observed within the system or structure. Within complexity theory, higher-level properties of a system of interacting agents are considered emergent, and these can be arranged in hierarchical order. A simple mechanical device such as a clock defines an emergent function of the individual parts that make it up. The capacity to tell time and pass on that information to another agent is a socially emergent characteristic, however, of the interaction of individual agents in reference to clocks—not an emergent behavior of clocks. The emergent behavior is recognized by new patterns that appear in the actions and interactions of independent agents and of the system relative to other systems. This characteristic is what makes the complex system adaptive.

The complex adaptive system is the unit of analysis in complexity theory. But, it is the interrelationships of the agents within it that define the system. The

> capacity of the agents to break with routines and thus initiate unfamiliar feedback processes is what makes the system complex … [and the] capacity of the agents to cope collectively with the new challenges is what makes them adaptive systems. Such, then, is the modern urban community, the nation state, and the international system.[6]

So we see that complexity refers only to systems that have a great number of autonomous agents, each having multiple interactions with both the environment (structure) and with other agents, and that are capable of changing in response to those exchanges. In every complex system, it is 'the very richness of these interactions [that allows] the system as a whole to undergo *spontaneous self-organization*.'[7] This self-organizing behavior is adaptive because the change is an attempt to tenaciously overcome a barrier. This means it is not random, or chaotic, but *purposeful*. It is an active attempt by the *system*, regardless of the intent of the individual agents, to achieve a continuing advantage.

The now classic example is a neural network, like the human brain, which 'constantly organizes and reorganizes its billions of neural connections so as to learn from experience.'[8] Heavily studied organic adaptive systems include ants, bees, and urban societies.[9] These systems tend to seek a sustainable equilibrium, and to the extent that their environment is relatively constant, they are successful. There is a point, however, where complex adaptive systems remain in a constantly changing flux, where individual components of a system have not locked into place, but neither do they succumb to entropic randomness. This balancing point is commonly known as the *edge of chaos*.

Systems on the edge of chaos are at a point where small changes in the environment can cause critical system properties to change *suddenly*. The change will be to a more rigid form (towards order) or a less discernible one (towards chaos). A simple example is the transition from a liquid state (dynamically stable) to solid (order) or gaseous (chaotic) form. In the full range of temperature, water exists as a liquid only in a very narrow band. Stability at the edge of chaos comes from the system's capacity to change to a more orderly state when the environment is moving toward chaos or to a more changeable one when the environment is becoming static. The impetus for change does not come from within, but from the application of an external force; heat. The capacity to repeatedly move in either direction allows the system to achieve *dynamic optimality*.

The pressure of maintaining dynamic optimality is the starting point for emergent properties in a system. In organic and social systems, the effort produces rules that ultimately constitute a higher system or structure. This higher structure will then organize and interrelate with other systems in a manner that exhibits its own emergent properties, and so on. The emergent properties are so radical that after only a few generations of emergence, the characteristics of the larger system may bear no resemblance to the ones from which it emerged. Nor are the higher and lower organizations necessarily (or even likely to be) aware of the other as having an impact on their actions. Again, the illustration here is of neural cells organizing into brains, which produces consciousness, which, among other things, produces literature. So removed are the system's constituting elements that not only is prediction nearly impossible, anthropological deconstruction is staggeringly difficult. One simply could not discern the causal chain that leads to *Moby Dick* from a dissection of the neural cell, nor reconstruct the neural network of Melville's brain from a reading of the same. There may even be an inherent form of irreversibility in the process of emergence. Just as stirring sugar into a cup of coffee makes it sweet; reversing the agitation does not stir the sugar out.

Complexity in the system does not come simply from a great number of rules or agents, or varieties of interaction, but from the *density* of the interactions. The more actors, the greater the potential for interrelations, but it is not the actors that make the system complex—it is the *organizational structure*. A system could have an infinite number of agents, arranged in a chain such that each one could interact only with the one below it and the one above. If the function were to pass along information directionally, that is if A passes information to B, and B passes the same information to C, C to D, *ad infinitum*, no matter how long the chain, the system is hopelessly static. Without an external impetus, the chain will simply be a transmission line. If, however, the information could be *changed* as it is passed, following a simple rule, the chain could begin to exhibit patterns. This is the essence of Steven Wolfram's startling work.

Wolfram insists that all the structural diversity in the universe can be explained as the output of innumerable interactions by rule-guided agents, and these rules may be remarkably few and simple.[10] What results is an incalculable array of intricate constructions. This intricacy has obscured the fundamental nature of the universe, he claims, as it has caused scientists to focus on the details (or output) of the relationships and not the organizing principles of those relationships.

Wolfram's method has been to study the patterns that result from simple interactions of cellular automata in computer programs. The concept was developed in 1952 by John von Neumann, who devised a simple self-reproducing program that could copy its initial base 2 (0s and 1s) configuration.[11] The program would color in a cell (or a pixel on a computer screen) one at a time as it moved from left to right on a graph. As the idea developed, rules were substituted to have the program write different configurations depending on its initial configuration (state) and the configurations (states) of adjacent cells. The new program repeats the process. When graphically displayed, and the program self-reproduces continuously (automatically), a bewildering array of patterns can emerge.

Wolfram determined there are 256 possible rule combinations for cellular automata using a base 2 (on–off, 0–1, positive–negative) configuration in a simple two-dimensional space.[12] In this condition, an automaton is influenced by adjacent or touching automata, of which there can be a maximum of two (before and after). The rule is for the automata to reproduce in its current form or its alternate state, depending on its initial state and those of adjacent states. Each time the automaton assesses its own state and the state of others, it has the potential to transition. The sequences of transitions occur in four categories or classes, numbered in order of complexity. Usually, the rules will dictate a simple stable order Wolfram calls *repetition,* or Class I rule sets.[13] Often, the repetition makes a complicated though symmetrical pattern of patterns, which he calls *nesting* or Class II behavior. Class III rule sets spawn a pattern of transitions that does not repeat, and the result, while it can be visually fascinating, is *random*. Last is a category that seems to exhibit macrobehavior. Class IV rule sets Wolfram dubs *localized structures*. These are characterized by transitions from nesting, repeated, and random behavior. The patterns themselves transition (not just the automata), and they do so without external influence.

The simplest forms of transition are heuristic enough, but Wolfram takes the next step by going to a base 3 rule set. Astonishingly, when the transition can be to one of three states (white, black, or gray) vice two, there are 7,625,597,484,987 possible rule sets![14] Wolfram could not possibly run and evaluate each rule set, and so to compensate, he first looks at 'totalistic' rules, ones in which the color of the new (replicated) cell takes the color of the average of the current cell and its neighbors.[15] For three color transitions, there are 2,187 possible totalistic rule sets. But, despite the more complex rules, the basic set of structural behaviors is little changed. The four classes identified in base 2 automata remain.

While the totalistic rules reinforce the essential point that complex rules do not make for a greater variety of aggregate or macrobehavior, Wolfram persisted. He developed a notion of *mobile* automata rules. Instead of moving continuously in one direction, changing its state depending on the rule set, the mobile automaton determines its state *and* the *direction* of the cell to be replicated. If we can think of the cells as squares on a piece of graph paper, the automaton can move in one of eight directions, to any cell that touches it (a compass would direct the automata to move north, south, east, west, northeast, northwest, southeast, or southwest). Totalistic rules and mobile automata allow for 65,536 permutations, and not one displays more complex behavior than the original 256 rule sets. [16]

Wolfram then allows the totalistic mobile automata rule sets to change not only the active cell color, but the color of all eight adjacent cells. With more than four and a quarter *billion* possible rule sets, Wolfram decides to sample them. More than 99 percent display simple repetitive (Class I) macrobehavior. Every 'few thousand or so' the rule sets display Class II nested macrobehavior.[17] About every 50,000, a rule set displays purely random (Class III) macrobehavior. After 'searching through a few million rules,' Wolfram found a set that displayed truly complex macrobehavior with an apparently randomly moving mobile automaton. The macrobehavior displayed was visually stunning.

The preceding highlights the extraordinary comprehensiveness of Wolfram's study. He forged on by examining rule sets with simple and sequential substitutions, simple and cyclical 'tag' configurations, register and Turing machine formats, and symbolic systems. All together, the fundamental structure held. Extremely complex macrobehavior can be generated from very simple rule-guided microbehavior, and complex behavior is exhibited in every type of rule set. The simplest rule sets, like the one in the chain example above, will only ever produce repetitive microbehaviour and macrobehavior. Slightly more complex rules can produce apparently random behavior, while truly complex macrobehavior requires rule sets that are slightly more complex again. Nonetheless, the complexity level of the underlying rules, even for localized structure macrobehavior, is quite elementary. 'Once the threshold for complex behavior has been reached ... adding complexity to the underlying rules does not lead to any perceptible increase at all in the overall complexity of the behavior that is produced.'[18]

Wolfram explains an astounding array of natural and contrived behavior to drive home his point. It is hard not to be convinced by his rigor and his passion. Much of his work then seeks to determine the original rule sets that result in Class IV constructs. More interesting for strategists, the sequences of randomness observed in Class IV macrobehavior appear to be transitioning states for the overall structure. When one looks at the larger Class IV constructs, it is impossible to see these patterns of embedded randomness within order without thinking of the

118

edge of chaos. Indeed, it appears the transition requires a spasm of chaotic activity to undergo the transition from one state to another, regardless of the systemic activity. In human social (macro)behavior, for example, the movement from an ordered political system to a more chaotic (though still functional) one is often punctuated by war or revolution. Even in dynamically stable political systems like liberal democracy—especially in the Westminster parliamentarian model—the electoral mechanism takes on the vibrant characteristics of potential chaos, returning the extant regime to power or ushering in a more progressive or conservative reformist one.

The more interrelations a system has, and the greater their variety, the greater the potential for emergence of an adaptive systemic behavior. Complexity is found in the relationships of actors, in the structure of organization, and in 'the incessant urge of complex systems to organize themselves into patterns.'[19] Even when the interactions are extremely simple, like those of bees or ants, when carried out simultaneously and relentlessly, the straightforward relationships change the system. And change is the key to everything.

Power, change, and feedback

Adaptation and emergence do not occur in a perfectly stable system. Change is required, and fortunately in socio-political systems, change and surprise are persistent. Master strategists will not only adjust to unforeseen change, they will construct a strategy that manipulates and advances change. The more rigid and inflexible the opponent's plans, the better the relative advantages that will accrue. The strategist cannot, of course, anticipate with clarity the unknown or unforeseeable. These are by definition beyond our current comprehension. What can be attempted, nonetheless, is to prepare for the unforeseen.

In nature, systems incorporate change through adaptation. The system that can adapt quickest and best survives. Adaptation in these instances is not contingent upon conscious assessments of utility value, a capacity humans have but do not always do well, but on structural factors built in to the system. Hence the good strategist builds adaptability into the structure of the strategy. Recognizing change and incorporating it, or manipulating it, or rejecting and dispensing of it (all of these are forms of adaptation) requires the capacity to *learn*. Learning is the ability to confront change and be surprised once, and thereafter be better prepared.

The immune system is an exceptional adaptive learning system that is purely structural. When a new threat to the body is recognized, a new antibody model is adapted and remains in the system. If the threat is realized early enough, when the invasion is small, the body can adapt its defenses to defeat it. Moreover, when similar (though not identical) threats appear in the future, the body is better prepared to meet the new manifestations of the threat. The immune system, without consciousness or intelligence, has learned to recognize certain types or forms of threat, and is able to categorize them for future reference.

It does not require a thinking agent with free will to learn. Structurally, systems evolve and adapt over time in a series of unguided reactions to external and internal stimuli. Successful systems do so by quickly *recognizing* meaningful change and adapting to new conditions. This is a capacity that is built in to the complex system, and a successful strategist seeks to build similar capacities into the systemic structure of military forces. The key to an adaptive structure construction is the incorporation of *feedback*.

A relationship exists when the action of one agent affects the behavior of another. This is called a power relationship: hence, power is a relationship between autonomous agents. Indeed, power is only discernible in relative context, so much so that the measure of power is often calculated in resistance to the application of it. Therefore the amount of power expended or demonstrated is measured via the engineer's notion of *feedback*.

Robert Dahl's definition of the power relationship is simply, 'A has power over B to the extent that he can get B to do something that B would not otherwise do.'[20] This simple definition works as a point of departure. 'First, let us agree that power is a relation, and that it is a relation among people.'[21] Second, 'the *amount* of an actor's power can be represented by a probability statement: e.g., "the chances are 9 out of 10 that if the President promises a judgeship to five key Senators, the Senate will not override his vote."'[22] In other words, power relationships are always expressed in probabilistic vice deterministic terms, because the interactions of people are not akin to the predictable interactions of inanimate objects such as billiard balls. Third, what Dahl calls the first property, and 'a necessary condition' of his power relation, 'is that there exists a time lag, however small, from the actions of the actor who is said to exert power to the responses of the respondent.'[23] This time-lag allows for the measurement of power and is the basis for assertions of the *necessity* of feedback in both strategy and power relationships. Fourth, it is vital to understand that *meaningful*, or what are often termed *political,* power relationships exist only when the exercise of power is *intended*. Clearly, unintended power is important, and many potential actors are affected by it, but until and unless it is recognized by *either* or both agents in the power relationship, it is not a power relationship.

A power relationship without a feedback loop is equivalent to the notion of a null relationship. It is *theoretically* possible, but it is an artificial notion that cannot exist in the real world. David Easton is sympathetic: 'the concept "feedback loop" is [a way] of identifying not only information that returns, but *all the other actions* directed toward taking advantage of this action.'[24] Power and feedback are in this manner at the core of all military planning and strategy.

The critical function of feedback is the ability it provides to recognize change over time. Henry Teune is pointedly aware of the importance of change in any concept of power and strategy. To be sure, asserts Teune, 'explaining change is at the core of any social theory.'[25] He shows that without change to assess social relationships, the relationships themselves would go unnoticed. And this is too often the problem in existing power models, as they attempt to describe power relationships as a frozen moment in time, a snapshot, if you will, of a complex social association. In such models, power is measured *within* the actors, either as it is contained in A (as potential power or power expended) or in B (as resistance). Classic Balance of Power models explained the relative power of one state versus another in terms of numbers of troops, tonnage of ships, monies in reserve, and the like. Power is in this view held by a state.

In a dynamic power model, at least two snapshots must be taken, far enough apart in time to demonstrate change (or stasis where change was expected). In reality, the first snapshot is of the world we expect. It is *prediction*. The second snapshot occurs as we assess the world as it has become. The difference is feedback. When *change* is incorporated into the model, the focus of measurement on either actor is potentially more accurate, despite the lack of a base or foundational power rule. Rather than an arbitrary measurement of power, for which we still have no yardstick, *relative* levels of power between actors can be assessed. Indeed, *resistance* may prove to be the fundamental unit of analysis in a future power theory (e.g. power = resistance × change). Resistance to A's efforts may be contained within B, but is meaningless if it is not related to B's motivations, cognitions, and perceptions of capability and A's perceptions of and reactions to B. *The focal point of power analysis should therefore be the feedback loop itself, the point where resistance is evaluated.*[26]

Most definitions of power also include some notion of the power *to do* or to act, and potential power over some one or some thing. Any analysis of the power one actor holds over another necessarily includes these two components: extant power and potential power. When that distinction is imported into a relational model between two or more actors, the behavior described is that of *control* or *attempted control*. Control is politically indistinguishable from power, both actual and potential. When A has at least partial control of the actions of B, A is in a power position over B. The amount of power is discernible only because of feedback.

It is generally recognized that the concept of feedback has its origins in engineering, as the first recognized feedback applications were mechanical.[27] Otto Mayr, who has written extensively on the subject of mechanical feedback systems, dates their origin to at least the third century BCE, to the water clocks of Ktesibos.[28] These sophisticated and highly accurate clocks regulated the flow of water (by which time was marked) with an ingenuous system of float valves that counteracted the disruptive effect of varying water pressure in holding tanks.

Mayr cites the definition of the American Institute of Electrical Engineers, that feedback is a 'control system which tends to maintain a prescribed relationship of one system variable to another by comparing the functions of these variables and using the difference as a means of control.'[29] The classic example of the first intentional or conscious use of a mechanical feedback control system is James Watts' celebrated centrifugal governor for the steam engine.[30] In Watts' contraption, a change in the speed of the engine would cause a set of weights to move up or down, opening or closing the steam conduit. Despite these earlier prototypes,

Mayr credits James Clerk Maxwell, because of an 1867 paper 'on governours,' as the father of automated control systems, and more importantly, as the inspiration for Norbert Wiener's cybernetics.[31]

The first academically recognized attempt to link social sciences and the engineer's feedback mechanism was provided in a 1943 article by Arturo Rosenblueth, Norbert Wiener, and Julian Bigelow.[32] The authors contended that any action that was 'purposeful [may] be subdivided into two classes: "feedback" (or teleological) and non-feedback (non-teleological).'[33] In other words, any action that was not encumbered with feedback was either unintended or random. The authors also made an early distinction between *positive feedback*, which 'adds to subsequent input signals, it does not correct them,' (similar to an amplifier, in which 'the fraction of the output which reenters as input has the same value as the original input') and *negative feedback*, which is 'the behavior of an object controlled by the margin of error at which the object stands at a given time with a reference to a relatively specific goal, that is, the signals from the goal are used to restrict outputs which would otherwise go beyond the goal.'[34] All biological feedback systems, according to the authors, are negative feedback systems.

It is important to note that Rosenblueth, Wiener, and Bigelow admitted certain conscious or purposeful biologic actions could be thought of as non-feedback, or non-teleological. This was due to the speed with which these actions take place, presumably limiting if not eliminating the processing time necessary for feedback. Their examples were a snake striking at a frog, or a frog striking at a fly. This is a fairly primitive view of the feedback process (for which the authors are more than excused). If the action is understood to be part of a larger meta-action or series of actions, and, in these cases, the notions of strike preparation (positioning, waiting, targeting, etc.) and learning are factored into the behavioral description, it is difficult to conceive of any conscious or intended action or behavior that is not affected in some measure by feedback. Of course, this kind of analysis is predicated on behavioral emphases on actions.[35]

While the notion of intended action without feedback is difficult to conceive, it is not necessary to assume that received feedback will hold any value for the actor. Held and Freedman developed the concept of 'decorrelated feedback' in their work on astronautics.[36] They asserted feedback must be correlated or corroborated to be useful, 'for example, bodily movements are, for the most part, the resultants of muscular exertion against the counterforces of objects and gravity.'[37] An astronaut experiences decorrelated feedback in the weightlessness of outer space. Charles Osgood furthered the key conception of 'representational feedback [which] selects among alternative perceptual organizations' such that 'recognition times [vary] with such things as values, attitudes, previous rewards and punishments, and the like.'[38] Indeed, feedback can be misinterpreted, misleading, or baldly inaccurate.

The founding moment for the widespread application of feedback mechanisms came in 1948, with the publication of Norbert Wiener's *Cybernetics*.[39] Wiener's basic model intended to show that communication (or information transfer) and control occur in the functioning of many different kinds of systems, and that *all types of systems ultimately control themselves with feedback* designed to disclose error in accomplishing goals and initiate corrective action.[40] 'Feedback' he asserted, '[is] the property of being able to adjust future conduct by past performance,' and there were two kinds of feedback, negative and positive.[41] The negative feedback approach was simpler and more sensitive to a changing environment, argued Wiener. By using negative feedback, much as a home thermostat, the mechanism can home in on the most desirable conditions and maintain a dynamic equilibrium—what Wiener called homeostasis—within tolerable limits. For this reason, it is adaptive, and can handle random changes in the environment. 'Negative feedback, then, is a way of reaching an equilibrium point despite unpredictable—and changing—external conditions. The "negativity" keeps the system in check, just as "positive feedback" propels the system onward.'[42]

Wiener was searching for 'the relationship between control and feedback,' and for him, 'negative feedback is a way of pushing a fluid, changeable system toward a goal. It is ... a way of transforming a complex system into a complex *adaptive* system.'[43] Adaptation occurs because of a system's desire to follow a specific pattern. The difference between the ideal pattern and actual performance is a new input for the adaptive system. It responds by making a move or correction in the desired direction of homeostasis, and then takes a new measurement.

Negative feedback systems were desirable for a number of reasons. They were utilitarian and to some extent predictable, and they handled random change quite nicely. But they were not observable in most social systems, and Wiener singled out political activity as especially lacking in negative feedback processes. Indeed, social systems tend toward positive feedback mechanisms, which add additional input to already moving or correcting behavior. This allows for extremely disruptive and violent change within the system. If negative feedback is the means of balancing, positive feedback creates bandwagoning behavior. An example is the rumor, or the e-mail legend, which starts as speculation and can spread through a social system until it is more than a confirmed fact, it is a phenomenon.

Negative feedback was for Wiener the font of learning, for it had a tendency to control error en route to a discernible goal. Such activity is purposeful. But negative feedback was also remorselessly leading the system to the ends of entropy, movement to the most probable state homeostasis, undifferentiated and chaotic.[44] Entropy was, for Wiener, the enemy of life and living, and life is defined by the ability to challenge entropy, to roll back the deleterious effects of decay, and open the closed system to new challenges and innovations. For this, only positive feedback will do. In the tactical model so far described, negative feedback is the mode of preference. Tactical genius seeks the most probable state of battle, victory by one side. Strategy seeks to reverse entropy, to increase the set of probable states and to create options for action by opening the system and loosening control.

Cybernetics is thus indistinguishable from control. The term itself has its roots in the Greek word for 'steersman.'[45] The difference between mechanical and social feedback systems is, of course, the presence of human judgment in the 'chain of feedback.'[46] When this chain is drawn schematically, feedback loops inevitably emerge, and it is the feedback loop that provides the input data to affect control. Power, as has been shown, is a notion indistinguishable from control. To have the ability or potential to influence another actor is simply to assert control over that actor. If all *intended* power relationships are in some measure, if not entirely, control relationships, then feedback looms as the operant concept for analysis and is the logical point of departure.

Karl Deutsch immediately recognized the value of cybernetics for political analysis and expanded on the early models, adding the notions of learning and purpose, values, consciousness, free will, autonomy, and integrity.[47] His belief that social theory was dependent on a well-grounded understanding of communications networking and feedback was amply presented in his 1963 classic, *The Nerves of Government*.[48] According to Bernard Susser, Deutsch's text, which takes up the challenge raised by the cybernetic ideas of 'learning, control and self-monitoring,' asks the questions:

> What are the implications for our understanding of the political system if we conceive of it as a vast information storing, receiving, processing, and transmitting network? If we compare the political process to what we know of learning, responding to new stimuli, self-correction, and self-regulation, are our traditional assumptions about politics still adequate and serviceable?[49]

In *The Nerves of Government*, Deutsch corrects Rosenblueth, Wiener, and Bigelow's erroneous notion of the existence of non-feedback intended action. No conscious act can be isolated from a process which ultimately includes some feedback mechanism. As an example, Deutsch describes the operation of a 'modern radar tracking and computing device, the series of actions and decisions based on feedback that it takes, and I cannot help but recall the image of the striking snake or frog.'[50] The biological action described by Rosenblueth *et al.* is more cleverly portrayed by an electro-mechanical device in Deutsch. Even so, '[n]one of these devices approaches the overall complexity of the human mind.'[51] Ultimately, Deutsch relies on the concept of feedback to make his model work, and he defines feedback as 'a communications network that produces action in response to an input of information, and *includes the results of its own action in the new information by which it modifies its subsequent behavior.*'[52]

Moreover, Deutsch brought positive feedback, or 'amplifying feedback,' into the social equation.[53] Such a phenomenon exists in crowd panics, runaway inflation, and arms racing. Specifically, in the latter example, if each side in a classic security dilemma perceives that it must maintain a measure of superiority over the other, a spiraling and dangerous amplification of destructive behavior can result. Understanding and managing the positive feedback input, however, suggests the escape from such dilemmas. In the case of arms racing, both sides monitor the simultaneous de-escalation actions of the other (made in small, incremental steps), never accepting a clear inferiority to a rival.[54]

Signaling thus becomes an integral component in social feedback. While it is conceivable that across levels of analysis the action of one actor could affect the behavior of another, even though the influencing actor is unaware of the impact, such a relationship still exhibits feedback characteristics. A fanciful example is the President of the United States signing a trade bill that is ruinous to a farmer in Madagascar. Clearly the relationship is political, and without doubt a causal link is evident. Several strategic and tactical repercussions are applicable. The first is what I call *anti*-feedback, or the misperception that since no feedback is received, everything is OK and current behavior can continue unchanged. Plainly, it seems, one could argue that the lack of feedback in this situation is still feedback. Anti-feedback will in most cases be mistaken or corrupted feedback, but in some it may be quite appropriate. By not complaining about a behavior, an actor is implicitly approving of it. By not being *able* to complain, a deeper level of feedback is at work, but a strand of feedback nonetheless. It is also quite possible, in the example given, that the President could someday become aware of the plight of the Madagascar farmer. As soon as this happens the relationship becomes intended, for the President must consciously decide to continue with the same policies or modify them. This type of feedback can be called latent feedback. It is the process of making a relationship conscious, and therefore intended and political, as soon as the actor becomes aware of the relationship. Even so, latent feedback is not the emergence of feedback in the relationship, it is the potential for a change in the perception of feedback over time (anti-feedback already was present).

An additional type of feedback must be identified because some systems have a time-lag problem that makes feedback entirely impractical in real-time control situations.[55] There is, therefore, a useful distinction between feedback and *feedforward*.[56] Feedforward systems monitor the inputs of a process to ensure they are going as planned. If they are not, the inputs (though sometimes the processes) are changed. This idea, too, ultimately derives from the engineer, where 'feedforward is accomplished by analyzing the inputs to a process, seeing how they interact, and monitoring the inputs so the adjustments can be made to them *before* output from the system occurs.'[57] Of course, in analytic terms, the problem with feedforward is anticipating the unanticipated. Not all variables can (or should) be accounted for in advance. Therefore, a combination of feedback and feedforward systems working in tandem is most efficient.

Feedforward in humans is exemplified by the motorist who accelerates in anticipation of an upcoming hill, preferring not to wait until the speedometer registers a decrease in speed; or by the hunter who leads the quarry when aiming, in anticipation of the lag time between a shot and the hoped-for hit. Feedforward in power terms is useful because it highlights the concept of potential power or power *over* another. In a power relationship, one actor may weigh the advantages or disadvantages of an action before it is undertaken, in effect anticipating feedback and modifying inputs before actions are taken (or not taken). For example, a student may anticipate the answer an instructor wants before responding to a question asked in class. In this context, the student is responding to an exertion of power (perhaps unintended) by the instructor.

Change and surprise in strategy

Any strategy that does not incorporate change is not just a poor strategy; it is no strategy at all. To accept the status quo as the baseline of the future or to promote it as the goal of strategy is to lose sight of the potential beyond the horizon of the known. The best that can be achieved is a rigid stasis that denies all change, buying time for an inevitable and sudden catastrophic collapse. To be sure, acceptance and tolerance for change and surprise may be the most efficient discriminators when separating tactics from strategy.

But how does one incorporate the notion of surprise into strategy? In other words, what surprises can we expect? It is a moot question, as stated, for if we can expect them, they are hardly surprises. We can only state what has surprised us before, not what will. For the tactical thinker, who seeks certainty of the outcome, no surprises can be planned. All contingencies are to be accounted for, or reacted to at the time of action. Surprises that occurred in the past can be studied, explained, assigned a probability, and integrated into the plan. If completely accounted for, they are no longer surprising. Likewise, things that have not happened before but *could* happen can be incorporated if they are imagined. The master tactician draws on experience, grasp of the situation and the means available to both sides, knowledge of the opponent, and innate creative abilities to think of every contingency. Changes are only surprises if they have not been thought of and prepared for in the plan. Despite the admonition that no plan survives contact with the enemy, when carrying out the plan, the tactician dreads the inevitable surprise.

For the strategic thinker, who sees no finality in the outcome of events, surprises must be expected. They must be embraced and seized upon as opportunity. The strategic thinker manipulates the boundaries of context so that change—or newness, in whatever its form—is accepted and incorporated seamlessly. A strategy that cannot embrace new technologies, new alliances, and a wide range of tactical victories and defeats, is not truly a strategy.

The difference between strategy and tactics is thus observed in the process of planning. The tactician deals with what *is*. The strategist copes with what *is not*. As Lao Tsu said when describing a ceramic storage jug, it is the clay that gives the jug its shape, but it is the hole that is the *purpose* of the jug. Therefore, utility is had from what there is, but value and meaning come from what there is not. To carry the analogy, the tactician crafts from the materials available the means to go to war; the strategist determines its best use.

We return, then, to the meaningful differences of strategy and tactics that animate this study. The tactician seeks to culminate events, both in victory and in exit strategies or endgames. This is appropriate. But only that which is capable of

126

change is capable of continuing indefinitely. Thus the realm of the strategist, which has no end or culminating point, is the realm of change. It is the strategist's purpose to manipulate the boundaries and rules of competition, to make them fluid, to change them as readily as needs dictate. In such a realm of the possible, the strategist enters into a relationship with the goal of continuing it, on favorable terms, and accepts that every choice made and acted upon redefines the rules and boundaries of the interaction. And this is anathema to the tactician, for if the rules and boundaries of the conflict change in mid-conflict, the carefully made plans are disrupted. Imagine a game of chess in which, halfway through, pawns were allowed to move as queens. The master chess player would be frustrated to no end. More important, when the conditions of conflict are not fixed, it will be impossible to agree on a victor! The conditions for victory could change at the moment of triumph, and then the winner is determined not by skillful play but fortuitous interruption.

Hence it is vital to the tactician that the rules do not change during the course of battle, and many of the tactician's actions are toward that end—a consistent combat environment that is in accordance with the strengths and knowledge of the tactician. Expecting and adapting to change is the essence of the strategic thinker's planning, however. Without *at least the possibility of change* the strategist has no function *within the conflict*. In the chess analogy above, once the terms are agreed upon and the decision to begin the game is made, strategy is set aside. Prowess within the rules will determine a winner. Play may conform to an overall strategy, to win decisively for example, or to lose credibly, but neither outcome is predicated on a future change in the structure of the game. If the future will be like the past, then boundaries are set and immutable. Master tacticians can hone their craft through experience and study of history alone. Everything important is already known.

In the game of chess, the master does not seek to take the king. The master forces a situation in which the king must move, and that move can only be to a vulnerable square. The master looks to dominate the space next to the king, not the king's space, and then forces the king to move into it. The chess master is thus a tactical thinker. When the opposing player understands that within the rules and boundaries of chess, the outcome is certain, resignation occurs before the final moves are made. When there is no action allowed in the rules that would reverse the coming defeat, surrender will be offered.

If chess has master strategists, they would not be concerned about the outcome of a particular game or tournament. The outcome of each game establishes new conditions and boundaries for subsequent play. The desire is not to win, but to continue playing chess. If I were to teach my daughter the rules of chess, so to have a ready opponent available to indulge my pastime, and then won every game quickly and decisively, she would soon grow bored and refuse to play. I would have demolished my opponent, satisfying the conditions of victory, but I would have lost my strategic *purpose* of playing a challenging game with my daughter. If I were thoughtful, I would carefully develop my daughter's skills so that she becomes an able opponent—so that she develops a taste for the game and may become a master herself—in order that someday she can teach me new options, ultimately enhancing my play and enjoyment of the game. No matter how much more skillful we mutually get at chess, there is no meaningful point the games *must* end. As I get older and my skills erode, my daughter will continue playing for enjoyment and as an excuse to spend time with me in my dotage. At that point, she may even let me win now and again. Even upon my death, the game continues. My daughter may teach her children, and they will play on.

The metaphor for conflict and war is not clean. It is possible to find warriors who seek battle for the purpose of continuing play, such as the ritualized combat and counting coup of the North American Plains Indians. But this type of perpetual war is properly maligned when the weapons of war allow violence escalation to achieve genocidal proportion. Some theorists, following the lead of Machiavelli, argue that perpetuating small conflicts is in the best interest of the long-term health of the state.[58] It seems a bit strained to try to equate the desire of the chess player to play chess in the future and the state strategist's desire to continue positive future interactions with other states, but the mental leap is not overly wrought. The tactician plays chess to win, the strategist to play in the future. The tactician wages war to win. The strategist *anticipates* waging war in the future.

Hence the ideal tactical decision-making situation is one in which all courses of actions are known (surprise is impossible) and the rules and boundaries are clearly established. Battle is a foregone conclusion and so entering into it (or not) is the initial strategic decision. The game of tic-tac-toe provides an analogy. Between skilled opponents, the side that goes first will win. While there is no best strategy *for* playing the game, there are infallible tactics *within* it. It would even be possible to create a short guide that would list all possible moves and the optimum counters to each. All the tactician must do is recognize the situation on the board and counter appropriately. In a few iterations, it becomes apparent that the side that moves will attempt to put the opponent in a position that requires a choice: block one of two winning moves. Since either block allows the other to win, it is not even a meaningful choice. It is interesting, I suppose, from an historical perspective, but the outcome is not in doubt. Therefore neither how the game was played nor its outcome is relevant to the strategist. What is important is how the decision was made as to who goes first. This critical competition *outside* the boundaries of the field of play is what connects the tactician to the strategist.

The tactician strives to eliminate choice, to ensure that no surprise can occur. All possibilities are included in the ideal battle plan. The best of these anticipate an outcome that is foregone, a surety. The perfect plan is therefore perfected prediction. Accordingly, if the outcome is not in doubt, then choice has been eliminated. If whatever action the other takes will not forestall victory, then those actions are meaningless. The strategist strives instead to expand options, even for the opponent (by leaving an honorable exit, perhaps), to maximize the available choice-set. The tactician seeks closure, the culmination of the plan. The strategist rejects closure, seeking instead to continue planning. It is the interaction of war, its dual nature, which forces this view. No matter how careful my planning, no matter how comprehensive my plan, the opponent *could* do something unantici- pated. The boundaries *could* change. The rules *could* evolve. The tactician seeks to force the opponent to choose an option that will lead to defeat. This is done by taking options away, by removing the possibility of free choice.

Choice again becomes the operational descriptive of power and meaning. As human beings, we reference our lives not by the boundaries that begin and end them, notions of birth then death, but by the major events that shape them; gradu- ations, marriage, the births of children, new jobs, and the like. These are events and accomplishments that define us, and they are always subject to change. They are representative of the free choices made and rejected that continuously shape our existence. So long as life goes on, there is choice, and where there is choice, hope. A single act can redeem a life of evil, or condemn the good person to ignominy. More than this, a life ends in death only in the physical sense. The choices and accomplishments of a profound life can shape the future long after the body is dust. Birth, too, is not a sudden creation of life. Each person is the result and extension of generations before, the manifestation of a physical, cul- tural, and political evolution that gives shape and meaning to the newest life.

The state is a manifestation of this logic. Its decisions are based on a past his- tory and accomplishments. It is understood not as a simple descriptive of its existing characteristics (size, population, resources, etc.), but as a culmination of these and its culture, ideology, mythology, and more. Since it is the state that makes war, its power has meaning only in the context of its accomplishments and the events that shaped it. But history is not deterministic for the state any more than it is for the individual. It shapes and guides behavior, but the likelihood that a certain action will or will not be taken is a probability only. It is in fact this mutability of time that makes strategic thinking incompatible with the notions of victory or defeat. For the tactically defeated, this means the possibility of rising to challenge again exists. For the tactical victor, it means there will be new chal- lenges, and new challengers. Nothing is ever truly finished.

Strategy is always *about* the game or competition; *within* it are tactics. The absurdity of a strategy within a game is highlighted by the example of a solitaire card game. The only unknown, the order in which the cards are revealed, is tacti- cally all-important and strategically meaningless. The conclusion of the game is immaterial to the play or outcome of subsequent ones, with the exception that pat- terns might emerge that could reveal or prompt a preference (or habits) for certain moves. Since no others are required to engage in solitaire, and the decision to play is entirely internally motivated, strategy is absent. It is a time-filler.

On the other hand, in interactive games with players of differing skills, strategy is always present, even if only implicitly so. Poker is the exemplar here. When and where to play, what limit on bets, which variation of the game, what opponents to engage; these are all serious strategic questions. Once *in* the game, knowledge of odds, skills of card-counting, awareness of other player's 'tells' (and one's own) are critical to increasing the chances of winning. Even a decision to throw some games once it is recognized that the other players are outmatched, so as to increase the take at the end of the night, is a tactical move toward ultimate victory. To throw some games because the other players are friends or family, and the most important thing is to keep them playing week after week, is a strategic choice, however. Examples abound. A poor player who engages in poker to win, by playing to the best of his or her ability, may lose repeatedly, yet still desire to play on. In this case, the external strategy may be to gain experience. Future advantage is the goal, *to become a better player*, and so current reversals are expected as part of the process toward that end.

The act of becoming is central to the development of the strategist. A tactician is trained. A strategist becomes. In his differentiation of the purpose of finite and infinite games, James Carse uses the innocuous example of gardening, an analogy I extend for strategists: 'To garden is to design a culture capable of adjusting to the widest possible range of surprise in nature. Gardeners are acutely attentive to the deep patterns of natural order, but are also aware that there will always be much lying beyond their vision.'[59] The garden itself is a perpetual thing, and a 'successful harvest is not the end of a garden's existence, but only a phase of it … gardens do not "die" in the winter but quietly prepare for another season.'[60] Like a gardener, who creatively monitors and cares for a parcel of ground, the strategist perceives a continuity of interactions that must be tended to from one generation to the next. Just as master gardeners creatively and experimentally draw all the sources of nourishment and variety to enhance the continual output of the garden, master strategists must take an active part in maintenance and health of the many political systems that encompass military actions. It is necessary to prune the tree to keep it healthy, but too vigorous a cutting will kill it.

> Inasmuch as gardens do not conclude with a harvest and are not [planted] for a certain outcome, one never arrives anywhere in a garden … [one] does not bring change to a garden, but comes to a garden prepared for change, and therefore prepared to change.[61]

So important to strategy are change and surprise that they could easily be justified as enduring principles of war. At the tactical level, the decision-maker anticipates every conceivable action of the opponent. The actions that are not anticipated are surprises. As a rule, the more an opponent surprises the tactician, the less likely the tactical goal of victory will be achieved.[62] The logic is so compelling that the master tactician who has prepared for all reasonable contingencies has to a limited extent predetermined the future. The opponent can do nothing (within the boundaries of the battle) that has not been foreseen. The opponent's *meaningful* choices, those that could put the outcome in doubt, have been eliminated.

It seems likely that perfected knowledge is impossible, and therefore at least some possibilities will always be unknowable. Clausewitz called the infinite number of things that can go awry in battle the friction of war. The term is encompassing and intuitively accurate. While the tactician struggles to eliminate friction, a practical impossibility that is still worth pursing, as any limit to the amount of friction favors the side that is more prepared, the strategist embraces friction and surprise. Surprise forces the strategist to look anew at the situation. The superior strategist is the one that recognizes new choices and emerging options faster than the opponent does. Surprise alters the context of war. Surprise allows for the boundaries of war to change.

To forgo surprise, and to inflict it on the opponent, the tactician engages in deception. The master tactician desires the maximum amount of accurate information while denying that information (or providing misinformation) to the opponent. Deception in this way maximizes surprise for the opponent, who at the tactical level is degraded in direct proportion to the effectiveness of the deception. This is the aspect of war that is so heavily weighed in classic guides like Sun Tzu's *Art of War*:

> Warfare is the Way (Tao) of deception. Thus although [you are] capable, display incapability … When committed to employing your forces, feign inactivity. When [your objective] is nearby, make it appear as if distant; when far away, create the illusion of being nearby.[63]

To keep one's intentions unknown, location secret, and appearance humble is the greatest tactical (and for Sun Tzu, strategic) advantage. Between equally skilled opponents, however, the level of misinformation and deception is the same. Both are trying to garner accurate information while spreading deception. Taken together, there is a significant total loss of accurate information on the tactical battlefield. In the effort by both sides to reduce the influence of friction, the combined outcome is a massive increase in friction. Such devotion to secrecy dominates the tactician's planning and expectations, and greatly influences the outcome of battle and of wars.

The strategist generally eschews secrecy, however, preferring instead the maximum flow of accurate information to all sides. The greater the flows of accurate information, the more plausible options are made plain, and the greater the likelihood there is for meaningful choice. The availability and dispersal of accurate information throughout the system in this way provides the surest foundation for responding to change. Since the strategist anticipates change, there is no surprise when it occurs. The state or military that can most quickly adapt, and then integrate change into its strategy and operations, is the one that will reap a relative advantage.

And so, strategists do not fear the spread of accurate information, even to their enemies. It needs to be spread evenly to all decision makers: friend and foe. Tactical details can be withheld, of course, and the battle space commander should make full use of deception, but deception does little to promote *continuance* of a situation of advantage. The strategy of the state should be to broadcast strategic information accurately and fully. Strategic intentions should be clear and understood by all. An argument can easily be made that if two states are in complete agreement about the situation, relative capabilities and force structures, and the stakes involved, that war would never occur. If both I and my opponent have the same assessment of the outcome of a future fight, the one who is about to be thrashed will likely work very hard to find an alternative settlement procedure. Perfect knowledge limits conflict and increases options leading to mutually beneficial compromise.

Symmetrical knowledge can also assist in the maintenance of continuing advantage. The case of blackmail can illustrate the point. If I have information embarrassing to another, I will gain no advantage from it in our relationship unless the other knows I have it. If I threaten to make the knowledge public, the other could rationally decide to agree to my demands. In a sense, I have achieved victory by suppressing the dispersion of accurate information. I might also decide rationally not to tell the other that I have this information, so as to wait for a more opportune moment. But that moment may never come, or could be undone if another finds out the information and releases it. Information withheld has only *potential* value, deception is thus a risk. I also run a very precarious gambit akin to the strategic conception of deterrence. I expect my demands to be met or I will release the information. But if I release the information, my efforts have failed! I no longer have leverage over the other. Thus the other may choose to release the embarrassing information publicly. Once available to all, it can no longer be used as blackmail, and a panorama of new choices is revealed.

Embracing perpetual novelty

One of the earliest efforts to create a structural means for dealing with change was the TOTE plan, for 'Test-Operate-Test-Exit,' that was developed for business by Miller, Galanter, and Pribram in 1959.[64] In the TOTE design, a test is performed to see if an intended goal is met. If not, an operation (or action) is undertaken/performed in order to approach or meet the goal. Another test is made to check for goal accomplishment. If the goal is met, the loop is exited. If not, the loop continues. TOTE is important for power analysis because it was the first attempt to make the feedback loop itself the base unit of empirical measurement.[65] Initial work on TOTE was an attempt to explain reflex actions, or simple cause-and-effect models in organisms, but the TOTE model had applications far beyond this initial descriptive, and proved useful in understanding and measuring gradually increasing and decreasing power application in the face of resistance. Specifically, TOTE allowed analysts to understand incremental exertions of power. In an example of probing, R exerts an amount of power (to test E's resolve). E resists, and so R increases the strength of the current influential behavior. The process continues until E performs or R relents. This type of power behavior is common, and can be efficiently described in a TOTE model. The reliance on feedback is evident.

The TOTE method is especially useful as previous attempts to quantify resident power in the actors themselves proved problematic, as a common, fungible measurement of power (an equivalent, perhaps, to money in economics) has not been isolated. By measuring the increase in exertion and resistance over time as depicted in successive TOTE models, a relative power baseline for power behaviors in specific relationships can be established and potentially quantified. Additionally, complex maneuvers can be envisioned as a hierarchy of TOTE units, arranged in successive loops.[66] The idea here is that a simple feedback mechanism can be built into a complex activity, allowing for change and surprise to be adequately dealt with in the structure of the system.

The military equivalent of TOTE is evident in US Air Force Colonel John Boyd's concept of the OODA Loop, for 'observe, orient, decide, act,' what he equates to a system of adaptive command and control. What makes a system adaptive, capable of reacting and surviving in a changing environment, is its capacity to deal with surprise. The objective of the military commander is to 'get inside the enemy's OODA loop,' accomplished 'by simultaneously destroying the enemy's capability to sense, process, and act on information while preserving his own ability to do so.'[67] The intent is to cycle through the OODA loop faster than the opponent, thus ensuring that the other reacts to my initiatives. As time passes, the enemy's actions lose coherence, and vulnerabilities emerge. As such, this is a strategic practice, designed to gain and maintain the advantage in any conflict situation. In a complex, open-system environment, Boyd argues that command and control is a process of continuous adaptation.

Boyd's methodology is designed for the tactical fighter, and as such it is a rule-set to allow for the greatest amount of systemic adaptation. It does this by assisting the individual's ability to stay ahead of the opponent's decision and action process. If a large number of individuals are using simple rule-sets to assist in decision-making, and these individuals are capable of numerous, essentially random interactions, then the aggregate of individuals is likely to show patterns of activity that increase (or compound) the effectiveness of the individual decisions. This will occur if the adaptations made are swiftly and thoroughly transmitted throughout the system, via a neural-like structure for interaction.

Free-trade economic structures and the Internet are examples of neural-like complex adaptive systems, and in these systems the structure itself is what allows them to absorb and react to extremely heavy damage from external forces (e.g. swings in supply and demand; server or other equipment failure; and in the case of a military system, violent attacks) and yet still function, not unlike a brain after a mini-stroke. Without direction from a central authority, communications are maintained by rule-conforming adaptive behavior that restructures the network most efficiently. Lesser attacks are dealt with swiftly, with only marginal systemic adjustments required. Larger attacks can shut the system down for a time, but as corrective responses travel through the net the system can be repaired—without guidance or conscious effort from a decision-making agent. The process is automatic.

Moreover, attacks on neural systems are not necessarily cumulative (linear), and so a great deal of power can be exerted on the network without causing a noticeable effect. This can be an advantage to the net and a severe disadvantage to the attacker, who seeks the critical node that if damaged will have effects that cascade through the system, creating a victory with the greatest economy of force. A neural net has no single-point of failure. Only massive disruption can take it down permanently. But, this does not mean the complex adaptive system is invulnerable to lesser force or discriminate forms of violence. What the strategist must target when confronted with such an opponent is to *strike at its ability to adapt to change*. Mao Tse-Tung and Ho Chi Minh understood this principle, and made it the core of their guerilla doctrines. Lazare Carnot was fully aware that by introducing the *levée en masse* he was creating a new type of armed force that would dismantle the old monarchical militaries because the leadership of those states could not afford to incorporate the new military innovations without threatening the very existence of their hierarchical societies—the font and sustenance of the royal political system. It is precisely this ability to attack a superior force at points they will not or cannot defend effectively that is the basis of successful *asymmetric warfare*.[68]

Asymmetric warfare is the bane of high-technology military forces because the opponent chooses to fight in a low-technology manner, one in which the higher technology force may be extremely inefficient, and so the appearance is that lower-technology (and vastly less expensive) warfare has an inherent advantage. This is clearly not the case, and one is wise to remember the admonishment of Admiral Cebrowski, Director of Force Transformation: '… the rise of asymmetrical warfare is largely our own creation.'[69] The success of conventional American war fighting is such that its current enemies cannot successfully engage it in like manner. This is a good thing. But, as it also includes high standards of military conduct and adherence to international conventions, there are alternate ways in which to challenge the United States and its allies. What the users of asymmetric methods do is to make combat bloody, brutal, and against all rules of civilization and international law.[70] Leading states must be faced with severe losses or a threat to sovereignty before they are likely to respond in kind (with large-scale violence directed against innocent noncombatants, suspension of the rule of law, and adoption of low-tech methods). Until then, they are unlikely to radically change the way they respond to asymmetric threats, giving the less powerful side the perception of continuing success. The response does not (and probably should not) have to be to symmetrical warfare on the other side's terms. It should be to counterattack the ability of the other side to adjust to change. Today, terrorists challenge Cold War-designed militaries with tactics they were not prepared to confront in battle, and the manner in which they respond and adapt to those challenges will determine the success or failure of the Western effort.

To institutionalize change in the structure of the system, to move it closer to the edge of chaos, Steven Phelan has adapted Wolfram's categorization schema for business strategies, and there are clear parallels for military planners.[71] His logic is sound and I will follow it closely. Class I behavior is very simple, and leads to a uniform state of *finality*. Order is so strictly ingrained in the limited interaction of its agents that after only a few iterations, no change in systemic activity is possible from within. So rigid is this design, forced change from without collapses the structure. There is no room for adaptive behavior. Such a system is extremely stable, however, and quite useful for closed system functions intended to operate efficiently over a long period.

Class II behavior allows for a myriad of final states, but all of them are perfectly homeostatic or consist of simple repetitive patterns of behavior. In the process of reaching a final state, the system may *appear* to be adaptive as it reacts to external stimuli, but there are a limited number and intensity of outside influences that can be successfully encountered. The greater the number of influences that can be anticipated, the greater the number of patterns will be evident in the system. Thus, for a great many tactical planners, Class II thinking is the norm. It equates to a perfectly cyclical view of history, in which the actions of the past will be repeated in the future. The final state or homeostatic state is a perpetual repetition of known patterns and responses, and careful study of past repetitions should provide reasonable projections of the future. If the notion of inevitable cycles includes a concept of social progression, such as the Marxian politico-economic dialectic, then the final state will be stable after a series of punctuated cyclical patterns. It is a progressive transformation of a Class II system into a Class I structure. For strategists, however, Class II planning is a relatively trivial exercise in identifying repetitive historical patterns and projecting them into the future. The capacity to adapt to surprise is almost nonexistent.

Class III behavior is apparently random at the macro-level, although smaller discernible patterns may repeat at apparently random intervals. They display a sensitivity dependence on initial conditions that makes accurate predictions of future conditions virtually impossible. This is chaos. Even a small structure is difficult to erect, and all too easily torn down. It is a perfectly entropic system, constantly seeking and achieving its most probable state. It is eminently adaptable, if by adaptable one means the ability to return to a previous condition of randomness despite massive external influences. Both strategic and tactical planning are impossible in Class III structures, and any perceived successes are dumb luck.

For strategists, Class IV systems offer the most insight. Class IV behavior, the most complex, exists conceptually between Classes II and III. Patterns of both ordered and chaotic macrobehavior emerge for a time and then transition. The transitions themselves can appear random, and the macrobehaviors appear to move and interact with each other in both ordered and chaotic patterns. As Phelen states, however,

> To the extent that extended transients in Class IV systems display regular (i.e. predictable) behaviour for prolonged periods of time then it would seem that strategic planning is indeed possible in Class IV systems. However, planners in a Class IV world should attempt a Stoic outlook on life.[72]

At any time in the Class IV system a pattern may encounter unforeseen interaction with a chaotic element in the system that has the potential to overtake and disrupt the relatively stable one. Indeed, as the structure moves toward Class IV activity, as the level of turbulence in the system increases, the life expectancy of the structure goes down. Conversely, as the system moves toward Class II structures it becomes more stable, and less innovative. Strategic planning should attempt to identify and incorporate those transiently stable patterns and recognize that they will be overcome as long as the structure remains at the edge of chaos, but that the gains of adaptability and innovation for carefully perching the structure there will be worth the effort, and will keep the structure in its most viable position. Risk tolerance, to the extent it can be equated with strategic planning, consists in the amount of time the planner is willing to spend in the far edge of the Class III construct (toward Class IV chaos) where breakdowns and setbacks compete with innovation and gain, and away from the safer (though more subject to collapse through catastrophic surprise) edge of the Class II constructs. Ultimately, Phelen insists that successful organizations 'should then *direct resources away from trying to predict the future state of the system and towards learning new adaptive behaviours.*'[73]

Wolfram recognized that the existence of two fundamentally opposed classes of behavior, the ordered and the chaotic, required the existence of a third fundamental class, the phase transition space (just as A and B implies A, B, and A *and* B). This is the quantum equivalent of Schrödinger's cat in the world of Wolfram class behaviors, the structural equivalent of the coin toss after it has left the hand and before it has landed heads or tails. It is a realm of possibility and despair, where all things are possible and none have yet come to pass. Fundamentally opposed systems *must* have a phase transition space if they have the capacity to interact. This space is a narrow and precariously unstable position between the two elements of relative order and chaos, and in most systems it is a preferable or desirable place to exist. Figure 7.1 shows the phase transition space for society, information, and conflict.

Once a system goes over to chaos it cannot return without an external influence or forces to nudge it into order—the equivalent of Machiavelli's lawgiver prince or Hobbes's leviathan king. Once a system is perfectly ordered, (any) change can rescue it from stagnation—but only at the price of destroying it. Change comes in the spark of revolution, an idea that comes into the system to which it cannot adapt, and so it collapses. For a system to maintain its own viability and determine to the greatest extent possible its own fate, it must exist in the realms of Classes II and IV behavior, with an edge to Class IV—*if* the strategist or planner is able to accept change and surprise and incorporate it into the system design.

	Government	Information	Conflict
Class I Rigid or strict order	Totalitarian dictatorship	Dogma	Negative peace 'peace at any price'
Class II Order adaptable to projected change	Absolute monarchy through progressive republic	SOP and doctrine through 'rule of thumb' and knowledge	Neutrality through limited intervention and limited war
Class IV Phase transition or 'the edge of chaos'	Liberal democracy	Wisdom	Positive peace
Class III Chaotic or random state	Anarchy	Nonsense	Hobbesian state of nature

Figure 7.1 Government, information, and conflict

Summary

Complex adaptive systems, like human society, share a fundamental set of characteristics.[74] They are composed of a great number of *independently* acting agents that continuously interact with other such agents. The structure in which these agents interact is produced by a combination of initial conditions and the interactions of the agents themselves, the latter being vastly and increasingly more important as time progresses. This means that for all such systems, the operating environment is not fixed. There is no final state of order or chaos, only a continuing and perpetually changing milieu. Macro-patterns leading to finality of order or chaos are changed and revised. The system further remains dynamic by organizing and reorganizing at a great many levels, consistently creating new and higher (more encompassing) patterns of behavior.

The capacity of such systems to persist is due to their ability to adapt to unanticipated change. In complex adaptive social systems, patterns of *purposeful* macrobehavior can emerge from both the cooperative *and* competitive behavior of its agents. That the macrobehavior is purposeful is clear because learning occurs. Learning is demonstrated by the capacity of the systems to avoid the permanent pitfalls of rigid order and disheveled entropy.

The characteristic of complex adaptive systems to adapt to change and continue in a dynamic, progressive form, is the structural organization that allows the agents to continually interact, try new suborganizations, and disperse their knowledge and experience *throughout* the system. Wolfram showed the number of potential organizations from just a few simple rule sets. No individual agent or discernible subgroup of agents could anticipate or experience all possibilities, and it may be worse than useless to try to do so. John Holland says

> there's no point in imagining that the agents in the system can ever 'optimize' their fitness, or their utility, or whatever. The space of possibilities is too vast; they have no practical way of finding the optimum. The most they can ever do is to change and improve themselves relative to what the other agents are doing. In short, complex adaptive systems are characterized by perpetual novelty.[75]

8

PRINCIPLES OF WAR

The past is never dead, it is not even the past
William Faulkner, Requiem for a Nun[1]

Like all intellectual pursuits, military arts and science cannot exist in a vacuum. Strategy and tactics are influenced by the prevailing ideologies and rationalizations of the day, by dominant technologies and personalities, and by cultural and social preferences. Although the modern search for a mathematically precise theory of human interaction winds its way from the sixteenth-century philosophies of Niccoló Machiavelli and Thomas Hobbes, the potential to realize a true science of war does not come until the twentieth century, with the heuristic applications of the physical sciences to behavioral studies. But the century of physics is giving way to the age of space and information, and the mathematical precision of astronomy and Newtonian mechanics is finding new vigor in the unknowable realms of chaos and complexity. Profound changes in our understanding of social activities are on the way, and will be adapted by innovative strategists in due course. But the fundamental principles of war, which have been recognized for centuries, will not be invalidated in the cauldron of emerging knowledge and technology. The pure strategist seeks to isolate those principles, and adapt them to his or her own understanding of the world, for they are timeless.

Classic principles and the order of things

Clausewitz generally avoided strict principles of war in his published work, fearing they would too easily degenerate into rules for action: 'They aim at fixed values, but in war everything is uncertain, and calculations have to be made with variable quantities.'[2] The spasm of violence that is incorporated in war is overcome only by genius in the commander, whose judgment rises above all rules.

Still, Clausewitz provides maxims, or broadly applicable truisms, to assist us in ensuring the genius of military command will have a chance to prevail.

> The first, the supreme, the most far-reaching act of judgment that the statesman and the commander have to make is to establish [the] kind of

war on which they are embarking; neither mistaking it for, nor trying to turn it into, something that is alien to its nature. This is the first of all strategic questions and the most comprehensive.[3]

War will be decided by a 'paradoxical trinity' of primordial emotion, chance and probability, and reason.[4] The people, commander, and government play the predominant roles in these overlapping influences, with the military involved most in overcoming 'friction' and the government in setting sound policy.

On the problems in war, Clausewitz tells us:

> Everything in war is very simple, but the simplest thing is difficult. The difficulties accumulate and by producing a kind of friction ... Countless minor incidents—the kind you can never really foresee—combine to lower the general level of performance, so that one always falls far short of the intended goal.'[5]

The commander overcomes these barriers with two qualities: '*first, an intellect that, even in the darkest hour, retains some glimmerings of the inner light which leads to truth; and second, the courage to follow this faint light wherever it may lead.* The first of these qualities is described by the French term, *coup d'oeil;* the second is *determination.*'[6] *Coup d'oeil* is the ability of the commander to take in the entire sweep of battle in a glance, and to understand innately the actions that must be taken. This capacity is built through experience and a careful, intellectual study of war. With this comes the internal fortitude to recognize the path to victory and relentlessly pursue it. Clausewitz is quick to remind us that these are the critical qualities *in* war, but they are not the paramount necessities in maxims *for* war.

In war, the passions of the people can be elevated to great value. Lazare Carnot's manipulation of the French love of country, their *patrie,* allowed him to fashion the largest citizen-army the world had ever known, via the notorious *levée en masse.* Napoleon then forged this rabble into an efficient armed force, and almost seized the entire continent of Europe. The passions can also force the government into rash and importune policies. Both the emotional vigor of the people and the great game of probabilities undertaken by the military must be tempered and guided by the 'political aims [that are] the business of government alone.'[7] Here we have the first principle *of* war: 'war is not merely an act of policy but a true political instrument, a continuation of political intercourse, carried on with other means.'[8]

Clausewitz then undertakes a brilliant dissection of the meanings of law, principle, rule, regulation, and method in Book II, Chapter 4 (a set of distinctions previously discussed). *Of* and *in* war, he argues, laws are inappropriate because they are *objective.* That is, they apply in all places and situations. War is always to some extent *subjective,* or governed by *perceptions,* and therefore only the more malleable principles or methods are useful. These must be evaluated in terms of context and the preferences and emotions of the individuals involved. With this as a basis, Clausewitz tells us the best strategy is to be strong in all things, first in general and then in the particulars of the current context of capabilities and alliances.

Good advice, to be sure, but not always practical. It was intended for a soldier-king in the mold of Frederick the Great or a General Staff of the highest erudition. Unfortunately, the commander-in-chief would not always be a genius. For this reason, Clausewitz penned a brief essay on war and war-making in the tradition of Machiavelli's *Prince*. His masterpiece was *On War,* but the only work of his that was published in his lifetime was a simple essay on the principles of war.[9] Tasked with the military education of the future king, it was originally titled 'The Most Important Principles for the Conduct of War to Complete my Course of Instruction of His Royal Highness the Crown Prince.' Where *On War* is dense and forbidding, *Principles of War* is briskly written and accessible. It is a review of the most essential points distilled from his thoughts on the subject prepared in a manner to make it unmistakably clear. Still, and in keeping with the sophistication he would posthumously display in his opus, Clauswitz tells the reader that these principles 'will not so much give complete instruction to Your Royal Highness, as they will stimulate and serve as a guide for your own reflections.'[10] No finer statement of the purpose of strategic principles can be made.

There are three 'principles for war in general' that animate the essay.[11] First, while the student of warfare should pay close attention to gaining a material advantage at the decisive point, the capacity to do so is not always possible. There may be situations in which fortune, daring, and even desperation confound the most thoroughly crafted plans. Hence the principle of war that has primacy of place in all cases is the judgment of the commander. When judgment is based on experience, reflection, and reason, the decisions made will be 'heroic.'

Second, the probability of victory will not always be evident. Indeed, in many cases the probability of victory may be extremely small. But this does not mean we should fall into despair, and 'abandon the use of reason just when it becomes most necessary.'[12] Even when tactical victory cannot be achieved, the commander 'must act *against* this probability, *should there be nothing better to do.*'[13] Clausewitz is clearly not ruling out diplomatic or other efforts, but when these do not appear likely to gain a positive result, *the political leadership and military commander must act.* It is difficult to act when the outcome of war is unknown, more so when the outcome is not likely to be favorable, but this should not lead to paralysis. There is advantage to be gained even in defeat, so long as 'we familiarize ourselves with the thought of an *honorable defeat.* We must always nourish this thought within ourselves and we must get completely used to it.'[14] Thus the second general principle of war urges the strategist to see that war is never final, that a loss today—be it honorable—can translate into victory tomorrow.

Last, Clausewitz tells us that there is always a tension between the most carefully calculated and the most audacious solution. Choose the latter, advises Clausewitz. The various manuals on war-fighting that seek scientific rigor and predestined surety in the outcome of battle are based on physical calculations that cannot account for the moral and psychological factors of war. They tend to be methodical, lower risk assessments that may be comforting but cannot be completely prescient. The audacious solution is the decisive one, made by the leadership's 'inner force,' a trait made up of 'his own courage, according to his spirit of enterprise, and his self-confidence.'[15]

Consistent with the three general principles of war are three general principles of strategy.[16] While these principles are not enumerated as such, the following summary is consistent with Clausewitz's intent. As warfare has three main objects—destruction of the armed power of the enemy, possession of the enemy's material and other sources of strength, and the gain of positive public opinion—three *general principles* of strategy are paramount:

1   The main body (or most critical element) of the enemy force is the primary focus of operations.
2   Military operations to obtain material and other strength should be directed at concentrations of that support. This will have the added effect of drawing out the enemy's main force.
3   Public opinion is won through great victories and the occupation of the enemy's capital.

Subordinate to these general principles are four *rules*.

4   Use great effort ('utmost energy') in war to make the result unambiguous and to sustain/gain public support.
5   Force should be concentrated at the decisive point even if this means incurring disadvantages elsewhere.
6   Unless an important advantage is obvious in doing so, never waste time. Speed will overcome enemy measures by bringing about surprise, and will most efficiently gain positive public opinion.
7   Follow success. Pursue a beaten enemy.

From the rules of strategy Clausewitz determines that defense is the stronger form of war, for the defender can select and prepare the place of battle and in general has simpler and shorter logistics. This does not mean that offensive war should be abrogated and that the state should rely on a defensive military posture only, for this cedes the initiative. That tactical and operational defense is the stronger form of war is an admonishment to the strategist to take great care when preparing to face a prepared and fortified opponent.

At the political level, which is the true level of strategy, there is also a defensive form of war separate from the tactical and operational form. 'Politically speaking,' remarks Clausewitz, 'defensive war is a war which we wage for our independence.'[17] This political fact is what makes the defensive form stronger, much more so than any debatable battlefield advantage: 'Whether the *battles* we wage in this [form] of war are offensive or defensive, makes no difference.'[18]

Defensive war is chosen when (1) the enemy is superior in arms, (2) logistical concerns make it difficult to operate at full strength, and (3) when the enemy is superior in the *art* of war: that is to say, when the leadership and morale of the enemy is greater. The latter is selected because the span of control in a defensive form of war is greater, and reliance on subordinate initiative is therefore less.

The advantage of the defensive form of war is lost if the strategist does not pursue it actively. The husbanding of resources the defensive form allows is wasted if the enemy is not engaged in tactically offensive counterstrikes when and where it is weakest. The purpose of fortifications, according to Clausewitz, is to engage the bulk of the enemy's force in costly siege while the maneuver element of the defense persistently hounds the lesser concentrations of force. Clausewitz goes on to suggest a version of defense in depth. Rather than attempt to stop the opponent at the border, or along every point of the most defensible terrain, allow the enemy to break through in areas of little strategic concern and then strike at the incursions before they can consolidate their gains and re-supply their forces.

In a last word on strategic defense, Clausewitz insists that the purpose of it is to hold back superior forces only until such time as a strategic counteroffensive can be mounted, or until early battlefield victories allow a peace to be negotiated that is advantageous to the defensive state. Submitting 'to the blows of its adversary without ever striking back [will lead it to] become exhausted and succumb.'[19] Thus the defensive form of war sets up the offensive form, which is to be pursued when the state holds superior forces, leadership and morale, or logistical capacity.

The offensive form of war will follow the rules and procedures described in the elaboration of the general principles of strategy above, with two additional caveats. First, the offensive form requires the capacity for a constant replacement of troops. Planning and organization for recruitment and supply must be thought out long before hostilities are initiated. Second, and this admonishment is entwined with the first, 'Even under the most favorable circumstances and with the greatest moral and physical superiority, the aggressor should foresee a possibility of great disaster.'[20] An assumption must be made that the war will continue well beyond the best projections for success. For if the enemy can delay the consummation of battlefield victory (and its re-supply and recruitment efforts are vastly easier on its own territory) then the offensive state will find itself caught short, and will have to negotiate a disadvantageous peace. The siren call of victory is ruinous in strategic planning, and should be shunned.

Modifications and flourishes

Clausewitz's contemporary rival was Baron Antoine-Henri de Jomini, whose books on war and strategy were far more accessible and readable and therefore more popular.[21] Jomini had a keen appreciation for late eighteenth- and early nineteenth-century warfare, having served as longtime aide to Napoleon. He attempted to distill the art of war into rules, and was the butt of Clausewitz's harangue in opposition to doing so. Still, the maxims of Jomini were widely accepted as insightful and reliable. He provided dozens of rules for the planning and conduct of battle, and practitioners found his guides much more useful than Clausewitz's more ethereal prose. He wrote on the necessity of concentration of forces at the decisive point of attack, the advantages of interior lines and the requirement of unity of command, the value of surprise, and the necessity of logistics. All of his rules were subordinate to the

> one great principle underlying all the operations of war, ... embraced in the following maxims:
> 1   To throw by strategic movements the mass of an army, successively, upon the decisive points of a theater of war,
> 2   To maneuver to engage fractions of the hostile army with the bulk of one's forces.
> 3   On the battle-field, to throw the mass of the forces upon the decisive point, or
> 4   To so arrange that these masses shall not only be thrown upon the decisive point, but that they shall engage at the proper times and with energy.'[22]

The difficulty, admits Jomini, is in precisely recognizing the decisive points to be engaged. This hardly sours the principle, and it is from this discussion that a number of fundamental principles of war that still resonate today are founded. Moreover, these 'invariable scientific principles ... prescribe *offensive action* to *mass forces* against weaker enemy forces at some *decisive point.*'[23] To this is sometimes added a fifth maxim: 'The lesson was clear: a government should choose its ablest military commander, then leave him free to wage war according to scientific principles.'[24] The statement was (and is) popular, but nothing could more clearly distinguish Jomini from Clausewitz. In his first proof that war is an act of policy, Clausewitz insists that if it were anything else, 'war would of its own independent will usurp the place of policy the moment it had been brought into being; it would then drive policy out of office and rule by its own laws ... '[25] Such would be a grievous error, for 'this view is thoroughly mistaken ... policy, then, will permeate all military operations, and in so far as their violent nature will admit, it will have a continuous influence on them.'[26]

The influence of politics in war is not the primary divide, however. It is the search for scientific principles of war that methodologically separates Jomini from Clausewitz. The effort, begun with Machiavelli and flowing through Jomini, continued a long tradition of such published guidebooks that tended to have the same title—*The Art of War.* For Jomini, strategy was 'the art of making war on a map.'[27] The definition tended to reduce strategy to a game, like that of chess, or better yet, miniatures, where rules and movements could correctly determine the outcome of any situation, limited only by the intellects of the competing players. The abstraction from battle to map was useful for Jomini, similar to the scientific model-building abstractions then occurring in physics and the social sciences, and the promise for a scientific schema of war was palpable.

144

The notion of a set of scientifically derived and immutable principles of war is clearly in opposition to the Clausewitzian emphasis on judgment and chance, but it is a seductive aspiration. 'Simplifying, reducing, prescribing—these had become the inescapably dominant qualities of Western military thought at the turn of the century.'[28] Following the slaughter of World War I, an exercise in human irrationality at a previously incomprehensible scale, military theorists would seek the principles of war that would make combat decisive, and brief.

J.F.C. Fuller would raise the study of war to its most precise, if occasionally more mystical than scientific, physical description. Fuller, working on a supernatural assumption of the power of threes, developed three fundamental *spheres* of war—moral, mental, and physical. These are quite similar to Clausewitz's triptych (see Figure 8.1), with the exception that Fuller's scientifically derived military realm could not incorporate the notion of Machiavelli's *fortuna* and Clausewitz's friction. Chance, for Fuller, was simply the lack of complete knowledge.

Each sphere is divided into three elements, equating to nine principles of war, and each of these in turn is divided into three functions, for a total of twenty-seven rules or procedures of strategy (see Figure 8.2). Of the nine principles, one was so comprehensive that Fuller elevated it to a law. The *law of economy of force* states that 'whatever force might be at our disposal, we should expend it at the highest profit.'[29] This law could not have been formulated so clearly, however, without a more fundamental assumption: that war is a science, which can be subjected to systematic categorization, observation, and analysis.

Fuller's work was pervasive, and representative of then current thought. The US Army's fundamental principles of war are based on them, and in 1921 differed only in that unity of command was absent, and maneuver was called movement. By 2000, the Army's principles of war had been rectified, and are as shown in Table 8.1.

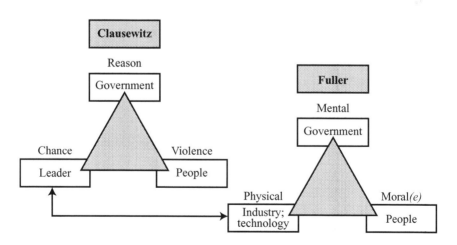

Figure 8.1   Clausewitzian and Fullerian trinities

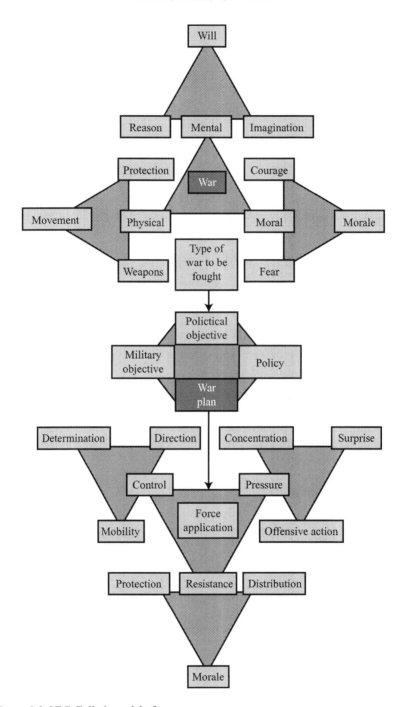

Figure 8.2 J.F.C. Fuller's model of war

Table 8.1 The US Army's nine principles of war

Mass	Concentrate combat power at the decisive place and time
Objective	Direct every military operation towards a clearly defined, decisive, and attainable objective
Offensive	Seize, retain, and exploit the initiative
Surprise	Strike the enemy at a time, at a place, or in a manner for which he is unprepared
Economy of force	Allocate minimum essential combat power to secondary efforts
Maneuver	Place the enemy in a position of disadvantage through the flexible application of combat power
Unity of command	For every objective, ensure unity of effort under one responsible commander
Security	Never permit the enemy to acquire an unexpected advantage
Simplicity	Prepare clear, uncomplicated plans and clear, concise orders to ensure thorough understanding

Principles of strategy were not limited to ground forces, of course. American Captain Alfred Thayer Mahan wrote that 'The considerations and principles which enter into them belong to the unchangeable, or unchanging, order of things, remaining the same, in cause and effect, from age to age.'[30] Mahan insisted that in order to be a truly great power, a state needed to be a great *naval* power. Sir Julian Corbett found Mahan's work lacking, and attempted to bring the principles of war espoused by Clausewitz to the seas. He rejected the Mahanian notion that naval warfare is a thing unto itself. Instead, it is part of the larger concept of maritime warfare, inextricably tied to land operations. Naval strategy as a separate realm of action was unthinkable. The navy's purpose was to secure lines of supply and communication for the army:

> By maritime strategy we mean the principles which govern a war in which the sea is a substantial factor. Naval strategy is but that part of it which determines the movements of the fleet when maritime strategy has determined what part the fleet must play in relation to the action of the land forces: for it scarcely needs saying that it is almost impossible that a war can be decided by naval action alone.[31]

Mahan was in complete disagreement here. He insisted that naval forces could not only operate independently, with independent principles in war, but that they could become the supported force.

> If it is merely to assure one or more positions ashore, the navy becomes simply a branch of the army for a particular occasion, and subordinates

147

its action accordingly; but if the true end is to preponderate over the enemy's navy and so control the sea, then the enemy's ships and fleets are the true objects to be assailed on all occasions.[32]

The basis of Mahan's insistence was in the notion that a state could gain broad and general command of the seas without having to occupy the whole of them. The seas had an equivalent of the dominant ground on land, and Mahan identified these as chokepoints, the control of which could ensure the state a decisive advantage in commerce (lines of communication and supply) and maneuver.

Corbett directly challenged Mahan's conception of general command of the sea, too. He proclaimed that the natural state of the seas was uncommanded, and that the purpose of seapower was to gain command in a specific place for an intended time. Command of the sea was thus local and temporary: 'command of the sea is only a means to an end. It never has been, and never can be, the end itself.'[33] Nonetheless: 'The object of naval warfare must always be directly or indirectly either to secure the command of the sea or to prevent the enemy from securing it.'[34]

Corbett then begins a discussion of three 'inherent differences' between land and sea 'conditions' that obviate identical principles in war.[35] The first principle in land war is to seek out and destroy the enemy's main force. In naval war, the enemy can withdraw the opposing fleet to the high seas where its movements are difficult to monitor or to a defended port, for example, 'where it is absolutely out of your reach without the assistance of an army.' Corbett perhaps should have foreseen the coming effects of airpower on naval engagements, and the end of the defended port as a safe haven from attack, but this is not the fruitful point of his argument. What is important is the corollary. If the enemy chooses to withdraw forces from battle, due to actions on your part, then command of the sea is achieved without an engagement. The effect of a naval victory is achieved … for now. The down side is that the enemy fleet remains in being. Without a blockade or other active measure, the fleet retains the potential to sail out at any time and contest command of the sea.

Second, on land the lines of communication are fixed. Roads and obstacles are fixed; according to Corbett, these determined the lanes of movement and commerce, and thus the points of battle. The seas had no roadways or obstacles, at least tactically, and so terrain had little impact on operations. Mahan had already argued the opposite when he noted that, although the seas were 'a wide common upon which men could pass in any direction,' strategic geography created trade routes and lines of communication that were as distinguishable and fixed as roads. No matter—for Corbett, naval lines of communication were as fluid as the medium.

This second principle leads directly to the third. Without point locations or fixed roadways to defend, yet saddled with the requirement of protecting commerce over the long haul from port to port, the notion that forces could be effectively concentrated for mass was foolish: 'the more you concentrate your force and efforts to secure the desired decision, the more you will expose your trade to sporadic attack.'[36]

Corbett's transformation of the principles of war for naval warfare is highlighted not because it makes the case that the classic principles do not operate there, but because it reinforces the notion that the negative of proper principle is always plausible and useful, dependent only on context. This proves the enduring value of the principle as surely as the positive, and in combination even more strongly. In the third Corbettian example, the principle of massing of force at the decisive point is maintained; it is simply that the decisive point is elusive. Dispersion gives the greatest possibility of engaging the opponent at a time of your own choosing; bringing forces to bear once the decisive point is determined that will locally and temporarily have the advantage of concentration over the opponent's own.

The essential elements of strategy and war are detailed in land and maritime studies. Air and, to date, space power and strategy have followed their lead. Though the operating media of air and space have their own tactical and operational requirements, the essential principles of strategy, where they are involved at all, follow the patterns already established. The classic search for timeless or immutable principles of war has been the guiding effort in attempts to establish both a teachable science and an apprenticable art. The essential elements are no longer in serious doubt, but their proper influence remains a source of tension. When should force be concentrated and when should it be dispersed? Under what conditions is economy of force not desirable? How does the element of maneuver fit into modern information warfare?

Enduring principles of war

Do the principles of war change with the times, or they are immutable? Clearly, tactics change with technology, politics, culture, and more. But is *strategy* so malleable? As a severe binary question, it is poorly framed. Such core strategic queries should not be set up as either-or, unless one is doing so to drive a competitor into a decision trap—for there is *always* another option. The mind that accepts the choices presented cannot break the bonds of the endeavor at hand. It has accepted its fate. The initiative has been ceded, and the battle or war is lost.

The question highlights the matter of duality that is ingrained in our patterns of thought, both Western and Asian. We accept that there is a yin and yang, a heads and tails, to every issue. For every plausible course of action, there is an equally plausible and precisely opposite course. The tragedy of humankind is that we *must* choose. Selecting either option will lead to advantage for some and to misery for others. Neither outcome is preferable over the other. There is no calculus that will help us, no higher authority to take away the responsibility of choice. But there is a way out; it is only tragedy when no other options are available—and there are always more options. For every coin tossed there is in addition to two sides a sense of the *edge*, a situation *in being*, in which both options are in competition. It is this edge, not unlike the edge of chaos, where outcomes are not yet set and so neither—or both—remain possible. In military strategy, one edge of chaos is the battle or campaign. The outcomes are victory and defeat, and neither is yet sure. Actions there create a flux, roiling and unsettled, influenced by continual external inputs. There is a tug and pull that continues until the tactician brings events to a close, establishing the conditions for the next rounds of interaction. The coin is in the air and neither heads nor tails has yet occurred. It is this point of interaction and possibility that the strategist must occupy.

So, I do not accept one or the other answer to my opening question; I choose one *and* the other. The immutable principles of war *adapt* to the times, and are strengthened in the process. Previously I identified principles as *beliefs* of causation, and argued that a few examples to the contrary do not necessarily make them void. A principle to which no counter examples could be found should be elevated to the level of causal law, and in war no such law yet exists. Moreover, while principles are broad enough to cover all known contexts, and encompassing enough to cover unknown futures, they do not have a monopoly on truth. Opposing and plausible principles exist that also account for all known and unknown future contexts. Massing force at the decisive point is a principle even when certain contexts require dispersing force when no decisive point is apparent. Such principles are adapted to new situations, and they persist.

Rules and practices that are inextricably tied to temporal and spatial context do not adapt, and so they cannot be principles. They can, however, be sound tactics. What one accomplishes with a long bow or blunderbuss is eminently tied to the time and situation. If I have a shotgun my efforts to engage the enemy will be different than if I have a rifle, and absolutely conditional upon how the enemy is armed, the terrain, and any number of other contingencies. Maurice of Nassau's manual of arms for musket troops allowed the greatest concentration of firepower of his day, proved time and again for more than a century. But it has little practical value today. It was, nonetheless, an *extrapolation* of sound principles of war that persist today, as all good tactics are, including concentration of combat power, economy of force, and dominant maneuver.

The notion that tactical rules must change and adapt to the times is well known. According to Arthur Cebrowski and Thomas Barnett: 'Across the 1990s, global *rule sets* became seriously misaligned, with economies racing ahead of politics [and] technology racing ahead of security (e.g., the rise of transnational terrorists exploiting globalization's growing network connectivity).'[37] While it may seem that the face of warfare has changed immeasurably from its earliest, organized form, it is clear from our understanding of the hierarchical nature of knowledge, rules, and power that the fundamental *principles* of war have not. They have been refined, adjusted, and adapted to evolving conditions, morals, and technologies, but the core characteristics of strategy endure.

It is useful in a work as far-ranging as this to keep terms precise and consistent. In the previous discussion of regimes, principles resided at the top of a structural pyramid. If we can view war as a regime, we see that the tactical or lower levels equate to rules and decision-making procedures. Higher up, the operational and strategic military levels equate to norms, and at the top level are the grand strategic principles. At the top, we deal with general concepts, capable of encompassing a vast array of innovations and adaptations. As we move down the pyramid, the requirement for detail and decision is accentuated. Moreover, in regime theory, principles are malleable to the extent that for every statement of causation or rectitude there is a plausible counter. If the principle is truly unchallengeable, it becomes a law. The key, however, is that if the principle changes, the regime collapses.

What follows are norms and rules of thumb that should prove heuristic in the development of a consistent framework for strategy in the current century. It is not an exhaustive or encompassing list. I do not propose that any of the norms of war described below be elevated to law. There are candidates, the equivalent of the Newtonian physicist's triptych of mass, energy, and velocity, or the quantum equivalent of momentum, charge, and spin, but it is not necessary to do so to highlight the enduring quality of the principles. As an example, the first principle of war that I offer is time. This includes the norms of speed and tempo; the side that can move faster and adapt to changes quicker should prevail. This may not always be the case in practice, but isolated counterexamples are likely to have an explanation that proves the rule. The tortoise just may win a race now and then. Nonetheless, when the hare and the tortoise line up at the starting blocks, the bookmakers will gladly take your bet on the tortoise.

Time

It remains a universal axiom that the side capable of outmaneuvering the other will have an advantage, all other variables held constant. Maneuver is a function of speed, in most cases, the capacity to traverse distance at a rate greater than that of the opponent. Speed is thus a function of movement over time. It is also useful to see speed as a function of change over time, and the side that adapts to change faster than the other will have a distinct advantage. Technology plays an intricate role in this process, and at the strategic level is the equivalent of shrinking the earth.[38] Not only is battlefield maneuver increased, but the time it takes to move information and power from place to place is decreased. As the span of distance becomes smaller in time, the conception of what is linked becomes greater, and the strategist can export a wider array of variables into the tactical situation. This is the principle that so clearly points to space as the future realm of dominance in war. The side that can operate freely there, and can prevent the opponent from doing so, has effective instantaneous movement of information and (someday) power around the globe. Maneuver will have been accomplished in advance, as no time is consumed to prepare for conflict.

Time is the most critical limitation on the power the tactician can yield, and the most malleable enabler that the strategist can manipulate. It becomes incumbent on the strategist to provide as much time as possible for the tactician, just as it is critical for the tactician to use all time available wisely. The difference is that the tactician is in a situation bound by temporal context—one that has a conceivable beginning and an anticipated end. Actions take place within temporal limits, and efficiency is measurable in time. Knowing the criteria under which a conflict is considered over, how to know when the end has been reached, is of vital importance to the tactician. Without it, no assignment of victory or defeat can be made, and the tactical logic is confounded. This is precisely the reason strategists cannot sanction the notion of victory for themselves, for it *requires* there be an end. From the strategic thinker's perspective, temporal boundaries are always shifting. Every action creates change. Meaningful change creates options. Increasing options produces time.

All strategy is necessarily *shaped* by time. Time closes down options at the tactical level, as the rush toward victory compresses the decision-making parameters. For the strategist, time is constantly expanding, both into the past and the future, as history and horizon. In most real situations, time is perceived as a *vector*. It has a single direction as it goes by, always into the future. As such, it is amenable to scientific study. It is a component of our perception of the world around us, a physical dimension as binding as the spatial three-dimensionality of our perception. And as it goes by it fixes the past, even as the future remains probabilistic. This setting—if not settling—of events is important for the planner, and has consequences not readily apparent. When one mixes flour, water, and yeast with heat, one gets bread. Mixing bread and heat does not produce flour, water, and yeast. These processes are irreversible in the sense of time.

To be sure, if one could reverse the flow of time, physical and moral dilemmas would instantly result. In a gruesome example provided by Robert Charles Wilson, we would 'see the United States sign a peace treaty with Japan and then drop an atomic bomb on Hiroshima; we see the Nazis extract bullets from the skulls of emaciated Jews and then restore them to health in camps.'[39] If morality can have such a time-dependent vector, then it is easier to see that strategy must comply with the dictates of an irreversible flow of events. The moment we are in is made comprehensible by what has happened before. The logic of our current situation must work itself into the decisions to be made.

Thus, time compresses as it passes. The long term becomes the short term. Pressure mounts for action—any action—to mitigate the reckless consumption of it. This occurrence is useful when a desirable end is sought, and so the tactical decision maker searches for the action that will result in a favorable culminating point. Such a bias can have the compounding effect of making events increase in certainty as time compresses, and the process of planning itself becomes a culprit. As early as the 1920s, for example, American military planners were preparing for a war with Japan. As time passed, the likelihood of such a war increased, despite a series of diplomatic and economic actions intended to head it off, and planning became more urgent. As 1941 approached, choices were set aside, new options were shunned, and war became assured. At the strategic level, captured by the tactical understanding of time compression, a perversion of time's arrow is the result. Time moves in reverse as the effect (war) precedes the cause (war preparation). An action is taken because of—in response to—what the opponent is going to do.

Tactical decision-making, because it seeks a conclusion, always takes place within temporal constraints. Time itself is a diminishing commodity; it flows past and is lost. As the tactical scenario proceeds, the supply of time declines and its value rises. The less time available to make decisions, the more essential it becomes to make sound ones. Errors are magnified because there is less time for recovery. Choices become limited because there is less time to develop and explore options. As the end looms, decision makers are pressed to take specific actions that seem less choice than a necessity. Backed into a corner, out of time, the decision maker perceives that there is a very limited number of options. Time is a scarce and ultimately depleted commodity.

To this end—the conservation of time—decisions are often made in advance of events. This is an economizing device, the essential role of habit, preference, standard operating procedure, and doctrine. Potential decisions are categorized and resolved beforehand. Decision-making is made swift and consistent with the expectations of others working toward the same ends. The decision maker simply has to recognize the context or situation, and follow the established rules associated with it. This allows training and practice to hone the capacity for action, increasing the efficiency of violence. When done well, doctrine simply overwhelms minor variations and unexpected reactions. Where such doctrine fails is when it is *surprised,* when the situation has changed enough that doctrine or standard operating procedure (SOP) cannot efficiently overcome resistance. When this occurs, the decision maker must adapt, and master tacticians are those who can adapt quickly and effectively, retaining and incorporating useful elements of doctrine with new or additional means to achieve the desired end.

Both strategist and tactician can further extend the amount of time available through effective *prediction.* The tactician relies heaviest on prediction, for it is with sound forecasting that the tactician gains *control* of the situation, in effect gaining more decision-time than the opponent. The more accurate the prediction, the more control over the situation is expected. When the opponent reacts in a way that was anticipated, the effect is as a tightening noose. By compressing the decision-time frame of opponents, the capacities to assess (measure) and react using standard methods and means is made faulty. Increased *tempo* produces error. The side that can increase tempo and maintain decision-making clarity is the one more likely to prevail. This means to do so is to *continuously adapt* to the emerging situation. In the fluid edge of chaos that is combat, efficient command and control is maintained through vigilance and adaptation in the face of increasing tempo. John Boyd's OODA loop was an attempt to do precisely this. For the strategist, time is acquired as the structure or system adapts to change. Change expands the event horizon and creates fresh possibilities, indeed, time seems to slow down as more meaningful choices are made, it is fuller and richer than time passing when stability and stagnancy reign.

The principle of time in the new century can be encapsulated in the notions of tempo and vector in decision-making and action. The norms are that the side which can recognize and adapt to change quickest is most likely to prevail, and the side that retains the most options in a compressing time frame will have an advantage over the side with fewer options. The strategist's function is to construct an operating structure or rule set that increases the time available for decision-making, through effective techniques like OODA or through disseminating accurate information quickly through the system. The capacity to operate in compressing time is *speed*, and acquisition and training must be geared toward those ends. Faster decision-making processes, faster equipment and streamlined training, in-depth learning and skills acquisition all assist in making the agents of the structure act in ways that will allow the entire system to adapt effectively to change.

Noise, entropy, and friction

Hans Von Bayer relates that entropy was essentially invented as a counterpoint to energy.[40] In military terms, entropy—the gradual running down of closed systems to a state of chaos—is akin to the Clausewitiztian notion of friction, the innumerable number of things that can break down and go wrong in the course of war. The perception is astute. To the extent that the real world of war is closed, it is tactical. To the extent that it is open, it is strategic. For the tactician friction, entropy, or noise (hereafter just noise) are the maddeningly inevitable glitches in the perfect plan. The more information, the greater the detail, the less the noise; the more one trains and practices, the more experience that can be gained, the less friction thwarts the tactical plan. For the strategist, noise is the necessary limitation on information and vision that make it possible to perceive the bigger picture.

The world of the strategist is informed by statistics and probabilities. In such a world, noise is a particularly valuable commodity. It allows outlier events to be recognized and tossed out. Meaning is more accurately assigned. 'In a hundred tosses of a penny, throwing fifty-two heads instead of the theoretical fifty is said to be "in the noise."'[41] The strategist recognizes that information perfection is impossible, and even if it were not, it would not be worth pursuing. Noise is ubiquitous. It surrounds us. It is part of our existence. And it is reasonable to state that it is also necessary, not because perfection is impossible, but because perfection would be intolerable. Consider how the world would be without it. In theory, it is possible to mill a bar of gold to a length that is a precise fraction of the number one. The length could be measured as a tremendously long sequence of numbers (such as $0.9878343 \ldots n$), reflecting an exactitude of subatomic distance. Now suppose you transcribed the entire works of Shakespeare into a numerical code so that this very large number could be decoded by a recipient with the proper instrument and algorithm. The bar could be cut so as to equal in percentage the Shakespearean code. In theory, the number could be sent as a brief sound, the length of which (measured in time) could be perfectly measured to coincide with the encoded text. Without noise, one could send any amount of information in a single pulse. ' … in a noiseless universe, an infinite quantity of information could be encoded on a simple shape … to a friend equipped with a noise-free measuring device and knowledge of the [encoding system] employed.'[42]

We can conceive of noise as an economizing device for the strategist. It is the cut-off point when we can say that we have *enough* information, *enough* motivation, or *enough* advantage. Without noise, a single observation would take an infinite amount of time to fully describe. Without a discriminator to shut out all the variables in the real world we would be overwhelmed. Imagine trying to hear a conversation if our hearing was perfect for all ranges of sound, from the lowest to highest frequencies—and at all decibels! Even if we were not driven mad, we could not discern relevant words of a conversation from the billions that are being spoken at any given moment. Imagine trying to see a landscape with similarly perfect vision. It would be impossible as we would keep seeing deeper and deeper into the details of nature until all we could perceive is a mass of subatomic elements. How could the venerable *coup d'oeil* of genius exist without the capacity to take in the sweep of battle, seeing at once the totality of the situation and not a jumble of its many parts?

Hence some noise is valuable. By setting a level of importance before information can get through, noise covers or eliminates trivial or unwanted information so that the mind can focus on the essential. The lesson drawn from noise, entropy, and friction for the current world of strategy is that a lack of information is not inherently undesirable. Not all things need be known before the decision is made or the agent acts. Waiting for more information is an endless task, for there will always be more. Information may be the enemy of action. This is neither a call for recklessness, nor a preference for prudence over haste. Noise is what makes audacity possible, and audacity is more effective in a system that adapts well to change.

Relativity and symmetry

Clausewitz said the best strategy is to be strong in all things. Strength is a relative term, however. It relates to the other. The strongest power on earth a century ago would be swept aside by a mediocre power today. Thus we see that all strategy is relative.

Moreover, no strategy is possible without a thinking and reactive opponent. If the opponent is unthinking, as in the weather or the odds at a gaming table, then metadecision-making is the best tactic, a term that by definition separates this kind of thinking from pure strategy. There can be no strategy in a game of solitaire, either, unless the player is hopelessly schizophrenic. In the military realm the concept of relativity is paradoxically absolute. I have already asserted that no nation can go to war until it has found an opponent that can agree to the terms of the conflict.[43] To compete is to agree to act in a specified way vis-à-vis the other, because the other can always decline. The penalty for failure to compete may be severe, as in the mugger's request for your wallet or your life, but it is always available. For that agreement to occur, it is best to assume that the opponent has knowledge that you do not. It is further best to assume the opponent is cleverer than you, more adaptable than you, and stronger than you suspect.

The opponent is not the only concern for relativity and symmetry. Numerous other thinking agents or actors are impacting the war and constantly changing the boundaries within which it is fought. These are at least your allies and the enemy's, those states who have not yet chosen a side, and your domestic support and opposition (as well as those of all other actors). There are in addition contextual actors, including transnational movements and corporations, non-governmental organizations, and individuals of particularly strong following who can influence the conflict with their support or lack thereof. All of these actors are in the system to the extent that an action by any one of them affects and changes the others, and that these changes in turn establish new conditions of conflict. To the extent that these actors can inflict relatively minor changes that reverberate throughout the system, resulting in major modifications, the structure is chaotic. Those actors who respond to change best will survive, and are most likely to influence future structural conditions.

Moreover, *all strategy is relational.* It rests inextricably on the notion of *symmetry:* of power or force for military strategy, public support for political strategy, wealth for economic strategy, and perhaps morality for socio-cultural strategy. At the highest level, grand strategy, all of these must be considered in combination. Weakness in one area may be balanced by strength in another. In a single strategic realm, however, the stronger the actor in relation to the other, the more decisive and unilateral that power can and should be in its relationship. This is important for the efficiency maximization of the stronger power, and while it goes against the grain of magnanimity, it prevents subordinating the needs and capabilities of the strong to those of the relatively weak. This is not to say that the stronger or larger power cannot be generous, or thoughtful. It is just that, especially where the intent is to influence friends or allies, the dominant power must act decisively, consistently, and unilaterally if necessary. This allows all less powerful actors in the system to adjust their actions and expectations to those of the stronger power, assists in identifying actors who are opposed to the stronger actor's intent, and lessens distrust and animosity.

This does not mean the weaker actor must submit. Conversely, the weaker the power is relative to the other, the more cautious and deceptive that actor can and should be in its relationship with the stronger. Smaller and weaker states thus benefit from decisive and consistent actions by the stronger. This is because the weaker the state, the fewer options are potentially available. As options decrease, the state becomes cornered or forced into making tactical decisions, and will look for near-term gain at the expense of a longer view. By foreknowledge of the stronger actor's intent, the weaker actor can efficiently strive to create options that include niche-activity or specialization within the stronger's construct, increasing the value of the smaller to the stronger—or efficiently plan for the exploitation of the stronger as weaknesses appear.

When a state is interacting with another on roughly equal terms (militarily or in any power relationship), the state should act moderately toward the other. This means that a mix of bold action and cautious intractability are advised. The mix is informed by the context of the situation, but is not bound by it. To this extent—the relative power differences between actors—strategy is *contextual*. The effort of the strategist should be to maintain, gain, or move the conflict to a structure in which the strategist's state has continuing advantages; one where it is strong (or stronger).

The structure the strategist builds to take advantage of relative differences between actors is based on establishing the norms and rules that will be used as problem-solving devices. To the extent the actor is strong, these can be simply mandated. To the extent the actor is weak, they must be negotiated. Those which are mutually beneficial, whether dictated or agreed upon, will last longer with fewer maintenance costs than those clearly favoring one or more actors over others. The reality of the situation is 'to the extent that scarcity of time, of space, or of available "goods" exists, individual actors cannot achieve their goals without interfering with each other's pursuits and/or experiencing actual conflict.'[44] Such constructs link the individual behavior of agents to the general good of the system. 'On the one hand they leave each actor free to decide for himself/herself which goals to pursue—even to break the rules—while on the other hand they safeguard the conditions of social coexistence.'[45]

Every relationship is continuously redefined by the actions and reactions of the participants. Strategy does not succeed or fail so much as it is better or worse. Either it readily anticipates and incorporates change, or it does not. Either the state increases its power and influence relative to expectations in the absence of the strategy, or it does not. The only way this can be measured is by the reactions of and feedback generated by other states. Because there is no end in strategy, strategists require the response of the opponent to develop, update, and modify the strategy. How the opponent reacts to the strategy is in fact *the* critical measure of its value. Are relations getting better or worse? Is resistance getting stronger or weaker? Measuring success in terms of goal achievement implicitly denies the importance of the other; it is supremely egoistic. Because the goal of tactics is victory, the tactician can measure success regardless of, and in some cases in spite of, the responses of the opponent. Finality in goal-setting means victory can be declared and lauded whether the opponent fought poorly or well, bravely or cowardly. Defeat can be acknowledged whether outgunned or outmaneuvered. In retrospect, mistakes can be seen and blame assigned.

In war, and conflict in general, the relationship of highest concern is one of power. Power itself is a notion that has no meaning outside of its juxtaposition with others. Indeed, power is a concept that is notoriously difficult to define under any socio-political terms. The standard definition, that power is the capacity that A has to get B to do something B would rather not do, or to continue doing something B would prefer to stop doing, or not to begin doing something B would prefer to start doing, has already been used and justified. It is a utilitarian definition that has merit, but it leaves something to be desired in practical application. Power may simply not be measurable in isolation, and then it is only so to the extent that it encounters *resistance*. Power can be described as the capacity to overcome resistance, but this has nonlinear ramifications as well. If power is applied and resistance occurs, unless the resistance is overcome it is impossible to know how much more power is needed to gain the desired result. If power is applied and resistance is quickly overcome, it may have been just the right amount of power or it may have been too much, the overage being incalculable. Thus, power is never inherent in one actor, but is always a ratio of effort and resistance.

The measurements of power and the rules that constrain war also establish the conditions for determining who has won—whose resistance has proven superior. Until one side is eliminated (utterly) or surrenders, the conflict cannot conclude. When surrender is offered, the tactician lays claim to victory. The strategist simply discovers a new horizon of possibilities; the terms of the continuing interaction—which is the purpose of strategy—are constantly in flux. Note that the surrendering side is not defeated by the boundaries or conditions of the conflict. The weather, the rules of engagement, the meddling of politicians, these constraints do not defeat an armed force in the sense of culmination. In such a case, the force may insist that it has not been defeated, that it was in fact simply *prevented from continuing by external events.* Just as the opponent is unwilling to accept defeat, since it did not come in battle, the tactician cannot claim true victory, since it was a change in the rules or conditions that ended the conflict. So important to war is the agreement to participate that overwhelming power is not necessarily defeating. A military juggernaut that cannot be stopped is perceived as an external constraint. It is not attacked or manipulated, but accepted as given. The side that surrenders is not recognized as defeated: it chose not to compete in that way. Nonetheless, that conflict in that place at that time is over. It will never be repeated. The master tactician will immediately begin planning for the next war, under new conditions and limitations. The work of the strategist has not been interrupted, however. The interaction between states goes on.

Synchrony and simultaneity

In an age when 'massing or concentrating combat power at the decisive place' may mean a single, precise bomb placed on target from a platform launched 6,000 miles away, the fundamental issues of synchrony and simultaneity rise to the level of strategic and tactical norms. It may also mean coordinating a B-52 strike from continents away with an infantry platoon miles away and a supporting gunship from another district so that each arrives at the target at precisely the same moment. It also requires coordinating the operation with overhead satellite surveillance capabilities, refueling support for the B-52, and commencement of deception or compatible operations meant to draw attention away from the intended strike. At the tactical level, synchrony is well known and practiced. At the level of strategy, it means coordinating research and development efforts, budget priorities, popular and allied support, diplomatic negotiations, and force acquisition so that the right capabilities are available at the right time. Should technology or funding lag, the whole process is delayed.

Einstein's theories of relativity made obvious the notion that observers at different places might perceive events differently. More disconcerting was the possibility that events perceived from different locations might actually *be* different. Events which appear or are simultaneous for one observer may occur at different times for another. To the disparate observers, the two events are both simultaneous and distinct. Neither is imbued with greater reality than the other. Simultaneity is a local concept that has no meaning outside of some relatively small spatial confines. Even such obviously important tactical terms such as now, sooner, and later are localized notions that have no meaning in the larger sense of physical and time differentiated events unless they are tied to a specific frame of reference.[46] This notion will be integral to the call for a relaxed or flattened command and control network for future military structures, to take advantage of all the promise of network-centric warfare discussed in the next chapter.

Once one accepts that strategy always takes place in the context of relative interactions between two or more thinking entities, it is potentially disastrous to ignore the possibility that truth or reality is equally valid from the other's point of view. This does not mean that all points of view are equally valid, it is the recognition that some points of view may add to the validity and power of your own. The more perspectives that can be gleaned, the more likely the view of reality is shared, and the more likely it is to be useful.

Simultaneity as it is portrayed here is not the same as a classic interpretation held by the Soviet Union's General Staff. Here was the idea that if attacks could be coordinated across an entire event to occur with choreographed precision, a collapse of the entire 'tactical depth' of the opponent could suddenly and catastrophically occur.[47] The adaptation of this concept, born of the Russian Civil War but still bound by the constraints of a predominantly infantry style of warfare, would lead strategic genius Mikhail Tukhachevskii to advocate that the most advantageous position for simultaneity was maximum contact with the enemy. As technology develops and the most sophisticated weapons appear abruptly (if at all) on the battle space, maximum contact is no longer needed to enhance synchrony and simultaneity of effort. Planning, however, is vital.

Scope and scale

Scope refers to the breadth of vision the strategist can maintain, and for this it is critical not to telescope or scale down into the details of the specific. The ultimate advice is to know where you are, be aware of others at your level, and of those on levels above and below you. In this way one can make effective decisions and influence the regions that are most salient.

It is also important to understand the criticality of scope and scale in analysis. The simplest adjustments can mean all the difference in dissecting and understanding a problem. If we look at the day-to-day life of a city, we can learn a great deal about its inhabitants, traffic patterns, methods of construction, and the like. What we cannot get is a sense of its importance to the state. For that, the scope of the investigation must be spatially widened so that other cities can be analyzed in comparison, and so the state itself can be assessed for a common frame of reference. Even then we are not able to place the state into the context of the global economy or international balance of power. Such would require an additional widening. Doing so necessitates, however, that the individual preferences and activities of individual workers and families are taken out of the analysis— removed as unimportant noise—so that the whole can be distinguished from its parts. And still we would not be able to assess the vector of the city's importance: growing or diminishing. That would require a broadening of the scope of time. Historical trends become apparent as the temporal unit of time moves from days to weeks to years and then decades. The patterns that develop in the life cycle of a city at a scope of decades are completely indeterminable from the daily view. The richness of the city's existence is just as unknowable from the macro perspective. When dissecting a problem it is thus vital to know what level and what detail is useful, and what is merely interesting.

It is possible to use a factorial device such as a rule of ten to help determine scope and scale. This is not a definitive device; it is illustrative of the value of scope and scale only. If I lose my job I am devastated. There is little in normal or routine life that is more unsettling. The ten (or so) people closest to me (my family and dearest friends) have their lives impacted as well. If my home goes into foreclosure, the street I live on is affected.

If one person in the community of a hundred loses his or her job, it is interesting. It will be talked about, and may portend future problems, but is slightly more than inconsequential. If ten are laid off the effect on the community is significant, and palpably affects all members of that community. In the district of a thousand, it is of much less impact. In the town of ten thousand, it is not noticed by most people. In the city of a hundred thousand, it will not make the paper. In the city of a million, it will be unnoticeable, though the loss of ten thousand jobs will be noticed and the loss of a hundred thousand will be devastating. In the country of ten billion persons, a million out of work is quite acceptable. It is not even harsh, as it represents little more than normal worker turnover. The first person to have lost his/her job is less than trivial.

Efficient military operation requires a similar sense of scope and scale adherence. Clausewitz points out that what matters to a soldier is of little importance to a senior officer, and of no meaning at all to a commander. Moreover, it should not be of importance or meaning. This is the harsh truth of military life. If the general has a daughter in the armed forces, and that daughter is to engage in combat, concern over her safety (or promotion) may influence the decisions the general makes—usually to the detriment of the army.

Non-Commissioned Officers (NCOs) fulfill a vital and continuing need in every military organization. They are frontline supervisors. Without them, no armed force can function. The NCO is trained and prepared to train and prepare soldiers, and takes great pride in the ability to do so. The NCO is focused on the personal level war. To stop and contemplate the relative merits of a decision to attack here or there, or the policy that brought war or peace to this place, would be disruptive on the battle space, and good NCOs remove such matters from their thoughts *in* war.

Junior Officers guide and command at the tactical level, and their function is to learn and grow. They are guided by senior NCOs and allotted to tasks by superior officers. They absorb the tactical arts and gain proficiency in the habits of command, to include the most vital lesson of taking care of the soldiers, sailors, or airmen in their charge. This means ensuring their training is rigorous, their discipline honed, and that their food and essentials are fresh and plentiful. Mid- and upper-level officers command at the operational level. Their duties are to plan campaigns and battles, and it is here they should be instructed in the art of war as espoused by Machiavelli, Clausewitz, Mahan, and Mitchell. This is the transition zone from tactical to strategic ways of thought and action. Those who excel at the operational level will get their chance at the strategic, general level of operations. Most will bring their tactical baggage along, over-emphasize the weapons and techniques they learned as junior officers, and plan for victory. Some will transcend the operational level and rise to strategist.

Choice and response

The act of choosing is an essential function of tactical and strategic applications. Not choosing is itself a choice, and in no way abrogates responsibility for the results of inaction. In the norms of strategy, however, choosing has a specific function: ' … it is often only through the choosing itself—and through the perceived response—that actors become aware of their own utility function as well as that of their opponents.'[48] Making choices and observing the reactions in others is the foundation of analysis and the source of sound planning.

It is through choice and response that the strategist discovers the reality of the world, the efficacy of options, and correlation of events. When threatened by another's activity, for example, the strategist could simply do nothing, hoping the behavior will stop. This is poor strategy, as should be obvious, for there is little hope of continuing advantage in it. Moreover, the strategist is responsible for the choice-set this action provides for the other, which may be markedly increased based on the perceived response to hostile actions. As such, choosing reveals the embedded psychological differences and similarities in actors, and assists in establishing appropriate strategies in the appropriate context of relationships.

In the previous example, the strategist chose inaction in the hope that this would induce the other to refrain from increasing the level of threatening activity. Let us say it had the opposite effect, and the threatening activity increased. The strategist then attempts to establish a deterrent threat, say, a warning that if the activity did not cease, war would be the inevitable result. The deterrent threat may cause the other to cease the threatening behavior, or it may not. The other may simply have not been aware the behavior was threatening, and is cordially stopping. The other may also see the threat as retaliatory and escalatory, and may make a point of continuing the unwanted behavior to demonstrate resolve and independence. Whatever the context,

> When deterrence fails, [it is] because one actor did not believe the other would retaliate, because he hoped [he] could remain undetected, [etc.] … Note in this context that 'irrational' actors like terrorists cannot be deterred and that therefore a strategy of deterrence crucially depends upon normative understandings.[49]

Such understandings are revealed through an analysis of choice and response to choices. Strategists hone their strategies through them.

Choice has a vital negative function in this realm of modern norms as well. It is the point at which doctrine is defied, and it can be an extraordinarily important moment in strategy. At the same time that the capacity to micromanage the battle space has never been greater, momentum for increased choice is driving the ongoing shift from strict hierarchical military control to a dispersion of command and control, and increased decision-making authority to frontline combatants.

Prerogative is divergence from doctrine. When a commander follows the book, it is understood that no penalty shall accrue from the actions of war. When the commander diverges from doctrine, the *action must be explained.* A rationale is given that normal doctrine was not useful or appropriate in this instance. Such a choice is justifiable if the action was made in the absence of higher orders, because of the appearance of an unexpected high-value target, or due to external factors unavailable to the higher commander (the target was shielded by a school bus, for example). The divergence will either be commended or condemned, and the commander will be rewarded, punished, or ignored. If the choice was valid *for this instance,* it may be used to tweak doctrine. It may also be the exception that solidifies the rule of doctrine. If the choice was superior to doctrine in all instances like this one, then the doctrine will be changed. Thus choice is a valid option *if it can be explained.* Convergence with doctrine needs no explanation. If convergence with doctrine is unsuccessful (over time), then it will be changed through its own mechanisms. If an action in opposition to doctrine is taken due to instinct, visceral reaction, or fatigue, it is not a choice: it is a response. If it is randomly derived (by tossing a coin, say), or taken because the commander was unaware of proper doctrine in this context, then it will only affect doctrine if it can be explained after the fact—it turned out well. Doctrine is not invalidated simply because it is not used. It is invalidated when it no longer makes sense for normal operations.

The American way of war

When Russell Weigley identified the American Way of War in 1971, it was characterized by the use of overwhelming force, either through attrition or annihilation, to achieve 'crushing' victory.[50] It was, in its fashion, an attempt to overcome the influence of chaos in war. An overpowering preponderance of arms and materiel assured that failures here and there would not be fatal. It was, more-over, an attempt to overcome the long tradition and many advantages of most of its adversaries in the study and art of strategy. And the strategy of massive overkill is not such a bad one in the case of a state chock-full of amateur soldiers and pro-fessional entrepreneurs. In a half serious aside, military historian Tom Hughes has remarked that 'the reason Americans are so bad at strategy is they are so good at logistics.' When one's strength is production, it is a good idea to engage the enemy in a war of *matériel*.

With the end of the Cold War, and arguably by the end of the Vietnam War, America had begun to change its emphasis on massive victory and territorial occupation to one on preemptive and preventive strikes using precision attacks and measured violence. Some of the emphasis for this change is moral, some technological. America is perceived to be casualty averse in its post-Vietnam sen-sibilities, both for its own combatants and for those of the enemy, although no reliable study has been able to show that casualty aversion is a particularly American trait, and in fact when the cause is just and the nation's vital interests at stake, Americans may be less casualty averse than most others. But when the capacity to fulfill objectives is possible in more than one way, and if one of those ways involves far fewer casualties, American moral and ethical standards tend to value human life above all other considerations. The latter emphasis, technology, may be the more decisive in the change to precision warfare, however. Guns do not make it possible to use violence; they affect the way in which violence is pro-jected. Jet aircraft do not make it possible to go to war; they make it possible to contest war in a different way.

Developments in the technological means of US combat power, particularly air and space power, 'have made possible a new way of war for the United States entailing entirely new concepts of operations. Owing to precision, stealth and expanded information, airmen are now paradoxically able to apply airpower as first envisioned by the early advocates, but not in a way that they could have fore-seen.'[51] The new American way of war is increasingly understood as domination of the information battle space, enhanced by a lethal combination of precision, speed, and stealth.[52] It is the adaptation of notions of complexity—not chaos—into the peculiarly American method. These technology-spawned tactics have permitted the American liberal conscious to accept war as an increasingly viable tool in international relations. As the twenty-first century opens, the United States can anticipate a future of war that is surgically clean, superbly efficient, and mon-strously deadly. It can also anticipate that its main rivals will not cooperate into entering conflicts that are so one-sided. Still, these are the tactical aspects of the new way of war, and while there are severe moral implications from the applica-tion of such technology—yet to be fully understood—the impact on American strategy has already been extensive. The use of force in the world becomes predi-cated on a calculation of anticipated casualties, economic disruption, and political response. By limiting the first two drastically, the third is assuaged. It is an awe-some change wrought by the preeminent position of power the United States wields in the world today. And this form of war suits it. The temperament of the United States appears such that it may be politically impossible to go back to another kind of more visceral and widespread warfare. As long as the capacity exists to limit destruction of lives and property, it becomes immoral not to make every effort to do so.[53]

The explosion of information available in the modern era reinforces the dominance of this distinctively American mode of fighting. Increased volume and breadth of information, and the speed with which that information can be collected, analyzed, and disseminated, gives the wielder of information superiority a significant edge. In-depth knowledge of an opponent's strengths and weaknesses exposes a much wider range of targets than may have been previously considered, be they diplomatic, economic, psychological, or traditionally military. This knowledge facilitates the capacity to choose and hit the essential target (or targets, in proper order) that will most efficiently and effectively achieve desired objectives. Military reactions from opponents can be expected to arise more quickly, and across a broader range of potential future target sets as well. Thus, the capacities to evaluate situations accurately, inflict damage precisely, react to enemy counteractions, evaluate damage, and retarget if necessary are the keys to future combat. The side that does so with the greatest speed and skill is the side that will prevail. Warfare has become faster and is spread farther and deeper. It is, at the tactical level, the domain of highly trained, intelligent professionals.

Since efficiency (minimizing collateral damage and casualties) and effectiveness (maximizing target destruction, negation, or denial) are dominant requirements in the current political environment, the platforms of choice to perform most military missions must be stealthy, agile, swift, precise, and deadly. Attacks must proceed before the opponent can move or adjust. Precision is vital. Large-scale, wide area destruction of the type employed in World War II is no longer acceptable, reinforcing the need for speed and stealth. The target must be engaged before it is no longer critical, and especially before an unknown or collateral (unintended) target fills the void. Yet precision means war is also more lethal. In terms of efficiency and effectiveness, if not in the grisly calculus of total dead and wounded, ordinance is far more likely today to strike and neutralize its target than at any time in the past. The sniper's motto, 'one shot, one kill,' has become the implicit mantra of all modern weapon systems operators. It is also much, much more expensive.

Because the logic of politics, and not that of war, determines America's military actions, it is not out of place to use a million dollar bomb to destroy a mud hut, if that is what is necessary to do so with a minimum loss of life. The desire to minimize *all* casualties, most especially one's own but not insignificantly the opponent's, means the simple accounting of dollar values is not appropriate. Cost-utility accounting is a minor factor in the overall decision process. Here is where the most advanced stealth technology, designed as a penetrating force for a possible third world war, has evolved to symbolize American post-Cold War operations. Virtually unseen by enemy radar, the stealth aircraft moves in for surgical strikes extremely close to its target. It negates traditional models of command of the air because the enemy's air defenses cannot see it. Command of the air cannot be denied locally. By going in unseen to destroy the enemy's air defense network, stealth allows follow-on conventional forces to operate freely in exploitation.

Stealth operations encompass more than airpower, including Special Operations Forces (SOF) and super-quiet submarines, but airpower is the penultimate technological example. Stealth technology on aircraft also expands the possibility of a Mahanian-style global command of the air without having to constantly patrol or even monitor all areas of the sky. Mahan envisioned the sea as a 'wide common, over which men may pass in all directions, but on which some well-worn paths [emerge for] controlling reasons.'[54] These controlling reasons were predicated on the efficient movement of goods, and the geography of the earth provided natural corridors of trade. The state that could control these corridors would realize such enormous commercial benefits that through its subsequent wealth it would dominate other states both militarily and politically. Crucial to his theory was a discussion of *choke points*, globally strategic narrow waterways dominated by point locations. It is not necessary, Mahan argued, for a state to have control of every point on the sea to command it. In fact, such a strategy would be worse than useless. The military force required would drain every scintilla of profit from trade, not to mention every able-bodied sailor more usefully engaged in commerce. Instead, a smaller but highly trained and equipped force carefully deployed to control the bottlenecks of the major sea-lanes would suffice, and dominance of these few geographically determined locations would guarantee supremacy over global military movement and world trade to the overseeing state.

Stealth, in an admittedly convoluted way, is for airpower what the concept of chokepoints was in Mahan's seapower. It simply is neither necessary nor desirable to physically patrol or occupy all areas of the sky to have effective global command of the air. With the ability to move into previously controlled enemy air space virtually at will and negate the ability to deny American exploitation of airpower, at a minimum stealth provides areas of air contestability over the whole of the earth. With that power, that implicit if not continuously maintained command of the air, the United States is today's only true superpower. Moreover, a psychological advantage is introduced by maintaining the means to inflict massive punishment on another state's military forces, ultimately reducing the perceived security and viability of the state, with a weapon system that is incapable of physically occupying territory. To be sure, airpower cannot seize and control territory, conduct searches of personnel and property, or manage the surrender of an opposing army. The army and navy will always have value to the state. But there is a qualitatively perceived aggression difference in negating a target with an aircraft rather than with a squad of soldiers on the ground, and the diplomat can manipulate this difference to the state's advantage.

All of these capacities mean that warfare, at least what is termed here the new American way of warfare, will be subject to increased expectations of morality and ethical behavior. Because it is *possible* to strike specific targets, and only those targets, public expectation is that war will be surgical, clean, and limited. Only those directly deserving of attack will suffer, and that suffering will be doled out with little or no overspill of casualties or damage into innocent civilian realms. This overriding desire to reduce the loss of life in war, perhaps itself a Clausewitzian duality of the first order, is ingrained in Americans, and stands in stark contrast to fanatic or religious warriors of the terrorist and other military traditions, whose goal is to inflict as much collateral damage and terror as possible.

Today, airpower possesses precisely those characteristics that, with information superiority, translate to dominance in modern interstate conflict: stealth, speed, precision, and flexibility. Since air overlays both land and sea, air forces exploiting command of the air have the ability to deliver deadly force to virtually any point on the surface of the planet—much faster than either land or sea forces that are not already deployed on the point of application. With the accelerated nature of modern conflict, this is a vital capacity. In addition to speed, air forces can strike targets at long range with extreme precision. Long-range artillery and shore bombardment remain littoral area coverage weapons, and while traditional massed bomber formations have that capacity as well, newer generation aircraft can go close to the target, thousands of miles from their base of operations, and deliver a 500 to 2,000 lb bomb within scant meters of its objective. Such application of pressure to a specific point is crucial for resolving conflict along the entire scale of operations, from peace to war, from low intensity and non-traditional conflict to nuclear exchange. Thus, air forces maximize civilian leadership's options in the application of violence, a distinct advantage for the civilian leadership that ought to command military force. Dropping bombs is only one airpower option, however, when attempting to prevent the escalation of or implement the de-escalation of violence. Delivering humanitarian relief, evacuating endangered personnel, enforcing no-fly zones, and monitoring crises are just a few of the missions that can be most efficiently undertaken via the air, provided command of the air has been secured.

9

MAKING STRATEGY

' … our overall goal is to encourage a series of transformations that in combination can produce a revolutionary increase in our military capability and redefine how war is fought.'

Deputy Secretary of Defense, Paul Wolfowitz[1]

As the twenty-first century opens, American military horizons are firmly planted in the year 2020. Between then and now is the process called *strategic transformation*, a plan for 'large-scale innovation' intended to 'shape the changing nature of military competition and cooperation through new combinations of concepts, capabilities, people, and organizations that exploit … advantages and protect against … asymmetric vulnerabilities to sustain … strategic position [and] underpin peace and stability in the world.'[2] Four 'pillars' of transformation, 'strengthening joint operations, exploiting US intelligence advantages, concept development and experimentation, and developing transformational capabilities,' are the core of strategic guidance.[3] Though vague and occasionally obtuse, these directions are strategically quite serviceable, and are intended to 'create a new game with new rules.'[4]

State-of-the-art transformational strategy centers on the competitive advantage the United States holds in high technology information collection, processing, and (potentially) distribution. The term *network-centric warfare* has been adopted by the US Department of Defense to encompass 'military missions, operations, and organizations in the information age.'[5] It is the core of transformation, the center of the newest national strategy. It is based on an appreciation of the concepts of structural organization, rules and rule-making, chaos and complexity, and the enduring principles of war.

Transformation and network-centric warfare

Chaos and complexity theories are wholly convincing that complex adaptive systems can and do operate independently based on just a few simple rules. From this simple beginning, they can grow and evolve into extraordinarily wide-ranging metasystems. Moreover, as Wolfram has shown, it is possible to classify rules and determine in advance the probability of generating a system at the edge of chaos. This observation gives the explanatory capacity of the theories seductive appeal, especially for the strategist. But, what chaos and complexity theory cannot provide is precisely what is most wanted; perfect prediction and a guide to infallible action. The problem is that the rules of quantum logic dictate that we cannot know precisely how a battle, much less a war, will unfold. Even though complex adaptive systems behavior can be based on very simple rules, the strategist cannot manipulate those rules to achieve a specific outcome. We cannot know which agent's activities will cascade through the system unchecked to create a new, anticipatable structure. In other words, *we cannot know in advance all of the outcomes that are possible*. Novelty is inherent in the structure of nature.

We must satisfy ourselves that changes in the elements of the structure are not done to achieve a specific outcome, but to increase the probability of achieving a condition of future advantage. With understanding, we gain confidence, but strategy still comes down to making difficult decisions in stressful circumstances. Despite its basis in simple rules, complexity means that good strategy-making is *hard*. It is elusive. It rests on so many variables that the best we can hope for is an approximation, based on a desire for a better state of peace.

Information and networks

Norbert Wiener's work on and familiarity with the wartime development of radar, secret codes, and computing machines inspired him to view the world as *information*. Not like information, or as if it were information, but *as* information. 'Information is the name for the content of what is exchanged with the outer world as we adjust to it, and make our adjustment felt upon it. The process of receiving and using information is the process of adjusting to the contingencies of the outer environment, and of our living effectively within that environment.'[6] Information is the means of our existence, and everything we relate to is a conduit for information.

A thing is inherently information if it *reduces uncertainty, restricts choice, or controls something else*.[7] All of these are ways of conveying meaning. Information conveyed in a doctrinal manual gives instructions and guidance, thereby reducing uncertainty about the planning of battles and engagements. It further provides expectations of other planners' behavior, and enhances coordination. The fact that I have an air wing at my disposal instead of a tank brigade restricts the options available for tactical or operational planning. In both cases I am to a certain extent controlled, as my choices are funneled and restrictions to what I may or may not do are made explicit. 'Every action involves information. Every object contains information. And everything can't help but interact—exchange information—with the world.'[8]

Vital to an understanding of modern information-intensive warfare is what information *is*, because it dictates meaning and value. Information in the broader sense that is used throughout this discourse is the transmission of ideals or common understanding. The transmission can be from imposition by a higher or stronger authority, by detection, or by formal and informal communication. Because it shapes and forms ideals and expectations, information always connotes change. And this is the real power of information, the capacity to transform.

In pre-Information Age society, the power of information was understood to be coincident with the possession of it. Especially if I possess information that you do not, it may provide an advantage in some future context. The classic example is of the bureaucrat who becomes indispensable because he or she has knowledge of every intricacy of the organization. In highly compartmented intelligence bureaucracies, information is especially prone to power grabs. Secrecy rules dictate that only a few information specialists are fluent in every aspect of a certain operation, technology, or technique. Power emanates from this situation, as others in want or need of information must go to the guardian of it, who dispenses it in drips and dollops designed to maintain the necessity of the stewardship. This medieval arrangement is obsolete, and should be well on its way out. In the twenty-first century, information power does not accrue to the person who can hold it dear, but to the person who maximizes the spread of it: the one who disperses it most freely through the network. This is clearly the model for the Internet. Value added does not come from those recidivist sites that will only divulge information for a fee. There are innumerable examples and none of them are dominating the medium. The sites that have made their creators wealthy are the ones that give away information, that *enhance the ability to find more information*.

Modern business is replete with examples that show the value of information creation and dispersal, and the ruinous impact of holding onto information. In the mid 1980s, Apple technology was the best in desktop computing, and it looked poised to dominate the industry. By the end of the decade, it had lost much of its market share. Unlike Apple, which refused to license its operating system in the belief it would maximize sales as the only producer of its powerful computers and user-friendly software, its primary competitor allowed any and all manufacturers of home PCs relatively inexpensive rights to its operating system. As more manufacturers of the admittedly inferior operating system sprang up to fill the demand for home computing, more and more applications were discovered. More software was written, much of it distributed freely on the Internet. As costs tumbled and as applications soared, Microsoft became the industry giant.

The 1980s represent the transition from the old views of information power to the new, though it will be some time yet before the new ways are so dominant that the old are forgotten. Another, perhaps more pertinent, example of that ongoing transition was the remarkable introduction of Global Navigation Satellite Systems (GLONASS), a military-designed and intended navigation aid, to civilian use. The American GPS (Global Positioning Satellite) system was initially deployed with two accuracy modes: one for sensitive military applications, and another for civilian uses including air traffic and harbor control. The civilian accuracy was not very good, to within 100 meters or so, but it was good enough—and it was free. The GPS signal was broadcast unencrypted to the world. Within a few years, uses that had never been imagined were available worldwide. Entrepreneurs found ways to enhance the accuracy of the signal and soon GPS-enhanced applications became commonplace. Shipping of goods became vastly more efficient. The economic impact of GPS is now measured in the multi-billions of dollars annually. While the owner and operator of the system, the US Air Force, does not extract value directly from GPS (and to some, providing such a global public utility without recompense is seen as a burden), the resulting economic benefits have been more than recouped at the systemic level of the state. Adaptation and exploitation of the GPS capacity could not have happened as rapidly or efficiently if it had not been dispersed fully and evenly throughout the global system.

Information can be stored and locked away. It can be kept secret, but unless it is released at some point it can have no value. Even if the storage is meant to be temporary, waiting for the precise moment of maximum relative leverage for release, it may be overcome by events. Another might discover or infer the information and release it before it can be used by the original holder of it. 'If [information] were permanently locked up with no possibility of flowing in or out, it would be useless, and not really information at all.'[9] In order for information to have power, it must be free.

To be sure, exchanging information with the outside world is how systems survive, recognize change, adapt, and thrive. Since everything meaningful is information, and information is the filter through which we interact with reality, argued Wiener, then the maximum amount of information is the most beneficial situation of continuing advantage. Indeed, one can easily construct a hierarchical structure to demonstrate the benefits of information correlation. At the base or lowest level is *data:* a descriptive, detail, or statement, also called *fact.* When facts are correlated for *relevance,* that is, placed in reference to other facts, they become *information.* Once correlated, we derive *intelligence,* in the military sense of the word, an *information set* endowed with *meaning.* Meaning here refers to the association of information to action or intent. When information reveals patterns, we have *knowledge,* intelligence correlated to plans, or predictions, modified by feedback. With knowledge and *experience,* we gain *wisdom,* including the ability to form guides or policies. With wisdom and *insight,* comes the potential for *genius.* Growth of information, through the free dissemination of it, creates the greatest foundation for true information power. But there will always be those who attempt to block or corrupt information for their own uses, to stow it away and keep it secret. Information loses its value when it is contained; when it fails to circulate. Over time, information that is not circulated becomes useless.

This notion of the steady running down of information value spurred the concept of information entropy, what Wiener styled as the gradual dissolution of information and the source of the running down of systems: 'Just as entropy tends to increase in a closed system, so information tends to decrease.'[10] Entropy may be inevitable in a closed system, but it is easily staved off by opening the system to new or accurate information. The input of fresh ideas and knowledge returns dynamism and reverses—for a time—the process of information entropy. This is the emphasis of the ongoing effort of the first pillar of strategic transformation by the United States, creation of a system that rewards open discussion of new ideas, new operating methods, and the beneficial applications of new technology. To do this, the military must establish a hierarchical network with greater emphasis on the *connections* between nodes (or agents), and less on the nodes themselves.

As Steven Wolfram pursued the role of rules and information, prediction and feedback, on the fundamental structure of nature, he discovered that spatial concepts are best understood as a nodal network. The traditional three-dimensional view of space as a vast emptiness waiting to be filled must be replaced by a vision of space as 'a giant network of nodes.'[11] In such a vision, 'the nodes are not intrinsically assigned any position. And indeed, the only thing that is defined about each node is *what other nodes it is connected to*.'[12] With space as a vast fullness, a network-in-being awaiting information transmission rules and connections to make it meaningful, a new vision of nature is starting to form. The nodes are not things, or even places. They are simply the intersection of connections, placeholders for rules that direct the transfer of information. The connections are the key to making the network useful, and Wolfram finds that it takes very few connections to wire a network so that it can perform almost any imaginable function. With two connections per node, only the most trivial networks can be made, chainlike transmission lines that are subject to breakdown and collapse from external changes. But with three connections per node, an unlimited range of networks immediately becomes possible. Adding four or five connections does not fundamentally increase the range of networks that can be made. This is because 'any node with more than three connections can in effect always be broken into a collection of nodes with exactly three connections.'[13]

With space itself constructed as a vast network of connections, with at least three connections per node, the only thing needed to make something (or, as Wolfram describes, virtually anything) happen is a rule set. The rule sets can be very simple, but as interactions increase between nodes, and the number of interactions becomes very large, the system itself can undergo spontaneous reorganization into a higher level system that operates on rules derived from, but functionally unrelated to, the rule sets at the lower level(s). Ultimately these higher order networks organize into consciousness and intelligence, and these in turn organize into social systems. One of the most studied of these naturally occurring social systems is that of ants. Insect colonies are especially useful because they are amenable to scientific observation—the entire colony can be encompassed and studied in controlled experiments and by direct observation—and they display all the elements of true social behavior: specialization, hierarchy, and both individual and group behavior.

From the study of ant (and bee) colonies, one particularly interesting behavior pattern that has been identified is called *swarming* or swarm logic behavior. The notion here is that 'ten thousand ants—each limited to a meager vocabulary of pheromones and minimal cognitive skills—collectively engage in nuanced and improvisational problem-solving.'[14] The fascinating thing about swarm logic is that the simple set of recognition tools and minimal rule-based responses allows a collection of independent agents (ants) who are individually unable to assess the broader situation to work in apparently coordinated unison. They do so without any direction from superiors, gathering all their information locally, and yet in the aggregate their individual actions promote the welfare of the colony.

> *Local* turns out to be the key term in understanding swarm logic. We see emergent behavior in systems like ant colonies when the individual agents in the system pay attention to their immediate neighbors rather than wait for orders from above.[15]

Swarm logic would become the first analogy from complexity theory applied to what is now recognized as the US military's transformation toward information dominant warfare.[16] However, it was the defects in swarming-style combat, and not its merits, that led directly to an improved notion of network-centric warfare. In the ant or bee colony, each agent has the ability to recognize a threat, move to it, and attack by biting or stinging. As information flows through the system from the source of the attack out, additional agents move to engage the threat until a swarm or mass large enough to deflect or destroy the threat is reached. While effective and efficient for rudimentary social systems, as those systems achieve greater complexity, it becomes less desirable. Adopting a swarming operational and tactical philosophy is difficult enough, as it would completely decentralize command and control. Every soldier, sailor, or airman would have the authority to engage a threat upon recognition. Mistakes and unwanted actions are bound to occur. Moreover, such a design is extremely vulnerable to feints or deception. Fortunately for ants and bees, most of their natural threats do not practice such things. Some do, however, and such procedures have allowed humans to perfect the art of beekeeping—or complete subjugation of the colony entirely for the use and benefit of the subjugators.

A more sophisticated swarming logic would be more like the analogy of a swarming defense in football. Players are well equipped and rigorously trained to react to specific formations and movements. Once the offense has committed, the defense reacts in such a manner that multiple players engage the ball carrier to make a tackle. In a military force, individual combatants would be equipped with the most sensitive detection devices and the most lethal weapons available. They would be meticulously trained and disciplined in the use of the equipment, their organizational responsibilities to include zones of operations, and in proper rules of engagement. Still, once the operation or war commences, the individual agents must be able to perform their duties without real-time guidance from superiors. This would occur in an environment where communications were unreliable or off-line (such as in a post-nuclear situation) or where communication could negatively impact the operation (as in special operations deep in enemy territory, or under cover). The image of a military composed of autonomous killing machines roaming the battlefield looking for targets is simply unacceptable under current American sensibilities.

Network-centric warfare

Network-centric (or net-centric) warfare is the American military's response to the challenges of an emerging information age. It 'broadly describes the combination of emerging tactics, techniques, and procedures that a fully or even partially networked force can employ to create a decisive warfighting advantage.'[17] Net-centric warfare is intended to provide advantages at all levels of war, including the strategic. It is based on the notion that as the amount of information available, analyzable, and usable increases astronomically in the twenty-first century, a revolution in military affairs will result. Wars will be fought differently in the information age, and the powerful will be those states that adapt and evolve quickest. Based on a series of National Defense University and RAND studies in the late 1990s, the concept of net-centric warfare was well presented—it is difficult to find a strategic theorist who doubts that the effects of information warfare will be profound—but it has been poorly understood by those in the defense establishment who seek to implement it.[18] What I argue in this section is that the concept of a revolutionary change in warfare that will occur because of the capacity to transmit and use electronic forms of information has been misplaced. True net-centric warfare will be based on the characteristics of the network itself, its interrelationships, and not in the robustness of command or authority control that war planners currently seek. I assert that almost all current applications of the concepts of net-centric warfare remain node- or platform-centric and not connection-centric, as the logic it is based on demands.

Properly understood net-centric warfare expects to set an organizational structure that duplicates the capacities of higher order adaptive systems that learn through feedback loops and reverberating circuits. The human brain is the model for systems where learning occurs because of the dense interconnection of the neural networks, not in any static circuit-board or layout of neural cells. These relationships are defined in nodal terms, via axons and synapses, but the potential of the brain is in its connections. Each cell or neuron is connected 'to as many as a thousand other neurons. When a given neuron fires, it relays that charge to all those other cells, which, if certain conditions are met, then in turn relay the charge to their connections and so on.'[19] Focus on the relationships of the network, and not the nodes, allows us to isolate the phenomenon of self-transformation. For a *system* to *learn*, it must possess the capacities to recognize new or different phenomena (discern change), and an infrastructure capable of responding to that change (adapt). The response is a modification that incorporates, rejects, or abides the change. It is adaptability, and the mechanism that calibrates adaptability is feedback. Increasing the capacity for systemic learning is the same as increasing the capacity of the system to adapt, and 'making an emergent system more adaptive entails tinkering with different kinds of feedback.'[20]

At issue in the current rush to find meaning in the flow of information now flooding the battle space is the *proper* construction of networks. To date, unfortunately, the emphasis has been placed on network nodes. To call the transformation currently underway net-centric is therefore quite in error. It should properly be called node-centric, as the theoretical underpinnings of platform-centric warfare have so far been retained. When network-centric warfare is properly understood and implemented, we may end up calling it link-centric warfare to underscore its proper function.

It is the relationship *between* agents that provides meaning and value to the entire system, or network, not the capabilities or technologies of those agents. Until this conceptual hurdle is crossed and left behind, it is meaningless to call network-centric or information warfare a revolution in military affairs. Today the effort still is based on increasing transmission and reception capacities of platforms and controllers, increasing bandwidth to make the command and control flow of information richer and more detailed, and enlarging the types or means of communication available in order to increase the robustness and reliability of current networks and links. These efforts are commendable, and should enhance the transition to truly net- or link-centric warfare when it occurs, but they are not revolutionary. They are evolutionary upgrades in capacities that commanders have always desired: better and more reliable communication in all phases of war. What still needs to be done is a systematic and concerted effort to dramatically increase the number of links.

In a primitive system, where communication is limited to physical contact between agents, the amount of data that can be transferred from one to the other is extremely restricted, and where redundant transmission methods are absent, the principle of increasing system capability through maximizing the number of potential relationships is vital to the system's health. The key understanding is that *advantages of networking* accrue to the *system*, and not necessarily (or even desirably) to the individual agents or nodes. In social systems, society is stronger, culture is richer, and innovation expands quicker the wider the set of agents that meet and interact. Diversity breeds innovation. Good ideas spread faster and are more likely to take hold than bad ones. And, if bad ideas do permeate the system, they are more likely to be identified and weeded out as the number of interactions expands, increasing the evidence against them and the likelihood that a better alternative will be found. The *fear* strategic planners have, that by giving up network control, errors or mistakes will inevitably occur, must be minimized. In a true net-centric form of war, efforts to assert direct control and limit or eliminate agent error will reduce the efficiencies of a net-centric architecture. The more interactions, the greater the likelihood of a deviant or unique interaction, but the greater the capacity for the system to overwhelm ineffective or corrupting influences. In return, the network will provide an increasing number of positive deviations and fresh ideas. The best way to determine which are good and which are bad is to let them move through the system.

Obviously, increasing the number of relationships or connections means losing a measure of control over the system. Unexpected things will happen. Mistakes will be made. In a military operation, especially in a high-technology military where stealth and precision dominate, the impetus to give over control and decision-making to lower order agents (a flattening of system control versus a restrictive command hierarchy) is resisted. Truly net-centric warfare must concede the probability of making some mistakes, even deadly ones, at the individual level in exchange for the probability of greater efficiency and effectiveness at the system level. And that is a lot to ask of a traditionally hierarchical military command structure, more so for a military whose personnel have been conditioned to eliminate all mistakes, as one screw-up can be the end of a career.

The tolerance for error that must be accepted if net-centric warfare is to be fully implemented is just one of the impediments delaying its appearance. Air Force Colonel Thomas Ehrhard argues that there are six essential obstructions in implementing high-technology structures in a military organization, especially germane to net-centric warfare but not limited to it. All six impediments are *cultural*, and therefore can be manipulated and changed, but they are deeply ensconced. The first three are general, and apply across all manifestations of military change. The last three are more specific, and while transferable to a number of changes in the current environment of military transformation, are here in direct response to current efforts to implement net-centric warfare in the US military.

The first broadly cultural impediment is a wide-ranging negative reaction to change, in particular change as a result of new technology. Any move to a high-technology network-centric organizational structure would necessarily rely on *increased combat automation*. The maximum view of such automation would be a network of autonomous killing machines operating in a swarm configuration, not unlike fire ants or wasps. From this inherent fear of combat automation, especially in the swarming metaphor, the second impediment is drawn; the natural resistance of the *diminishing warrior*. In military culture, the fear is that technology will run away with war; that it will become uncontrollable once unleashed. Duty, honor, and sacrifice are the military virtues the warrior possesses but that the machine can never know. That this is a nonsensical comparison is not debated. For the life-and-death decisions that accompany war, commanders are especially wary of relying on anything that reduces control over events. It is perhaps for this reason more than any other that the full implementation of any manner of net-centric warfare will be resisted, and that implementation to date has in fact been contrary to net-centric concepts. The effort has focused on increasing the number and reliability of transmitters and receivers on individual platforms and to specific points precisely in order to obtain a *more* robust command and control capability, not to disperse authority and judgment.

The third impediment is the reaction to any new technology that is essentially invisible. Communications links are not so apparent as are tanks and airplanes. To argue that the combat effect of increased relationships is worth the billions of dollars that could otherwise be spent on tangible arms and munitions is a tough sell. It is magic to the users, and they either *believe* in it or they are unshakably *skeptical* of it. Both are irrational manifestations that cannot translate their convictions to the opposite view. More confounding is that the nature of military communications is now increasingly so complex that explaining these high technologies is a daunting task. The pace of change is so rapid that only specialists can follow the implications of generational improvements. For someone who has just managed to learn the procedures for radio communications, the tactical value of laser relay and streaming video systems (much less the technical and operational aspects of them) may be incomprehensible. For these reactionaries, frustration may lead them to argue that all the technology in the world doesn't mean a thing if you don't have a dog-faced GI with a rifle to back it up.

This flows inevitably into the conundrum of error, the fourth impediment and the first of the network-centric implementation ones. Should an automated system or open network manage to target and blow up—or lead the human operator to target and blow up—a school bus, the incident will be seen as proof that the technology or system is bad. Certainly, tragic mistakes will happen, and I am in no way condoning the errors that seem inevitably to occur in war—but effective commanders and strategists know that an operation cannot be allowed to be crippled by error, no matter how much one tried to avoid it, and that the error might have occurred regardless of the extant technology or organizing system. The situation has changed and now one must deal with the new reality. Network-centric warfare, properly configured, allows individuals at the forward edge of the battle space to access an incredible array of information and opinion in the belief that this will not only enhance the combat power of individuals and individual weapon systems, but that it will increase the efficiency of the entire structure in prosecuting military operations. An objective increase in efficiency is a laudable thing, especially if it is defined as lessening the impact on non-combatants. Perfection is not required to validate it. What is critical is that the system learns from its mistakes, whether human or automated, and that it becomes more discerning and more efficient in the future. That a properly implemented net-centric architecture could incrementally reduce the inevitable errors by disseminating corrections rapidly through the system and allow for sophisticated learning to occur through the multiple examples of its independent agents is little comfort when the school bus is burning.

And so net-centric implementation proceeds apace, with a nod to the architects of change and much lip-service paid to the tenets of net-centric operations. In practice, however, it is little more than a concerted effort to upgrade the existing means and methods of command and control, to make them more robust. This is obvious in the fifth impediment (though this may be a poor choice of words), manifest in the observation that the most important and celebrated gain from the recent experience in Operations Enduring Freedom (OEF) and Iraqi Freedom (OIF) has been friendly force tracking.[21] Lauded as the function that drastically reduced friendly fire casualties (fratricide) as compared with the 1991 Gulf War experience, it is clear that centralizing command and control ('I want to know where my guys are and precisely what they are doing'), rather than flattening command hierarchies, is paramount in application.

Finally, there is an impediment Colonel Ehrhard calls the fundamental constituency problem. Communications networks, intelligence surveillance, and bandwidth just don't kill anything—at least not directly. They are relegated to second order importance regardless of any argument for the criticality or necessity of their function to battle space success. In the constant infighting that occurs in budget decisions, second order programs will only achieve adequate funding and efficient implementation if they are championed by a commander or leader of sufficient clout. Otherwise, they will be widely acknowledged as a good thing, if only we had the money.

Of all the impediments to change that are slowing the implementation of true net-centric warfare in the US military, the most troublesome is the unwillingness to relinquish top-down command and control. The requirement for disbursed authority and responsibility to forward agents is holding back the process of *proper* implementation of net-centric concepts and ideas—and this may be an unavoidable part of the adjustment to an entirely new way of thinking about waging war. The two services that should be the most adept at implementing such concepts, as they have a tradition of ship and aircraft commanders acting independently in battle, are the Navy and Air Forces. Both are hindered by current doctrine drawn from classic military interpretations of effective fighting mode, described rather oxymoronically by the Air Force as 'centralized command, decentralized execution,' and more accurately by the Navy as 'centralized planning, decentralized command and execution' ('trigger-pulling,' what I will call action).

As the capacity to reach down into the tactical realm from the highest levels of strategy has matured, it is easy to argue that the mode of fighting we actually use today is centralized planning and centralized action. Pilots on bombing runs are made to hold release until authority comes from national command. Instant communications allows for real-time control of tactical engagements, and the highest levels of command authority have been increasingly willing to meddle. What is needed to make net-centric warfare work is a simple rule set that instructs combatants in clear, precise language (proper Rules of Engagement [ROE]), and then the fortitude to stand back and allow the fighters on the scene to make decisions and take allowable actions. Such a concept would be decentralized planning (with centralized or standardized *guidance* through ROEs) and decentralized action. Unfortunately, before the US gets to true net-centric operations it will likely go through a period of decentralized planning (as decision makers at the top delegate operations to those closest to the engagement) and centralized action (as the increasingly robust and redundant communications system makes it possible to control every move and action of the combatant from rear command centers). The less time spent in this entirely improper combination of control and execution, the better.

Maxims for a new age

The unprecedented and essentially uncontrollable explosion in the amount of information available today is truly unique in the history of humanity. Never before has it been possible for the majority of a single state, and perhaps soon the

world, to instantly access the global bank of knowledge, misinformation, advertising, archived data, inane trivia, and real-time events that are available on the
Internet. Today, it is difficult to argue that for any plausible application or investigation imaginable, there is not enough information available. What is clear is that
there is often no efficient means of gathering the information that is pertinent to
the inquiry or application. As the amount of information readily available doubles
every few months, the ability to *sort* and *retrieve* pertinent, usable, reliable information is the key to maintaining an edge in speed and tempo of information
processing over a potential opponent.

In the new strategic paradigm, it becomes useful to think of increasing rather
than restricting the amount of information in the system, to the point of flooding
the infosphere with data—all manner of data; right, wrong, dubious, and arcane.
Allow as many agents as possible to access it and create new information. Do not
try to hold back fresh information for it will quickly lose its power. Focus instead
on retrieving, processing, and using the information faster and better than anyone
else. Speed in all things, precision in data retrieval through enhanced technology,
increased *shared awareness* of problems and solutions throughout the system via
maximum and redundant dissemination, increased self-synchronization, greater
compression of operations through increased tempo, and enhanced learning will
accrue to the side that masters the techniques of truly network-centric warfare.

To a significant extent, the slowly transforming American military structure is
well behind in this race with its current enemies. The more successful terrorist
organizations are employing a modified swarming strategy with many of the sub-
tleties of network-centric operations. They recognize that the global war on terror
is at its base an information war, and the means they employ use information to
paralyze response. They attack directly at the ability to adapt. They piggyback on
open information networks to spread propaganda, recruit additional members,
and provide intelligence to a widely dispersed network of cells. Only the details of
their tactical structure are withheld. Direct links from terrorist to terrorist are minimized so that the capture of one cannot be used to roll up the entire organization.
But they are all still linked through myriad indirect connections and anonymous
intermediaries. Websites provide information to anyone who logs on. Orders are
published openly in the classified advertising of newspapers and magazines.
These information links are numerous, and wide open to scrutiny. Their planning
and execution is completely decentralized. Local cells determine the best ways to
inflict terror on the surrounding population, and take action at locally determined
moments of opportunity. The top may not even be aware of the plans and operations of the lower levels—and this is by structural *design*. It is the flattest of
formal organizations, barely above the non-organization of anarchy. And it works.

The world does not need to respond to the terrorist threat in kind, by becoming
a brutal terrorist-like counter-organization. Although this could work, in the tactical sense of increasing the terrorist body-count, it would of necessity transform
the basic social structure, at levels lower than needed. There are lessons to be
learned and realities to be accepted, however. The terrorist organization will be

more flexible and adaptable than the traditional military hierarchy. In a war of conventional combat the US has the world's premier fighting force, by orders of magnitude. In an unconventional war, the same force is proving cumbersome and prone to low-technology attack. The US must strike a balance between its traditional capabilities and the organizational requirements of information warfare. It must flatten its organization and expand the connections in its network. It must transform at least a part of its force into 'a system designed to learn from the ground level, a system in which macro intelligence and adaptability derive from local knowledge.'[22]

Network-centric systems design

To design a strategy with a complex, adaptive system structure, for military or any other purposes, there are four fundamental principles to consider:

1 *Maximize Nodes* The fewer agents in a network, the less likely it is to attain useful levels of adaptive behavior at the systemic level. The statistical law of large numbers—*more is different*—is the intellectual source of this tenet. Predicting the outcome of a single coin toss is an interesting activity, but one that will do no better than random selection over the long haul. Predicting the occurrence of heads or tails in a sequence of ten throws is more accurate, but the prediction of heads or tails thrown in a thousand coins tossed tends toward precision. The capacity to predict how any individual will act in a future context is extremely difficult, though less so than how a small group, say ten people, might act in a given situation. And although social group dynamics are not a factor in coin tosses, how a thousand people might react, in the aggregate, is highly predictable. The more nodes a network has, the more flexible and adaptable it will be, and the more accurately one can assess aggregate reactions to external change.

2 *Maximize Connections* 'Local information can lead to global wisdom.'[23] The primary mechanism of systemic adaptation is the interaction between independent agents. Good ideas are spread, bad practices are rooted out. Establish as many opportunities for agent-to-agent interaction (across levels, specialties, and missions) as possible. The greater the number and variety of potential interactions designed into the structure of the system, the greater the capacity of individual agents to be adaptive and dynamic, and for the system to be efficient. Diversity brings unique insights to long-standing problems. Channeling or funneling of interactions needs to be avoided.

3 *Maximize Response Sets* The real key to agent efficiency is the inductive ability to recognize patterns. In the ROEs for independent agents, use this to advantage. It is not necessary to describe every type of enemy equipment, for example, as the basis for identification and engagement. In fact, this decreases adaptability and efficiency, should the enemy be using equipment not on the list or slightly modified. Better to provide a short description of enemy behavior

patterns that the agent can apply to any situation, and allow the agent to independently interpret, modify, react to, and provide feedback on the utility of the pattern recognition rule. The widest latitude of response capability in decision-making is desirable, and a tolerance for assessment error is essential.

4 *Minimize Top-Down Control* The desire to control lower-level activity is deeply rooted, but must be systematically reduced. The capacity for one designated agent to control the actions of individuals is harder and less efficient the larger the network. It leads to telescopic vision, a focus on details, and abandonment of strategic generalities. Even if enhanced technology makes multiple agent control more efficient, it is still undesirable. Single-point control allows for the maximum amount of failure if the decision maker misinterprets information. It is better to build a densely interconnected system of agents guided by relatively simple rules, and allow positive emergent behavior to happen spontaneously. Moreover: 'Having individual agents directly capable of assessing the overall state of the system can be a real liability.'[24] A pilot ready to engage a target does not need to be encumbered with the weight of all the possible grand strategic repercussions of the action. Allow agents to operate freely within the parameters of assigned rules as informed by *local* conditions. They will be more efficient at their level and thus less detrimental at higher ones.

When building network structures designed to enhance adaptability and flexibility, it is a good thing to keep the design simple. Rules should be plain and as limited as possible. Information should be made available but not forced into use. Perhaps above all, action should be rewarded. Nothing is more paralyzing to a decision maker than a surfeit of information, or the hesitancy attributed to a search for that last bit of vital information. It is a truism of decision-making theory that the less one knows about the subject at hand, the easier it is to make decisions … and the fact is that individuals in battle space conditions often have to rapidly make decisions on the basis of extremely limited information.

Ideally, in a traditional military hierarchy, decisions should be made on the basis of sound deduction. Pure deduction, in the most rigorous mode, is the arrival at specifics of knowledge from the existence of known generalizations or premises. If the premise is true, and the rules of logic and rigorous analysis are applied, then the conclusion is true. In traditional military hierarchies, policy and ROEs are the generalizations that apply, from which the decision maker is to deduce proper actions. 'Do not engage the enemy unless directly threatened' is a sample ROE; since I am currently under attack, I may engage the enemy. Deductive reasoning is normally equated with logical thinking and clear rationalization. It is therefore difficult to apply in rapidly changing situations or in contexts where information is lacking. In these cases, induction—the arrival at general knowledge from specific incidents or fragments of knowledge—is the method of reasoning that prevails.

Induction is what allows us to infer the existence of a cat from the glimpse of a tail vanishing around a corner. Induction is what allows us to go into a zoo and classify some exotic feathered creature as a bird, even though we've never seen a scarlet-crested cockatoo before. Induction is what allows us to survive in a messy, unpredictable, and often incomprehensible world.[25]

Since inductively arrived-at generalizations, by definition, reason beyond the evidence, they are speculative and quite often wrong. But unlike deduction, inductive reasoning *is* based on evidence, no matter how fragmentary. Conclusions are arrived at not because of a single bit of knowledge or information, but because that new fragment is correlated with known or experienced patterns of behavior. A series of past engagements may have shared patterns such as a forward element of fast-moving aircraft and a lag time of two hours from first contact to the main body attack. Inductively one might generalize that these are characteristics of the opponent's doctrine, and so the situation here is enough like past experience to extrapolate a pattern of attack. Clearly induction has created new knowledge through inference, something that deduction cannot do. The trade-off, of course, is that an inductive conclusion may be based on irrelevant or misleading information, and in this case is simply wrong. Deduction will preserve the truth of the premise, but it will not generate new information, it merely provides detail. The conclusions of inductive reasoning, based as they are on logical leaps of faith, are always contingent on the validity of those leaps. Nonetheless, inductive reasoning is how new information (in the form of statements or theories) is created, as those leaps can have the heuristic quality of revelation. The new information can then be tested and formalized through deduction. The essential weakness of deduction is that it can never really say anything new because the conclusions are already contained in the premises.

Perfect or complete information is not only impossible, it is not desirable, as was demonstrated in the discussion on noise. Still, it is widely perceived that to have more accurate information is better than less. This is an extremely difficult notion to abandon, and yet it may have to occur, for the sake of increasing the amount of *new* information, in order to enhance the capacity *for the system* to respond and adapt to change.

Diversity and strategy

Information is not an end unto itself. It has no physical properties, it cannot be occupied, and many individuals can possess the same information simultaneously. Of utmost importance to the validity of net-centric warfare, different individuals can obtain different information from identical data. As more individuals examine the information, and transmit their interpretations to others, the more likely it is that the information will be accurately described by one or a combination of several individuals, and efficiently used.

Multiple interpretations increase the likelihood that one or a combination of solutions to a problem or responses to a change will be found most effective or efficient. Since we cannot know in advance which interpretation is best, the more that can be brought to light and allowed to compete, the better. This is a straight-forward means of increasing adaptability, but what if the best option or most desired response is already known, and the intent is to spread accurate information and tested solutions throughout the system? Should individual agents be allowed to test alternate or innovative solutions when the doctrinal ones work quite satisfactorily? Are the marginal gains possible with experimentation and maximum dispersion equal to the potentially disastrous setbacks that could occur?

The answer is yes, to all three questions. The system requires adaptability for its health, and there are always surprises, unanticipated events that cannot be accounted for in a strict command structure. Moreover, it is extremely unlikely that accurate information or solutions will be transmitted and received intact. If, as Wiener insists, we are defined through communication connections and feedback, and the act of using or observing information fundamentally alters it, then the act of communicating a message necessarily transforms it. The more the message reverberates through the system, the more it is altered. The solution is not to limit the transmissions, apparent in classically linear thinking where inputs equal out-puts: the more transmissions of a message, the more corrupted it becomes. If this were the case, then a simple formula could be derived that would assign an amount of error to each transmission, until the message was garbled. But this is not what happens in a robust network. The intent of the message can remain intact through multiple transmissions *because* it is interpreted at each node. Minor changes at one node are corrected after passing through several more nodes. Rather than cringe at the potential for corruption at any one point, it is better to embrace and harness the changes its transmission inevitably makes. It is more useful to think of these multiple iterations of change and alteration as a process of *refining* the message, of adapting it more perfectly to the agents who use it and the medium in which it is to operate. In the norm of choice in the previous chapter, I made the case that a conscious decision to go against doctrine must be explained, and that an explanation that is valid can effect positive change. The more that individual agents are exposed to situations in which doctrine is expected to apply, the more refined the doctrine can become. The more agents that receive and retransmit a message, the *more* likely it is to get through in an *intended* form than if it went through a strict, minimal chain from sender to recipient. In the latter case, a single misinterpretation of the message alters it permanently and irrevocably from the original intent, and its passage to the next recipient in the chain is unlikely to correct it.

It is the interaction of countless independent agents acting to properly interpret and retransmit a message that ensures multiple interpretations of the message are received and tested, and that the best interpretations will tend to dominate. In like fashion, the interaction of countless small agents makes the system flexible, ' ... if a pair of agents can't agree, a third agent can usually solve the conflict ... instead of getting stuck trying the same approach over and over, the agent can try something new.'[26] This is the real power of the network approach. Rather than attempt to command the interpretation of all messages, or to dictate the actions of every agent, the networking of the maximum number of independent agents allows the maximum number of solutions to a problem to be considered and attempted. While mistakes are made at the lower levels, the rapid spread of information allows for rapid corrections and swift adoption of the most effective techniques. In the aggregate, the system is able to adapt and adjust to change and surprise in the most efficient and effective manner.

Truth is a thorny subject, already broached. Without recounting the arguments in full, it is not generally valid to say that all viewpoints are equal. Some are good or considered, while others are misinformed, deluded, or ill-considered. Nonetheless, the greater the number of perspectives that can be brought to bear on an issue, the more likely the truth (or reality of the situation) is to be revealed. Omniscience, in this construct, would not be the knowledge of all things. Rather, omniscience would be the amalgam of *all* points of view. Strategy and strategy-making is best served when all valid perspectives have been discussed and analyzed, and the strategist uses this knowledge to construct a framework in which the actions of tactical agents are likely to lead to a condition of continuing advantage. How strategy *is* made and how strategy *should* be made are two different things, however. There are, in essence, three methods for making strategy using multiple perspectives. Two are practiced and the third ought to be.

Most strategies are developed in a perverse form of cost-benefit analysis. Options are gathered and the merits and weaknesses are tallied up. The options are then weighed and the heaviest (or lightest, depending on the value assigned to strengths and drawbacks) is selected. This is the trivialization of strategy-making, as proponents of any particular option must find as many details in favor of their own and as many details in opposition to the others as possible. When done correctly, cost-utility analysis is used as a *discriminator* between viable or otherwise preferred options. In other words, each of the options has obvious benefits and clear costs, and none is noticeably better than the others. The preferred process is to work through the logical *ramifications* of implementation. If this strategy is accepted, what are the likely outcomes, reactions, and spin-offs? Cost-utility analysis is thus a fine decision-making tool. It is not a valid *generator* of options, nor a particularly useful tool for fine-tuning strategy.

A second, rampant strategy-making technique is to conduct a survey of desired outcomes and attempt to match extant capabilities to the achievement of them. Similar to this is to undertake an analysis of extant capabilities and determine suitable objectives given the means available. While the former may sound reasonable at first glance, it is no more strategically sound than the latter. War and battle may of necessity be come-as-you-are parties, but strategy-making requires far more vision.

The proper way to make strategy is to generate views of the world as it is and as it should be from multiple perspectives, those of the most prominent actors and most critically from outside the system—a look at the structure of conflict itself. A plan that promotes the interests of *the greatest number* of these actors without damaging or impinging on the continuing viability of the actor for whom the strategy is being made—and keeps that actor relevant and viable in future decision-making—is the best. The prominent actors include any whose institutional interests can or will affect the conflict. Domestically, these include state political leaders, the various branches of the military (each with its own motivations and concepts of force employment), and shapers of public opinion (to include mass media). The perceptions of the equivalent agents in the opponent's state and any influential third-party states should also be simulated and analyzed if they cannot be otherwise collected. The structural perspective is the most difficult, but the most critical. From outside the system we remove ourselves from the interests and intentions of the actors just canvassed. We see the structure as intrinsically important and viable. We see that the world system is not maximized by the dominance of one agent over another, but on the continued interaction of all its members, on patterns of systemic accommodation and adaptation. 'So the question is how you maneuver in a world like that. And the answer is that you want to keep as many options open as possible. You go for viability, something that's workable, rather than what's optimal.'[27] Sound strategy maximizes the viability, robustness, and survivability of both the entity for which the strategy is developed and the global structure within which the entity operates. Such a strategy would likely have the following norms:

- Maximum dispersion of *accurate* information into the system to allow the maximum adaptation through inductive reasoning of individual agents; and the maximum redundancy and robustness of connections to allow the optimal subsequent flow of experiences to disseminate.
- Maximum interaction and competition between domestic agents, and maximum interaction between all others, with a minimum amount of centralized or top-down control required to maintain a systemic homeostasis. Think of the conditions necessary to establish a robust and continuing free market, and then adapt those conditions to the varying levels of domestic military activity.
- Maximum capacity for agents to express and make public their interests and views. This will require that each constituency develop advocates for their positions, based in the faith that the best courses of actions are derived from multiple perspectives offered in an open environment of intellectual competition.
- Suitable conditions for the spontaneous creation of multiple levels of hierarchical organization to allow for the maximum outputs of complexity (emergent adaptation and multiple problem-solving methods).
- Rules and incentives that keep the structure at the 'edge of chaos,' neither falling into disorder nor plodding toward stagnation. Simple rules of *mutual* feedback seem to be the key. Complex adaptive systems, like ant colonies, are not anarchies. 'They obey rules [defined] in advance, but those rules only govern the micromotives. The macrobehavior is another matter' that cannot be controlled directly; all that can be done 'is set up the conditions that you think will make that behavior possible. Then you press play and see what happens.'[28]

The US Department of Defense appears to share an affinity for most of these tenets of strategy-making. Its nine 'governing principles' for network-centric warfare are, in the main, quite compatible:[29]

1 *First fight for information superiority* The initial principle is in fact an enabling operational purpose, the core of operational strategy as described in Chapter 3. The purpose of information operations is to control the infosphere. If superiority is not possible, it is imperative to contest an opponent's attempts to dominate there. Actions taken in pursuit of information superiority will enhance access to information by friendly agents while increasing the costs of information retrieval and disinformation dispersal by enemy agents.

2 *Develop high-quality shared awareness* Through maximum dispersion of accurate information, common understanding and situational awareness will build. This requires an information network of networks, capable of disseminating raw and finished data, and quality intelligence and open-source reporting. It also requires that every agent capable of accessing information is also capable of supplying information. Every user should be a sensor. This allows maximum recognition of change, the first step in adaptation. Where tradition does not relent, in opposition to the recommendations of the present work, is in the insistence that 'high-quality shared awareness requires *secure* and assured networks and *information that can be defended.*'[30]

3 *Dynamic self-synchronization* Maximize agent-level autonomy in decision-making and task-setting to increase adaptability and reduce channeled authority. This is accomplished by increasing operational tempo and rewarding subordinate initiative.

4 *Dispersed forces* Reduced emphasis on physical occupation of battle space in favor of functional control, the ability to rapidly apply combat power in the right time and place, through self-synchronicity and simultaneous arrival of multiple forces on target.

5 *De-massed forces* Coupled tightly with the previous principle, this refers to de-emphasis of the traditional concept of geographically contiguous massing of force preparatory to application in favor of alternative means of achieving desired effects.

6 *Deep sensor reach* Develop and deploy multiple intelligence, surveillance, and reconnaissance (ISR) networks to achieve global, persistent information collection. Sensors in these networks can be thought of as maneuver elements in the battle for information superiority, and may have a deterrent effect if information gleaned provides early warning of enemy intent.

7 *Compressed operations and levels of war* Increased connectivity between systems at the lowest possible levels is desired, specifically in reference to the military services.

8 *Rapid speed of command* The desire is to reduce 'sensor-to-decision-maker-to-shooter timelines. As a guiding principle this is at odds with the rest, due to its unfortunate focus on tactical actions. It requires the commander to

release authority to individual combatants for individual actions at the lowest levels, rather than pre-release authority through properly designed rules of engagement.

9 *Alter initial conditions at increased rates of change* Force a situation of perpetual novelty that requires the enemy to adapt, and exploit reticence or inability to do so.

In practice, and in rhetoric, however, the US military undercuts its network-centric transformation. Although the overarching 'organizing principle' of network-centric warfare is an '[acceleration of] our ability to know, decide, and act by linking sensors, communications systems, and weapons systems in an interconnected grid,' the advantages expected to accrue 'allows a *commander* to analyze the battlespace, rapidly communicate critical information to friendly combat forces, and marshal a lethal combination of air, land, and sea capabilities to exert massed effects against an adversary.'[31] All of the nine principles articulated in the previous paragraph are violated in the purpose statement.

10

IS STRATEGY AN ART?

Pure Strategy is more properly a *philosophy* of strategy than an historical or scientific investigation. It is an inquiry into the fundamental *truth* of strategy as defined above: its purpose, place, utility, and value. I recognize that this may seem an odd or circuitous way to impart the lessons and meaning of strategy, especially to military practitioners who must make decisions that will have strategic ramifications, but truth is an ideal that cannot be universally measured nor thunderously proclaimed. Implications and projections will be accepted only to the extent that the theory herein is consistent within itself, with experience, and to which it is persuasive. As such, it may prove frustrating to the military practitioner who sees that no manual for strategy, no doctrine for strategic design, is provided.

Most deficient, I suppose, is that nowhere will the reader find a claim to superior tactical or operational insight into the *conduct* of battle, campaign, or war. This does not mean that the following is a discussion of the unreal or ethereal. *Pure Strategy* is an eminently practical book, intended for practicing strategists. It will set the student of war onto a path of strategic thinking, and may inspire the strategist to expand the horizon of possibilities in meaningful ways. By understanding the place and purpose of strategy, and using knowledge of the structure of war so that structure can be manipulated to the advantage of the state, however, I believe the strategist can make a profound impact on the conduct of war.

The notion that science is the basis of a theory of strategy that in practice is an art is not altogether absurd. Chapter 3 of Clausewitz's *On War* is devoted to the question of whether war is an art or a science, and he finds elements of both in it.

> We have already argued that knowledge and ability are different things … A book cannot really teach us how to do anything, and therefore 'art' should have no place in its title. But we have become used to summarizing the knowledge required for the practice of art [by] the term 'theory of art,' or simply 'art.' It is therefore consistent [to] call everything 'art' whose object is creative ability [while] 'science' should be kept for disciplines [whose] object is pure knowledge.[1]

Theory shapes our perceptions of the world and experience hones our ability to interact in it. Both are needed. Likewise, both tactician and strategist, with their disparate viewpoints, are vital to the military health of the state. The tactician joins means to ends in a way that maximizes the achievement of goals within a given structure of rules and conditions. The strategist perceives the outputs of tactical decision-making as but one component in a continuously changing landscape of politics. As such, the strategist continuously evaluates the rules and conditions of the tactical encounter and manipulates them in such a manner as to increase the probability that tactical outcomes will support the political aim.

Tactical decisions are made within boundaries; strategists manipulate boundaries. In competition and conflict, the goal of the tactician is to limit the opponent's options, and in so doing, bring events to conclusion. The strategist expands options, opens doors, and denies the possibility of an end-state. The two are not in conflict, but joined in a profound unity of opposites. Hence, strategy and tactics are equally critical—if theoretically opposite—components of state decision-making in and about war, more akin to the Asian concept of yin and yang than of fire and water. The whole cannot be understood or appreciated fully without the diametric characteristics of both equally at play. What connects the two, and makes each comprehensible to the other, is operational employment.

Together, sense is made of the whole. This knowledge by negative association is the basis of the comparative method, the source of all true learning. We know a thing by what it is not. Hard is relative to soft, light to dark, long to short. Each is necessary to define and appreciate the other, but more importantly, both together create wholeness—a thing greater than the sum of its parts. When we envision a synthesis of opposites we create a capacity to measure *and* an ideal for which to strive. We cannot determine the relative success or value of a tactical victory without knowing the consequences of defeat, nor can we evaluate its impact on policy if we are ignorant of what the outcome ought to have been.

The strategist does not achieve victory. Rather, victory is one means to achievement. Victory is not an end for strategy, any more than a finished portrait is the end for art. The parallels between art and strategy, craft and tactics, are profound. Art is a never-ending journey toward perfection. Each object of art is an expression of that journey but is only a marker along the route, the end of which cannot be known, and may not be knowable. Strategy, like art, is about exploration and the development of new ways of seeing, thinking, and being. Although one may have mastered the skills of the craft, technical mastery does not make an artist. True art is original, whereas great craftsmanship is repeatable. True art is astonishing, surprising, and different. Tactical genius is the acme of skill. Strategic genius is the mastery of change.

There is a pervading belief that true artistry, like strategy, cannot be taught. It is innate in some individuals. In this view, promise is evident in the individual, recognizable by those who have achieved the status of artist, and the proper method of training is apprenticeship. There are also those who believe that everyone has the potential to be an artist, and all that is needed is the exact inspiration at the right moment. Its appearance is enhanced by exposure to a variety of materials and disciplines, but this is less teaching than nurturing. Either way, true artistry is a rare expression of genius. The same may be true for the military arts. If strategy and tactics can be demonstrated to the level of genius, then it is reasonable to say true artistry is possible in the conduct of war.

A certain level of craftsmanship or skill can be acquired through practice and apprenticeship in any profession, but no matter how great the technical skill of the craftsman, art is always an act of inspiration. Experience serves both the tactician and the strategist well, but is more directly applicable to the tactical mode of thought. Here the analogy is to the furniture maker. Years of experience and training can make almost anyone with an interest in the craft and a desire to do well at least minimally competent. At the very least, the person trained will show improvement over time. A few will be able to replicate items of extraordinary quality and natural beauty. They will become adept at identifying materials and maximizing the characteristics of wood, fabric, and metal. They will become efficient in their craft and be able to turn out superior products in short order. Some of them will be identified as master craftsmen, and will break the bonds of the discipline and create truly original, stunningly beautiful works of art.

For the most part, the analogy of tactical thinking to craftsmanship (or artisanship) and strategy to artistry holds. Any conscript of minimal intelligence and physical ability can be trained to perform basic combat functions. The vast majority can learn to be mid-level managers (junior officers and non-commissioned officers) and most will perform well. Many can reach the top of their professions, in terms of rank, and perform adequately. Some, especially in peacetime, can become extraordinary leaders and, within the boundaries of military law and custom, functional innovators. These practiced individuals are the equivalent of technicians: highly trained and proficient in the application of *known* skills and techniques. Technicians, like tacticians, deal with the known characteristics of the situation at hand. Their investigation is limited to finding gaps in knowledge and filling them with the tools of their trade. The rank to which they aspire is *expert*, the one who knows everything in the field.

This is highly desirable, of course. Every organization needs its master practitioners, but it tends to create a blinkered perspective. Focus is so great that the forest loses its meaning, so imbued is the technician with a particular tree. The opposite is often the case for the strategist, who operates in the realm of the unknown. The forest obscures the individual tree. Connections abound. Details become fuzzy, even unimportant. But it is from this perspective that the truly new is discovered, in the patterns that *emerge* from the broad view. Like the pointillist painter who creates a portrait that can be seen only from a distance, the mass of colored dots blending together to form a scene or story, the strategist must make sense of the mass of individual actions that blur into the distance. Of note, it is impossible to see both the individual dots and the portrait at the same time. It becomes increasingly difficult to determine which view discovers the other, or perhaps, which perspective *creates* the other. It may be that it is equally impossible to think strategically and tactically *at the same time.*

The transition to great tactical leader or strategist is rare, and is normally not evident until war or combat draws out the battle-planning and strategy-making artistry within. To some extent, training and education combine with the opportunity of war to stimulate or inspire creativity. In extreme combat situations, leaders tend to emerge from the ranks in a baptism of fire. They assume leadership of the unit by their actions, as opposed to the more time-consuming process of promotion according to established and demonstrable criteria. Combat and crisis are where the genius of the tactical thinker becomes apparent, and is refined. The tactical genius is every bit the master artisan *in* war.

The name we give to supreme mastery is genius. Tactical genius, which seeks an end within the rules and boundaries given, is hardly at odds with strategic genius, which seeks to determine those conflicts (and the conditions therein) that shall be joined and those that shall be avoided, in order to continue to make meaningful decisions in the future. Genius in one does not imply genius in the other, however. To the contrary, genius in one may have the effect of retarding genius in the other, as the skill sets and intuition of the two are not the same. Perfection in one is not a prerequisite, and may not even be desirable, in the quest for attainment of perfection in the other.

In separating the two kinds of genius, it is best to associate strategy with art and tactics with science. The strategic genius is an artist. The tactical genius is more of a scientist, what can be termed an artisan for distinction. Both normally begin as apprentices, learning the techniques and skills unique to their trade through observation and practice. For tactician and strategist, these techniques and skills are the tools of war. They include, at a minimum, knowledge of the capabilities and aptitude of combatants and their equipment, and of the rules and decision-making procedures of the organization. The tactical artisan excels in the *application* of these skills, and uses this talent to fashion the ultimate expression of war craft—perfection in battle. The strategic artist breaks the bonds of these skills and *creates new ways* of perceiving the battle, new connections to exploit in war, and new means of shaping the canvas on which the craft is performed.

To the artisan, the ultimate expression of achievement is the masterpiece, the finest example of skill of which one is capable, and the end of sustained labor. It is technical perfection. The masterpiece is beautiful in its precision, and a demonstration of paramount skill that can only be obtained through study, practice, effort, and talent. In like fashion, the master tactician's masterpiece is the ultimate victory, the utmost achievement at the end of a long struggle to become the best, the tangible embodiment of unsurpassable combat perfection. The artisan sees *the thing* as the apex of creation, the end to which art is directed.

The purpose of art, on the other hand, is artistry, the capacity *to create*. The artist sees perfection as an *ideal* that will never be made real. Though it may define the career of the artist, a portrait, no matter how technically perfect or magnificent, is not the end of art. It is not the purpose of art. It is a manifestation of great skill. But rather than see it as the apex of artistry, it is the newly realized path for a deeper, more meaningful investigation to come. Even though the artisan creates the perfect image, art has not been perfected. There will be more master-pieces, more ideals to explore and express in a meaningful way. To paint, to sculpt, to make; these are the ends of the artisan. To increase the scope of art, to change the definition of what art is; this is the purpose of the artist.

Art *and* artistry are essential, for the one is not better or more important than the other. Both are vital, and both are appreciated in varying degrees by observers, critics, and most certainly buyers and patrons. To the majority of these, the artisan's masterpiece will have greater and more enduring value, because the masterpiece is measurable, and sets a standard for artisanship that follows. It inspires awe in others, and elevates the craft. To other artisans, however, the cre-ation of a new perspective or the application of a new medium opens an array of possibilities, a realm in which the masterpiece still awaits completion. It inspires others to create, and leaves open the far end of measurement. The two taken together are indeed greater than the sum.

We see that the relationship of artist and artisan, or strategist and tactician, is like that between architect and engineer. The architect envisions the finished pro-ject; the engineer makes it possible. Without the master tactician to achieve *in* war, that is, to construct victories in battle, the plan of the master strategist cannot be advanced, and the capacity to manipulate the boundaries *of* war would be sorely limited. Tactical thinkers are vital to the state because they deal with the here and now. They make specific recommendations and decisions that are the practical point of violence, or the use of force. Strategists are vital because they define the boundaries within which the tactical genius can emerge. Yet so invalu-able to the state's present condition are master tacticians that they are often mistaken for strategists. So indifferent to the specifics of context is the master strategist that he is likely to be a poor tactician.

I have suggested that both tactician and strategist are formed from the same base, and for the most part this is so. Both should learn and practice the funda-mentals of the military skills and arts before being elevated to the level of master, but it is not always the case. Occasionally, strategists of enormous talent emerge from non-military backgrounds, thrust onto the pinnacle of strategy-making via the process of politics. Pericles and Abraham Lincoln are fine examples.[2] This is perhaps because the principles of strategy (detailed in previous sections) are few and apply to most competitive endeavors. Military strategists can be experienced and learned in fields other than war. Moreover, since war—not battle—is an extension of politics, politicians who have worked their way to the top of the polit-ical chain should have developed the necessary talents of strategists, and be able to apply them to the theory of war and the formation of strategy.

It also happens that combatants of extraordinary effectiveness will appear on the battlefield, and with innate talent alone perform extraordinary acts of heroism and leadership. Nonetheless, given the need for specialized training to gain a min-imal functionality in the intricacies of modern battle, it is much more difficult to conceive of the sudden appearance of a master tactician than a master strategist. Development of a minimum level of competence in the complex endeavors of the military art requires study, rote practice, and direct applied experience to become a proficient artisan or tactician. Skills are honed through repetition and learning. The techniques of past masters are scrutinized and copied. In this manner, anyone with average intelligence and physical skills can be trained to a minimum level of proficiency. Beyond that takes talent, of course, but it is a latent talent that can be nurtured.

It may seem surprising that artisanship is less spontaneous than artistry, but the genius of art is sometimes evident even when the skill of craftsmanship is crude. Whereas most people can be taught to achieve a respectable quality in the making or doing of things, there is no equivalent of *training* for artists that will produce a minimum level of creative competence. There is a faith that with enough exposure to the skills and techniques of artistry, the creative genius of art will emerge, but only where it lays dormant. In how many, and in whom, the genius of artistry waits is unknown. It is no doubt true these principles extend to war. One who has not been an active participant in battle is less likely to become an adequate, much less master, strategist than one who has. But, unlike skill or technique, which can be taught and which for any individual can be improved with training, there is no method known that will confer upon the average person a minimum level of competence as an artist. Perhaps this is because art, unlike skill, is an inherently immeasurable commodity.

Occasionally, folk artists will appear that can conjure art naturally, without the artisanship of the great masters, but with a vision that refuses to be held in check. Because they have not received even minimal formal training, their output is rough and unsophisticated by the standards of the craft. But it is undeniably *art*, and despite the ragged edges, inspiring and fresh. It also happens that a soldier will emerge from the most unexpected place to become a great leader and strategist.

Napoleon was one such example, and although he remained the crude Corsican in his personal life, his skill as a tactician *and* strategist was unparalleled in his time. He was taught the basic skills of combat, of course. As a junior artillery officer, he was moreover educated in advanced mathematics. But from where did his sense of strategy originate? The question is worth pondering, as there is a general perception that tactics can be taught, but that strategy is innate. Under the proper circumstances, the great strategist will emerge, but just as with great leaders, they are widely thought born and not made.

This presents quite a challenge for military education.[3] The rule of thumb in modern democratic militaries is to evaluate personnel upon entry and to provide the most promising a sustained military apprenticeship at a service academy. Studies are done of great leaders to determine if they share traits, and then to search for these characteristics in the applicant pool. This will provide the proper environment, it is thought, for good and great leaders to come to the fore before placement into active units. All are given intensive martial training, however, as even a merely competent leader has utility, and may improve with real-world experience. One can *learn* the techniques and skills necessary to command a battalion or fleet, but one *becomes* a leader. Where leadership originates is simply not known. Pre-service culling is done to increase the odds of leadership emerging among a particular subset of the population, and this select group does produce a higher percentage of military leaders relative to the general population, but it is hardly the only source of military leadership in war. I outline the process to highlight the general conception that the skill of great leaders, like great artists, is innate. It can be nurtured, but not taught.

Such a view should not deny the role of education for inspiring and improving strategic leadership, for education is starkly different from training. The point was brilliantly examined by Clausewitz, who averred,

> It is therefore consistent to keep this basis of distinction and call everything 'art' whose object is creative ability, as, for instance, architecture. The term 'science' should be kept for disciplines such as mathematics or astronomy, whose object is pure knowledge.[4]

Knowledge, in this example, is information passed on; training is the means of passage. Creative ability is inspired, however, and *education* is the means for it. In addition, training has a goal. An end-state is achieved; there is no more to be done. Expertise is conferred. A skill or technique has been mastered. But education has no end-state. It is nonsense to say someone is fully educated and has finished learning. Exposure must not be limited to the techniques and skills of the discipline for education to occur, it must be to a broad expanse of wisdom. It is equally absurd to think that artistry is best encouraged by avoiding training, by ensuring that the budding artist has no preconceived notions or techniques to shape and limit creativity. For creativity is not the ability to make something out of nothing, it is the capacity to make something new out of something else. It is the ability to transfer an idea from one realm of knowledge to another, and to adapt it to other needs.

Training and experience expose latent artistry in individuals, but we still have no means of training individuals to be artists, and perhaps we should not even try. Education and training are not the same, and the differences are meaningful.

> We have said in our observations on the theory of the conduct of war that it should educate the mind of the Commander for war, or that its teaching should guide his education; also that it is not intended to furnish him with positive doctrines and systems which he can use like mental appliances.[5]

Artistry is not the ability to repeat the past flawlessly. A strategist gains insight from exposure to past examples, not guidance. Doctrine and dogma are the foundations of tactics, and, if allowed to determine it, the ruin of strategy.

Ideally, the best generals are master tacticians *and* master strategists, but not at the same time. It may well be distracting to a junior officer to muddle the thought process of battle planning with greater issues of strategy-making. This is because the master tactician works within the rules and boundaries of the situation but does not attempt to challenge them. For example, a prohibition on the torture of prisoners should not be ignored or questioned at the tactical level. This may lead to tactical sub-optimality, as a trade-off for strategic optimality, but this is the reason combatants are trained not only to obey orders, but also to follow the commander's intent. Likewise, the civilian leader of the state, the military commander-in-chief, is, ideally, a master strategist only. It could be equally distracting if that highest authority acted to manage the affairs of combat, for the strategic view might be lost in the details. Certainly, the commander-in-chief needs to understand the tactical issues well enough to make sound strategic decisions. Likewise, it is useful for the combatant in the field to have a sense of the ultimate purpose of this particular battle or war, as it may assist in discerning value between options. But expertise *necessarily* overlaps only at the level of senior officers in the military and in liaison staffs in the civilian realm.

The artist learns by seeing and being inspired by great works of art in all manner of manifestations, through experience and practice, and by introspection and thought. The artisan increases skill through training, studying the actions and works of masters, and doing. Without continual practice and repetition, the skills of the artisan decline, and must be reacquired after an extended period of inactivity. The tactician sees battle not only as an opportunity for decisive victory, but also as a means to keep martial skills sharp. Combat, in this view, is useful in itself. The artisan becomes an artist, fully formed at the moment of inception, and is an artist ever after. The strategist, once the breakthrough to genius has been accomplished, has *become* a strategist and needs no periodic maintenance.

NOTES

1 THE PATH OF PURE STRATEGY

1 Fuller (1926), p. 23. Fuller was, of course, belittling the Romanticist notions of previous strategists. He would eventually change his mind, and move closer to the tempered views of Clausewitz concerning scientific certainty, but at the time was convinced that a true science of war-making was finally within humanity's grasp.
2 Wilmot (1952). I appreciate the many contributions of my father, Professor Aart Dolman, in the conceptualization of this idea of continuing strategic advantages, and in assistance with the historical examples to make the case.
3 See Shirer (1960), pp. 1011–13.
4 Bullock (1992), pp. 784–6.
5 Beevor (2003).

2 THE END OF VICTORY

1 Bassford (1994), p. 330.
2 General Douglas MacArthur, in an address to a joint meeting of congress, April 19, 1951. See *Bartlett's Familiar Quotations* (1992), p. 642.
3 'The armies separated; and, it is said, Pyrrhus replied to one that gave him joy of his victory, that one other such would utterly undo him.' Attributed to Pyrrhus, king of Epirus, after inflicting a series of defeats on the Romans at the cost of losing most of his men. See *Bartlett's Familiar Quotations* (1992), p. 82.
4 Sinnreich (2003). My emphasis.
5 Ibid.
6 Made obvious in the 2000 US Presidential election, when the outcome was in doubt until candidate Al Gore decided to stop contesting the ballot count in Florida, weeks after votes were cast, and accept defeat.
7 Sun Tzu (1994), p. 177.
8 Ibid., Sun Tzu disagrees. He advises to fight only when necessary. In so doing, 'Thus his weapons will not become dull, and the gains can be preserved.'
9 Clausewitz (1976), p. 128. The Howard and Paret edition is the definitive English translation. Original emphases.
10 An argument made far more eloquently by Dr Jon Kimminau in discourses with the author.
11 Clausewitz (1976), p. 605.
12 Maoz (1990), p. 5. Maoz is citing Luttwak (1987), pp. 239–41, which includes a survey of definitions. See also Gray (1999), pp. 17–23, for additions to the list.

13 For example, the definition of strategy in the current US Department of Defense *Dictionary of Military and Related Terms* (2000), is ' … the art and science of developing and using political, economic, psychological, and military forces as necessary during peace and war, to afford the maximum support to policies, in order to increase the probabilities and favorable consequences of victory and to lessen the chances of defeat.'
14 Clausewitz (1976), p. 127.
15 Ibid., p. 143. 'The original means of strategy is victory—that is, tactical success; its ends, in the final analysis, are those objects which lead directly to peace.'
16 One could imagine the battle that would end all wars, I suppose, if one counts Armageddon. Without anyone left to fight, no more wars would be fought, no more strategy would exist. Likewise, the tumult that will end history is imaginable—Hegel, Marx, and Fukuyama have all proclaimed the coming 'end of history.' Yet here we are. We endure.
17 Ibid., pp. 90–1. See also p. 143. 'The original means of strategy is victory—that is tactical success; its ends, in the final analysis, are those objects which lead directly to peace.'
18 Ibid., p. 90.
19 Ibid., p. 579.
20 Ibid., p. 577.
21 Ibid., p. 582. Original emphasis.
22 Ibid.
23 Ibid., p. 91.
24 Ibid., p. 92. Original emphasis.
25 Ibid., p. 156. Original emphasis.
26 Ibid., p. 179. Original emphasis.
27 Ibid., p. 159.
28 Clausewitz's account is supplemented here by Schom (1997), pp. 56–60.
29 Clausewitz (1976), p. 160.
30 Schom (1997), p. 59.
31 Clausewitz (1976), p. 147.
32 Ibid., p. 583.
33 Cohen (2002), p. 8.
34 Clausewitz (1976), p. 605. Original emphasis.

3 THE ELEMENTS OF STRATEGY

1 Clausewitz (1976), p. 177.
2 Wylie (1967), p. 14.
3 Clausewitz (1976), p. 177.
4 Mao Tse-Tung (1972), p. 9.
5 Clausewitz makes the case repeatedly in *On War,* but nowhere more passionately than in *Principles of War,* (1942).
6 Clausewitz (1976), p. 177. 'Strategic theory, therefore, deals with planning.'
7 Jomini (1862), p. 62.
8 Ibid. My emphasis.
9 Cited in Holborn (1986), p. 290.
10 Moltke (1994), pp. 220–1.
11 Ibid., p. 219. Original emphasis.
12 Ibid., p. 220.
13 Liddell Hart (1991), p. 321. My emphasis.
14 Ibid.

15 Ibid., pp. 321–2.
16 The indirect approach, or the 'road less traveled,' is a favorite among military planners. Strike where the enemy least expects is the boiled-down advice. This is problematic, of course, because the enemy could expect you to strike at the least expected place, and thus defend it. You, on the other hand, would expect the enemy to expect your approach from the least expected position, and so you would opt for the most obvious approach. It is a vicious cycle.
17 Ibid., p. 325. Original emphasis.
18 Gray (1999), p. 17. My emphasis.
19 Ibid. Original emphasis.
20 Schelling (1963), p. 15. My emphasis.
21 Strassler (1996), pp. 98–9. Kagan (1995), pp. 63–6, provides a concise and generally compatible assessment of Pericles' strategy.
22 Clausewitz (1976), p. 75.
23 Ibid. Original emphasis.
24 Peat (1987), citing Galileo, p. 47.
25 Ibid., p. 87.
26 Ibid.
27 Clausewitz (1976), pp. 76–7.
28 Ibid., p. 77.
29 Ibid. Original emphasis.
30 Ibid., p. 76.
31 Ibid., p. 77.
32 Ibid., p. 78.
33 Ibid. Original emphasis.
34 Ibid., pp. 80–1. Original emphasis.
35 Ibid., p. 87. Original emphasis.
36 Ibid.
37 Ibid., p. 87.
38 Ibid., p. 143. My emphasis. See also p. 147: 'strategic theory, dealing as it does with ends which bear directly on the restoration of peace.'
39 For this section, I am indebted to Col. Raymond O'Mara, for his insightful analysis and unwavering perspective. O'Mara (2002).
40 See for example, Van Riper and Scales (1997), pp. 14–15: 'Real war is an inherently uncertain enterprise in which chance, friction, and the limitations of the human mind under stress profoundly limit our ability to predict outcomes; in which defeat to have any meaning must be inflicted above all in the minds of the defeated; and in which the ultimate purpose of military power is to assure that a trial at arms, should it occur, delivers an unambiguous political verdict.' Also see US Army White Paper (1996), the purpose of military power is 'to *compel* any adversary to do what he otherwise would not do of his own free will.' Original emphasis.
41 This is a disputed view, but retains some credibility. See Mandelbaum (1999), pp. 79–94.
42 Aristotle believed the best form of rule was monarchy, but since the state could not guarantee a succession of good men to rule, good laws would have to suffice.
43 Wolfram (2002), p. 1185.
44 Clausewitz (1976, p. 76) insists that we do not shy from the notion of violence or extremes (maximization). 'It would be futile—even wrong—to try and shut one's eyes to what war really is from the sheer distress at its brutality.' This conforms with an empirical study of war and preparation for war in Dolman (2000), pp. 117–47 and Dolman (2004).
45 Ibid., p. 76: 'To introduce the principle of moderation into the theory of war will always lead to absurdities.'

46 This is the essence of deterrence theory.

47 Sporadic or isolated forays into the commanded airspace do not violate the definition of command of the air if operations are not significantly altered to account for it. For example, the likelihood of a shoulder-launched ground-to-air missile engaging and downing an aircraft within the Continental United States is a possibility today; it remains remote enough that routine operations are not hindered. Clearly, the United States has command of its own air space, despite such unique possibilities as and including the events of September 11, 2001.

48 Salter (1999). While it is hardly definitive, fiction can be tremendously heuristic in theory building. It is the equivalent of the thought experiment.

49 Numerous chronicles of the war are available, but Yuen Foong Khong's *Analogies at War* (1992) is among the very best.

50 'So the old word *observer* simply has to be crossed off the books, and we must put in the new word *participator.* In this way we have come to realize that the universe is a participatory universe.' John Wheeler, cited by Peat (1987), p. 4. Original emphasis.

51 I am indebted to Dennis Drew for this observation.

52 Carl Builder suggests this is the common perception (1994) p. 33. This statement was made by Lt. Col. William Stroud: 'the basic purpose of air power is to realize that it is not omnipotent, [it] is, purely and simply, a means to knock down the bridge.' See Stroud (1988) p. 26. Stroud was writing about tactical purpose, and not strategic, but the difference is not made clear in his article anywhere but the title.

53 Comments are made drawn from Corbett's *Some Principles of Maritime Strategy* (1988) and Mahan's *The Influence of Seapower Upon History, 1660–1783* (1987).

54 'It scarcely needs saying that a war cannot be decided by naval means alone … [the fleet must determine its] relation to the action of the land forces … since men live upon the land and not the sea, great issues between nations at war have always been decided [there].' Corbett (1988), pp. 15–16.

55 Corbett, too often credited with bringing Clausewitz to seapower, explicitly stated that the 'object of naval warfare must always be [to] secure command of the sea.' Of course, this is for the specific mission of supporting armies in the field. From Corbett's 1911 text, *Some Principles of Maritime Strategy* (1988), p. 91.

56 Ibid., p. 91. This is what differentiates land and sea, for Corbett. The natural condition of the land is occupied, hence controlled (p. 94).

57 Mahan (1987), pp. 28–9.

58 Ibid., p. 287.

59 Ibid., pp. 287–8.

4 WAR AND STRATEGY, GAMES AND DECISIONS

1 Dougherty and Pfaltzgraf (1996), p. 457.

2 For an interesting view that the lack of war between the superpowers from 1945–90 occurred *in spite* of the existence of menacing nuclear arsenals, see Mueller (1996), pp. 204–5.

3 The litany of tactical (and occasionally strategic) surprises that are *all* based on the target's inability (or indifference) to comprehend and prepare for the unexpected bending of the rules that are called deception, trickery, and even cheating, is enormous.

4 Riker (1986).

5 See Tuchman (1994).

6 Howard (1971).

7 Brams (1976), p. 87.

8 Styron (1999).

9 The story is related by F.W. Winterbotham in *The Ultra Secret* (1974), pp. 60–1. Several historians, including John Keegan in *The Second World War* (1989), p. 500, have disputed the claim, arguing that Churchill never would have allowed Coventry to be so heavily attacked, regardless of the cost. Still, it was routine for sanitized Ultra reports that to find their way into the hands of local fire and civil defense departments an attack was likely. No such report seems to have made it to Coventry. See also Allan Kurki, *Operation Moonlight Sonata: The German Raid on Coventry* (1995) and John Colville, *The Fringes of Power* (1985).

10 Kozaczuk (1984), pp. 166–7.

11 Dalberg, (1955), p. 335.

12 Ibid. My emphasis.

13 Schelling (1992), p. 343; see also Brams (1976), p. 81.

14 Ibid., p. 344.

15 Wilson (1990), pp. 76–7.

16 Wilson (1990), p. 81.

17 Suits (1978).

18 Wolfram (2002).

19 Axelrod (1984).

20 Ibid., p. 3.

21 Ibid., p. 4.

22 Ibid., p. 6. My emphasis.

23 Harsanyi (1965), p. 300, see also Lieber (1988), p. 243.

24 It is quite possible that a player may wish to lose a PD. Imagine a member of an organized criminal element, for example. To win the PD, that is, to get off without jail time by turning in another, would be a death sentence in the external world of criminal ethics. The winner would be identified as a rat. The one who takes jail time without saying a word is a stand-up guy and is likely to be rewarded after the jail term with higher payout jobs.

25 Axelrod (1984), p. 15.

26 Ibid., pp. 12, 21. Emphasis added.

27 Ibid., p. 63. See 'proposition 5.'

28 Ibid., pp. 64–7.

29 Pincus and Bixenstine (1977), pp. 519–30.

30 Schelling (1967), p. 519.

31 Von Neuman and Morganstern (1944), pp. 44–5.

32 Brate (2002), p. 148.

33 Easton (1953), pp. 225–6; see also Popper (1971).

34 Popper (1959), p. 105.

35 Brate (2002), p. 56.

36 Popper (1971), p. 104.

37 Peat (1987), p. 58.

38 Eco (1990), p. 132.

39 Schelling (1967), pp. 524–5, noted the weakness in 1966: 'Game theory is hardly in accord with history and is probably overweighted to the present situation and understanding.'

40 Made notorious by Marilyn Vos Savant in her popular 'Ask Marilyn' column in *Parade* magazine, and fully discussed in Vos Savant (1997).

41 A story attributed to numerous persons, including Benjamin Franklin and Shakespeare, but whose origins are obscure: 'For want of a nail the shoe was lost, For want of a shoe the horse was lost, For want of a horse the rider was lost, For want of a rider the battle was lost, For want of a battle the kingdom was lost, For want of a nail a kingdom was lost.'

42 Wolfram (2002), p. 1085.
43 Thomas Hughes, author of *Overlord: General Pete Quesada and the Triumph of Tactical Airpower in World War II* (1995), in an aside to the author while overlooking the carnage of Verdun, April 28, 2004.
44 For this insight, and a great many more throughout this work, I am indebted to discussions with Colonel Thomas P. Ehrhard, USAF.
45 Von Bayer (2004), p. 66.

5 PRINCIPLES AND RULES

1 Kratochwil (1989), p. 95.
2 Tuchman (1962).
3 Clausewitz (1976), p. 151. Original emphasis.
4 Ibid.
5 Ibid.
6 Ibid.
7 Ibid.
8 Ibid.
9 Ibid., p. 152. Original emphasis.
10 Ibid.
11 Ibid., p. 153.
12 Krasner (1983), p. 2.
13 Ibid.
14 Waltz (1979).
15 Thucydides, 'Melian Dialogue,' in Strassler (1996).
16 The emerging discipline of historical sociology covers this important field, and owes much to the rigor of neo-Marxist historians like Immanuel Wallerstein with his magisterial *Modern-World System* in three volumes (1990) and Charles Tilly with his deeply engaging *Coercion, Capital, and European States, A.D. 990–1992* (1990).
17 Jervis (1982), p. 357.
18 Kratochwil (1989), p. 48.
19 Ibid.
20 Krasner (1983), p. 6.
21 Kratochwil (1989), p. 6.
22 Austin (1962).
23 Ursula LeGuin uses this mechanism in one of the finest novels of political and science fiction ever penned, *The Dispossessed* (1997).
24 North (1981).
25 Kratochwil (1989), p. 47.
26 Ibid., pp. 8–9, 64. Original emphasis. Actors also resort to norms when they want to air grievances.
27 Ibid. p. 53.
28 Ibid., 72.
29 Kratochwil (1989), p. 98.
30 Ibid., p. 25.
31 'But no matter how much data of this sort we imagine our observers to collect and no matter how many inductive generalizations we imagine them to make from the data, they still have not described American football.' Searle (1969), p. 35.

6 CHAOS, COMPLEXITY, AND WAR

1 Waldrop (1993), p. 21.
2 Rosenau (1996).

3 Wood (1965), p. xxxvii. See also Dolman (1995), pp. 191–212.
4 See Nichols and Tagarev (1994); James (1995); and Alberts and Czerwinski (1997).
5 Alberts, Garstka, and Stein (1999); Arquilla and Ronfeldt (2000, 2001); and Murdock (2002), pp. 86–95.
6 Gray (2002), pp. 2–3. My emphasis.
7 A case made by Kuhn (1996).
8 The story is widely recounted. See Hawking (2001).
9 Zukav (1980), p. 138. Original Emphasis.
10 Cited by Steven Rinaldi (1997). See also Schmitt (1995), pp. 17–22.
11 Von Bayer (2004), p. 12.
12 Ibid.
13 A point made by Alan Beyerchen (1992/93), pp. 59–90, and Barry Watts (1996).
14 Clearly articulated by astronomer Pierre Simon LaPlace (1994).
15 Plato (1976), pp. 207–14.
16 Von Bayer (2004), p. 13.
17 Brate (2002), p. 54.
18 Van Doren (1991), p. 338.
19 Zukav (1980), pp. 34–5.
20 Ibid., p. 32.
21 If this is true, then every thing in existence may be made of nothing. Green (2000).
22 See Hofsteder (1979).
23 Ibid., p. 17.
24 Wolfram (2002), p. 1158.
25 Maoz (1990), pp. 65–6.
26 Ibid., p. 137.
27 This example, of course, refers to the American military experience in Vietnam.
28 Peat (1987), p. 54. Original emphasis.
29 Ibid.
30 Wolf (1981), p. 145.
31 This discussion comes from Zukav (1980), p. 66.
32 Ibid.
33 Waldrop (1993), p. 39.
34 Ibid., p. 40.
35 Brate (2002), p. 149.
36 Alberts and Czerwinski, 'Preface' to Alberts and Czerwinski (1997).
37 Peat (1987), p. 64.
38 Jervis (1997), p. 46.
39 Ibid.
40 See Peat (1987), p. 71.
41 Ibid.
42 Wilson (1999), p. 54.
43 Von Bayer (2004), pp. 56–7.
44 Ibid., p. 57.
45 Ibid.
46 Ibid., p. 59.
47 See Jervis (1997), p. 46. 'We are dealing with a system when (a) a set of units or elements are inter-connected so that changes in some elements or their relations produce changes in other parts of the system and (b) the entire system exhibits properties and behaviors that are different from those of the parts.'
48 Waldrop (1993), p. 11. Original emphasis.
49 See Lewin (1999); and Gladwell (2000).
50 Waldrop (1993), p. 12.

51 Lorenz (1993), Appendix 1: 'Does the flap of a butterfly's wings in Brazil set off a tornado in Texas?'
52 Johnson (2002).
53 Waldrop (1993), p. 88.

7 ADAPTATION AND EMERGENCE IN STRATEGY

1 Johnson (2002), p. 18.
2 Ibid., p. 19. Original emphasis.
3 In 1776; Adam Smith, *The Wealth of Nations* (1937).
4 Of note, it is redundant to delineate boundaries for a system. If the element or agent is influenced (or could be influenced) by actions or changes in or of another part, then it is in the system. If the actions of one agent do not affect another, then they are not part of the same system, regardless of any line we draw around them.
5 The second criterion is from Robert Jervis (1997), p. 46.
6 Rosenau (1996).
7 Waldrop (1993), p. 11. Original emphasis. See also Johnson (2002), p. 12.
8 Waldrop (1993) p. 11.
9 Johnson (2002) p. 20.
10 Wolfram (2002).
11 Von Neumann (1966), p. 121.
12 Ibid., pp. 51–9.
13 Ibid., classes of behavior are discussed more technically on pp. 231–49.
14 Ibid., p. 60.
15 Ibid.
16 Ibid., p. 73.
17 Ibid., p. 75.
18 Ibid., p. 106.
19 Waldrop (1993), p. 118.
20 Dahl (1957), p. 202–3.
21 Ibid.
22 Ibid. Original emphasis.
23 Ibid., p. 204.
24 Easton (1965), p. 366–7. Emphasis added.
25 Teune (1988), p. 25. See also Teune and Mlinar (1978), p. 15. Social change 'is the most perplexing problem in the social sciences.'
26 First suggested by George Miller, Eugene Galanter, and Karl Pribham, in *Plans and the Structure of Behavior* (1960), p. 27.
27 Brown (1967), p. 42. 'The electrician and the electronics engineer have been using the word, feedback, for a long time. To them, feedback means a return to the input part of the electrical signal. Sometimes the feedback shows that a healthy signal has been transmitted as intended, and sometimes the feedback is an undesirable squawk [sic].'
28 Mayr (1970).
29 Cited in Mayr (1971).
30 Based on the 'centrifugal pendulum' patented in 1787 by Thomas Mead, a device that regulated the speed of windmills by furling and unfurling the sails. The waterclocks of Ktesibos were recognized as control devices, but not in the modern context of feedback control. Otto Mayr cited in Richardson (1991), p. 17.
31 Mayr (1976), p. 169.
32 Rosenblueth, Wiener, and Bigelow (1943), pp. 18–24.
33 Ibid., p. 19. See also Forrester (1968), pp. 1–5. A 'non-feedback system [is] not aware of its own performance'.
34 Ibid.

35 Richardson (1991), p. 95.
36 Held and Freedman (1968), pp. 321–9.
37 Ibid., p. 325.
38 Osgood (1968), p. 201.
39 Wiener (1961).
40 Cited by Koontz, O'Donnell, and Weihrich, (1984).
41 Wiener (1950), p. 33.
42 Wiener (1961), p. 138.
43 Ibid., p. 139. Original emphasis.
44 Wiener (1950), p. 12.
45 Wiener (1961), pp. 11–12.
46 Ibid., p. 96.
47 Deutsch (1948), pp. 506–33.
48 Deutsch (1963).
49 Susser (1992), p. 271.
50 Deutsch (1963), p. 80. See also p. 86, where Deutsch describes the actions of targeting, aiming, and adjusting fire. These notions are equally applicable to the process of striking in the biologic model of Rosenblueth, Wiener, and Bigelow (1943).
51 Ibid., p. 80.
52 Ibid., p. 86. Original emphasis.
53 Ibid., p. 194.
54 Ibid.
55 Ibid., p. 554. '[For example,] historical data [tells] managers in November they lost money in October for something that was done in July. At this time, the information is only a distressingly interesting fact.'
56 Koontz (1958), pp. 45–61. See also Steward (1980), p. 37.
57 Koontz et al., (1984), p. 557. Original emphasis.
58 Machiavelli (1950), p. 16.
59 Carse (1986), pp. 152–3.
60 Ibid, p. 153.
61 Ibid.
62 B.H. Liddell Hart argues that the best strategy is the least expected one – the 'indirect approach.' Of course, knowing this, the tactician will expect the least expected move. A devilish circle, indeed. See Liddell Hart (1991).
63 Sun Tzu (1994), p. 136.
64 Miller, Pribram, and Galanter (1960).
65 Ibid., p. 27.
66 Ibid., p. 37.
67 Rinaldi (1997).
68 Cordesman (2002). See also Applegate (2001).
69 Cebrowski (2003).
70 Bell (2001).
71 Phelan (1995).
72 Ibid.
73 Ibid. My emphasis.
74 Drawn from Wolfram (2002); and Waldrop (1993), pp. 145–7.
75 Cited in Waldrop (1993), p. 147.

8 PRINCIPLES OF WAR

1 Faulkner (1975).
2 Clausewitz (1976), p. 136.
3 Ibid., pp. 88–9.

4 Ibid., p. 89.
5 Ibid., p. 119.
6 Ibid., p. 102. Original emphasis
7 Ibid., p. 89.
8 Ibid., p. 87.
9 Clausewitz (1942).
10 Ibid., p. 11.
11 Ibid., pp. 12–14.
12 Ibid., p. 12.
13 Ibid. Original emphasis.
14 Ibid., p. 13. My emphasis. Clausewitz was on his way to Russia to fight with the Tsar against Napoleon when he penned these thoughts, and was undoubtedly overburdened with the shame of Prussia's collaboration with the French Empire.
15 Ibid., p. 14.
16 Ibid., pp. 45–59.
17 Ibid., p. 53.
18 Ibid. My emphasis.
19 Ibid., p. 58.
20 Ibid.
21 Jomini's thoughts are primarily from Jomini (1862).
22 Ibid., p. 63.
23 Baron de Jomini, *Traité des grandes opérations militaires,* cited in Shy (1986), p. 146. Original emphasis.
24 Shy (1986), p. 161.
25 Clausewitz (1976), p. 87.
26 Ibid.
27 Jomini *Art of War,* p. 69.
28 Shy (1986), p. 179.
29 Fuller (1926), pp. 201–2.
30 Mahan (1987), p. 2.
31 Corbett (1988), p. 15.
32 Mahan (1987), p. 288.
33 Corbett (1988), p. 91.
34 Ibid.
35 Ibid., p. 155.
36 Ibid., p. 160.
37 Cebrowski and Barnett (2003). My emphasis.
38 See Dolman (2002).
39 Wilson (2001), p. 129.
40 Citing Rudolph Clausius, Von Bayer (2004), p. 91.
41 Von Bayer (2004), p. 91.
42 Ibid., p. 123.
43 'Because power is only measurable in comparative—that is, competitive—terms, it presupposes some kind of cooperation.' See Carse (1986), p. 37.
44 Kratochwil (1989), p. 69.
45 Ibid., p. 70.
46 Zukav (1980), p. 146.
47 Simpkin (1987), p. 34.
48 Kratochwil (1989), p. 48.
49 Ibid., p. 48.
50 Weigley (1971).
51 Lambeth (2000), p. 314.

52 Again, I am indebted to Raymond O'Mara for his insight and assistance in helping me envision the uniqueness that airpower brings to America's world vision.
53 For a full and insightful analysis of these effects, see Murray (2002).
54 Mahan (1987), p. 25.

9 MAKING STRATEGY

1 Testimony before the Senate Armed Services Committee, April 9, 2002.
2 Cebrowski (2003), p. 2. See pp. 20–7 for detailed descriptions of the four pillars.
3 Ibid., p. 3.
4 Ibid., p. 6.
5 Ibid., p. 13.
6 Wiener (1950), pp. 17–18.
7 Brate (2002), p. 12.
8 Ibid., p. 13.
9 Von Bayer (2004), p. 25.
10 Wiener (1950), p. 116.
11 Wolfram (2002), p. 475.
12 Ibid. My emphasis.
13 Ibid., pp. 475–6.
14 Johnson (2002), p. 74.
15 Ibid. Original emphasis.
16 See Arquilla and Ronfeldt (2000).
17 Garstka (2003), p. 58.
18 Including Libicki (1995); Alberts *et al.* (2001); and Alberts, Garstka, and Stein (1999).
19 Johnson (2002), p. 134.
20 Ibid, p. 137.
21 An entire issue of *The Army Space Journal* was recently devoted to OIF, and most of the articles highlighted the extreme value of friendly force tracking, particularly in bad weather and at night. See especially 'I Corps Perspective,' 'Warfighter's Perspective,' and 'Space and Missile Defense Command Contributions and Lessons from Operation Iraqi Freedom.' US Army Space and Missile Defense Command, *The Army Space Journal* Special Edition, Vol. 2: No. 3 (2003).
22 Johnson (2002) pp. 77–9. Johnson is describing desirable networks based on the 'swarm logic' of ants, but the advice holds.
23 Ibid., p. 79.
24 Ibid., p. 78.
25 Waldrop (1993), p. 253.
26 Brate (2002), p. 159.
27 Ibid, p. 333.
28 Johnson (2002), p. 69.
29 Cebrowski (2003), pp. 31–2.
30 Ibid., p. 31. My emphasis.
31 Ibid., p. 13. My emphasis.

10 IS STRATEGY AN ART?

1 Clausewitz (1976), p. 148.
2 On Lincoln, and others, see Cohen (2002).
3 For Clausewitz's comments on the education and training of generals and soldiers, see *On War* (1976), pp. 144–5.
4 Ibid., p. 148.
5 Clausewitz (1976), p. 282.

REFERENCES

Alberts, David and Czerwinski, Thomas (eds) (1977) *Complexity, Global Politics, and National Security*, Washington, DC: National Defense University Press.

Alberts, David, Garstka, John, Hays, Richard and Signori, David (2001) *Understanding Information Age Warfare*, Washington, DC: National Defense University Press.

Alberts, David, Garstka, John and Stein, Frederick (1999) *Network-Centric Warfare: Developing and Leveraging Information Superiority*, Second Revised Edition, Washington, DC: National Defense University Press.

Applegate, Melissa (2001) *Preparing for Asymmetry: As Seen Through the Lens of Joint Vision 2020*. US Army Studies in Asymmetry, Carlisle, PA: Army War College, online at: http://carlisle-www.army.mil/usassi/ssipubs/catalogs/catalog.htm.

Arquilla, John and Ronfeldt, David (2000) *Swarming and the Future of Warfare*, Santa Monica, CA: RAND.

—— *Networks and Netwars: the Future of Terror, Crime, and Militancy*, Santa Monica, CA: RAND.

Austin, J.L. (1962) *How to Do Things with Words*, Cambridge: Harvard University Press.

Axelrod, Robert (1984) *The Evolution of Cooperation*, New York: Basic.

Bartlett's Familiar Quotations (1992), Sixteenth Edition, New York: Little Brown.

Bassford, Christopher (1994) 'John Keegan and the Tradition of Trashing Clausewitz,' *War and History* Vol. 1: No. 3, (November) pp. 319–36.

Beevor, Anthony (2003) *The Fall of Berlin 1945*, New York: Penguin.

Bell, Coral (2001) *The First War of the 21st Century: Asymmetric Hostilities and the Norms of Conduct.* Strategic and Defence Studies Centre Working Paper, no. 364, Canberra: Australian National University.

Beyerchen, Alan (1992/93) 'Clausewitz, Nonlinearity, and the Unpredictability of War,' *International Security* (Winter), pp. 59–90.

Brams, Steven (1976) *Paradoxes and Politics: An Introduction to the Nonobvious in Political Science*, New York: Free Press.

Brate, Adam (2002) *Technomanifestos: Visions from the Information Revolutionaries*, New York: Texere.

Brown, Fred (1967) *National Security Management: Concepts and Practices*, Washington, DC: Industrial College of the Armed Forces.

Builder, Carl (1994) 'Roles and Missions: Back to the Future,' *Joint Forces Quarterly* (Spring), pp. 32–7.

Bullock, Alan (1992) *Hitler and Stalin: Parallel Lives*, New York: Alfred Knopf.

Carse, James (1986) *Finite and Infinite Games: A Vision of Life as Play and Possibility*, New York: Ballantine.

Cebrowski, Arthur (2003) *Military Transformation: A Strategic Approach,* an Office of Force Transformation Document, Washington, DC: US Department of Defense.

Cebrowski, Arthur and Barnett, Thomas (2003) 'The American Way of War,' *Transformation Trends* (13 January), an on-line newsletter of the US Department of Defense, http://www.cdi.org/mrp/transformation-trends.cfm.

Clausewitz, Carl von (1942) *Principles of War,* Translated by Hans Gatzke, Harrisburg, PA: Military Service Publishing.

____ (1976) *On War*, Edited and translated by Michael Howard and Peter Paret, Princeton: Princeton University Press.

Colville, John (1985) *The Fringes of Power*, London: Hodder and Stoughton.

Corbett, Julian (1988) *Some Principles of Maritime Strategy*, Annapolis, MD: Naval Institute Press.

Cordesman, Anthony (2002) *Terrorism, Asymmetric Warfare, and Weapons of Mass Destruction: Defending the U.S. Homeland*, Westport, CT: Praeger.

Cohen, Eliot (2002) *Supreme Command: Soldiers, Statesmen, and Leadership in Wartime*, New York: Basic.

Dahl, Robert (1957) 'The Concept of Power,' *Behavioral Science* Vol. 2: pp. 201–15.

Dalberg, John E.E., Lord Acton (1955) 'Letter to Mandell Creighton, April 5, 1887,' in Gertrude Himmelfarb (ed.) *Essays on Freedom and Power*. Magnolia, MA: Peter Smith, pp. 335–6.

Deutsch, Karl (1948) 'Toward a Cybernetic Model of Man and Society, From Some Notes on Research on the Role of Models in the Nature and Social Sciences,' *Syntheses* 7, pp. 506–33.

____ (1963) *The Nerves of Government: Models of Political Communication and Control*, New York: Free Press.

Dolman, Everett (1995) 'Obligation and the Citizen-Soldier: Machiavellian Virtú versus Hobbesian Order,' *Journal of Political and Military Sociology* Vol. 23 (Winter), pp. 191–212.

____ (2000) 'War and (the Democratic) Peace: Applications from State-Building and Civil-Military Relations,' *Citizenship Studies*, 4:2 (Spring), 117–47.

____ (2002) *Astropolitik: Classical Geopolitics in the Space Age*, London: Frank Cass.

____ (2004) *The Warrior State: How Military Organization Structures Politics*, New York: Palgrave.

Dougherty, James and Pfaltzgraf, Robert (1996) *Contending Theories of International Relations: A Comprehensive Survey,* Fourth Edition, New York: Longman.

Easton, David (1953) *The Political System: An Inquiry into the State of Political Science*, New York: Alfred Knopf.

____ (1965) *A Systems Analysis of Political Life*, New York: John Wiley.

Eco, Umberto (1990) *Foucault's Pendulum*, New York, Ballantine.

Faulkner, William (1975) *Requiem for a Nun* (1951), Act I, Scene II, New York: Vintage.

Forrester, Jay (1968) *Principles of Systems*, Second Edition, Cambridge: Wright-Allen.

Fuller, J.F.C. (1926) *The Foundations of the Science of War*, London: Hutchinson & Co.

Garstka, John (2003) 'Network-Centric Warfare Offers Warfighting Advantage,' *Signal* (May), p. 58.

Gladwell, Malcolm (2000) *The Tipping Point: How Little Things Can Make a Big Difference*, Boston: Little Brown.

Gray, Colin (1999) *Modern Strategy*, Oxford: University Press.

_____ (2002) *Strategy for Chaos: Revolutions in Military Affairs and the Evidence of History*, London: Frank Cass.

Green, Brian (2000) *Elegant Universe: Superstrings, Hidden Dimensions, and the Quest for the Ultimate Theory*, New York: Knopf.

Harsanyi, John (1965) 'Game Theory and the Analysis of International Conflicts,' *Australian Journal of Politics and History* 11, p. 300.

Hawking, Stephen (2001) *The Universe in a Nutshell,* New York: Bantam.

Held, Richard and Freedman, Sanford (1968) 'Plasticity in Human Sensorimotor Control,' in Walter Buckley (ed.) *Modern Systems Research for the Behavioral Scientist*, Chicago: Aldine, pp. 321–9.

Hofsteder, Douglas (1979) *Gödel, Escher, Bach: An Eternal Golden Braid*, New York: Basic Books.

Holborn, Hajo (1986) 'The Prusso-German School: Moltke and the Rise of the General Staff,' in Peter Paret (ed.) *Makers of Modern Strategy from Machiavelli to the Nuclear Age*, Princeton: Princeton University Press, pp. 281–95.

Howard, Nigel (1971) *Paradoxes of Rationality: Theory of Metagames and Political Behavior*, Cambridge: MIT Press.

Hughes, Thomas (1995) *Overlord: General Pete Quesada and the Triumph of Tactical Airpower in World War II*, New York: Free Press.

James, Glenn (1995) *Chaos Theory: The Essentials for Military Actions*, Newport, RI: Naval War College.

Jervis, Robert (1982) 'Security Regimes,' *International Organization* 36 (Spring), pp. 357–78.

—— (1997) 'Complex Systems: The Role of Interactions,' in David Alberts and Thomas Czerwinski (eds) *Complexity, Global Politics and National Security*, Washington, DC: National Defense University, pp. 45–71.

Johnson, Steven (2002) *Emergence: The Connected Lives of Ants, Brains, Cities, and Software*, New York: Touchstone.

Jomini, Baron de *The Art of War* (1838), Translated by G.H. Mendell and W.P. Craighill, Philadelphia: Lippincott.

Kagan, Donald (1995) *On the Origins of War and the Preservation of Peace*, New York: Doubleday.

Keegan, John (1989) *The Second World War*, New York: Viking.

Khong, Yuen Foong (1992) *Analogies at War: Korea, Munich, Dien Bien Phu, and the Vietnam Decisions of 1965*, Princeton: Princeton University Press.

Koontz, Harold (1958) 'A Preliminary Statement of Principles of Planning and Control,' *Academy of Management Journal* Vol. 1, pp. 45–61.

Koontz, Harold, O'Donnell, Cyril and Weihrich, Heinz (1984) *Management*, Eighth Edition, New York: McGraw Hill.

Kozaczuk, Wladyslaw (1984) *ENIGMA*, Washington DC: University Publications.

Krasner, Stephen (1983) 'Structural Causes and Regime Consequences,' in Stephen Krasner (ed.) *International Regimes,* Ithaca: Cornell University Press, pp. 1–21.

Kratochwil, Friedrich (1989) *Rules, Norms, and Decisions: On the Conditions of Practical and Logical Reasoning in International Relations and Domestic Affairs*, Cambridge: Cambridge University Press.

Kuhn, Thomas (1996) *The Essence of Scientific Revolutions*, Third Edition, Chicago: University of Chicago Press.

Kurki, Allan (1995) *Operation Moonlight Sonata: The German Raid on Coventry*, New York: Praeger.

Lambeth, Benjamin (2000) *The Transformation of American Air Power,* Ithaca and London: Cornell University Press.

LaPlace, Pierre Simon (1994) *Philosophical Essay on Probabilities,* translation of the 1812 Fifth Edition by Andrew Dale, *Sources in the History of Mathematics and Physical Science,* Vol. 13, New York: Springer Verlag.

LeGuin, Ursula (1997) *The Dispossessed*, New York: HarperPrism.

Lewin, Roger (1999) *Complexity: Life at The Edge of Chaos*, Chicago: University of Chicago Press.

Libicki, Martin (1995) *What is Information Warfare?* Washington, DC: National Defense University Press.

Liddell Hart, B.H. (1991) *Strategy,* Second Revised Edition, New York: Meridian.

Lieber, Robert (1988) *No Common Power: Understanding International Relations*, Glenview, IL: Scott Foresman.

Lorenz, Conrad (1993) *The Essence of Chaos*, Seattle: University of Washington Press.

Luttwak, Edward (1987) *Strategy: The Logic of War and Peace*, Cambridge: Harvard.

Machiavelli, Niccoló (1950) *Discourses on the First Ten Books of Titus Livy*, Translated by Lesley Walker, New Haven: Yale University Press.

Mahan, Alfred Thayer (1987) *The Influence of Seapower Upon History, 1660–1783*, Republication of the 1894 Fifth Edition, New York: Dover.

Mandelbaum, Michael (1999) 'A Perfect Failure: NATO's War Against Kosovo,' *Foreign Affairs* Vol. 78, No. 5, pp. 79–94.

Mao Tse-Tung (1972) *Six Essays on Military Affairs*, Beijing: Foreign Languages Press.

Maoz, Zeev (1990) *Paradoxes of War: The Art of Self-Entrapment*, Boston: Unwin Hyman.

Mayr, Otto (1970) *The Origins of Feedback Control*, Cambridge: MIT Press.

____ (1971) *Feedback Mechanisms in the Historical Collections of the National Museum of History and Technology*, Washington DC: Smithsonian Press.

____ (1976) 'Maxwell and the Origin of Cybernetics,' in Otto Mayr (ed.) *Philosophers and Machines*, New York: Science History Publications, pp. 169–80.

Miller, George, Galanter, Eugene and Pribham, Karl (1960) *Plans and the Structure of Behavior*, New York: Henry Holt.

Moltke, Helmuth von (1994) 'Doctrines of War,' in Lawrence Freedman (ed.) *War*, New York: Oxford, pp. 217–21.

Mueller, John (1996) 'The Obsolescence of War in the Modern Industrialized World,' in Robert Art and Robert Jervis (eds) *International Politics: Enduring Concepts and Contemporary Issues,* Fourth Edition, New York: Harper Collins, pp. 204–17.

Murdock, Paul (2002) 'Principles of War on the Network-Centric Battlefield: Mass and Economy of Force,' *Parameters* 32, No. 1 (Spring), pp. 86–95.

Murray, Scott (2002) 'The Moral and Ethical Implications of Precision-Guided Weapons,' SAASS Thesis (June), publication pending.

Nichols, David and Tagarev, Todor (1994) 'What Does Chaos Theory Mean for Warfare?' *Airpower Journal* (Fall), available online at http://www.airpower.maxwell.af.mil/airchronicles/apj/apj94/fa1194.html.

North, Douglass (1981) *Structure and Change in Economic History*, New York: W.W. Norton.

O'Mara, Raymond (2002) 'To Command the Air,' unpublished manuscript, May.

REFERENCES

Osgood, Charles (1968) 'A Behavioralist Analysis of Perception and Language as Cognitive Phenomena,' in Walter Buckley (ed.), *Modern Systems Research,* Chicago: Aldine, pp. 200–15

Peat, F. David (1987) *Synchronicity: The Bridge between Matter and the Mind,* New York: Bantam.

Phelan, Steven (1995) 'From Chaos to Complexity in Strategic Planning,' presented at the 55th Annual Meeting of the Academy of Management, Vancouver, British Columbia, Canada, August 6–9. Online at http://www.css.edu/users/dswenson/web/525ARTIC/ strategyresources.html.

Pincus, Jeffrey and Bixenstine, Edwin (1977) 'Cooperation in the Decomposed Prisoner's Dilemma Game: A Question of Revealing or Concealing Information,' *Journal of Conflict Resolution* 21, pp. 519–30.

Plato, *The Republic,* (1976) Book VII: Scrolls 514–18, translated by A.D. Lindsey, Toronto: Fitzhenry and Whiteside, pp. 207–14.

Popper, Karl (1959) *The Logic of Scientific Discovery* (1934), London: Hutchinson.

—— (1971) *The Open Society and Its Enemies* (1945), Princeton: Princeton University Press.

Richardson, George (1991) *Feedback Thought in Social Science and Systems Theory,* Philadelphia: University of Pennsylvania Press.

Riker, William (1986) *Heresthetics: The Art of Political Manipulation,* New Haven: Yale University Press.

Rinaldi, Steven (1997) 'Complexity Theory and Airpower: A New Paradigm for Airpower in the 21st Century,' http://www.clausewitz.com/CWZHOME/Complex/PropBibl.htm.

Rosenau, James (1996) 'Many Damn Things Simultaneously: Complexity Theory and World Affairs,' paper presented at the Conference on Complexity, Global Politics, and National Security, sponsored by the National Defense University and the RAND Corporation (Washington, DC, November 13).

Rosenblueth, Arturo, Wiener, Norbert and Bigelow, Julian (1943) 'Behavior, Purpose, and Teleology,' *Philosophy of Science* Vol. 10, pp. 18–24.

Salter, James (1999) *The Hunters,* New York: Vintage.

Schelling, Thomas (1963) *The Strategy of Conflict,* New York: Oxford.

—— (1992) 'What is Game Theory?' (1967) in Bernard Susser (ed.) *Approaches to the Study of Politics,* New York: Free Press, pp. 335–64.

Schmitt, John (1995) *Chaos, Complexity & War: What the New Nonlinear Dynamical Sciences May Tell Us About Armed Conflict,* Quantico, VA: Marine Corps Combat Development Command.

Schom, Alan (1997) *Napoleon Bonaparte,* New York: Harper Collins.

Searle, John (1969) *Speech Acts,* Cambridge: Cambridge University Press.

Shirer, William (1960) *The Rise and Fall of the Third Reich: A History of Nazi Germany,* New York: Simon and Schuster.

Shy, John (1986) 'Jomini,' in Peter Paret (ed.) *Makers of Modern Strategy: From Machiavelli to the Nuclear Age,* Princeton: Princeton University Press, pp. 143–85.

Simpkin, Richard (1987) *Deep Battle: The Brainchild of Marshal Tukhachevskii,* London: Brassey's.

Sinnreich, Richard Hart (2003) 'Winning Badly,' *Washington Post,* October 27.

Smith, Adam (1937) *The Wealth of Nations,* New York: Modern Library.

Steward, Donald (1980) *Systems Analysis and Management: Structure, Strategy, and Design,* New York: PBI Press.

210

Strassler, Robert (ed.) (1996) *The Landmark Thucydides: A Comprehensive Guide to the Peloponnesian War,* Revised Edition of the Richard Crawley Translation of Thucydides, *History of the Peloponnesian War*, New York: Free Press.

Stroud, William (1988) 'The Use and Misuse of Tactical Airpower,' *Aerospace Power Journal* (Summer) pp. 26–7.

Styron, William (1999) *Sophie's Choice*, New York: Modern Library.

Suits, Bernard (1978) *The Grasshopper: Games, Life, and Utopia*, Toronto: University of Toronto Press.

Sun Tzu (1994) *Art of War*, Translated by Ralph Sawyer, Boulder: Westview Press.

Susser, Bernard (ed.) (1992) *Approaches to the Study of Politics*, New York: Free Press.

Teune, Henry (1988) *Growth*, Volume 167, Sage Library of Social Research, Newbury Park, CA: Sage Publications.

Teune, Henry and Mlinar, Zdravko (1978) *The Developmental Logic of Social Systems*, Volume 60, Sage Library of Social Research, Beverly Hills, CA: Sage Publications.

Tilly, Charles (1990) *Coercion, Capital, and European States, A.D. 990–1992*, New York: Blackwell.

Tuchman, Barbara (1994) *The Guns of August*, Reprint Edition, New York: Ballantine.

US Army Space and Missile Defense Command (2003) *The Army Space Journal* Special Edition, Vol. 2: No. 3.

US Army White Paper (1996) *Force of Decision ... Capabilities for the 21st Century*, Washington, DC: US Government.

US Department of Defense (2000) *Dictionary of Military and Related Terms*, Washington, DC: Government Printing Office.

Van Doren, Charles (1991) *A History of Knowledge: Past, Present, and Future*, New York: Birch Lane Press.

Van Riper, Paul and Scales, Robert (1997) 'Preparing for War in the 21st Century,' *Strategic Review* 25, pp. 14–20.

Von Bayer, Hans (2004) *Information: The New Language of Science*, Cambridge: Harvard University Press.

von Neumann, John (1966) *The Theory of Self-Reproducing Automata*, Urbana, IL: University of Illinois Press.

Von Neuman, John and Morganstern, Oscar (1944) *Theory of Games and Economic Behavior*, Princeton: Princeton University Press.

Vos Savant, Marilyn (1997) *The Power of Logical Thinking: Easy Lessons in the Art of Reasoning ... And Hard Facts About Its Absence in Our Lives*, New York: St. Martin's.

Waldrop, M. Mitchell (1993) *Complexity: The Emerging Science at the Edge of Order and Chaos*, New York: Simon & Schuster.

Wallerstein, Immanuel (1990) *Modern-World System*, three volumes, New York: Academic Press.

Waltz, Kenneth (1979) *Theory of International Relations*, Reading, MA: Addison-Wesley.

Watts, Barry (1996) *Clausewitzian Friction and Future War*, McNair Paper No. 52, Washington, DC: Institute for National Strategic Studies.

Weigley, Russell (1971) *The American Way of War: A History of United States Military Strategy and Policy*, Bloomington: Indiana University Press.

Wiener, Norbert (1950) *The Human Use of Human Beings*, New York: Anchor.

____ (1961) *Cybernetics or Control and Communication in the Animal and the Machine*, Second Edition, New York: John Wiley.

Wilmot, Chester (1952) *The Struggle for Europe*, New York: Harper.

Wilson, Edward (1999) *Consilience: The Unity of Knowledge*, New York: Random House.

Wilson, R. Rawdon (1990) *In Palamedes' Shadow: Explorations in Play, Game, and Narrative Theory*, Boston: Northeastern University Press.

Wilson, Robert Charles (2001) *The Chronoliths,* New York: Tor.

Winterbotham, F.W. (1974) *The Ultra Secret*, New York: Harper & Row.

Wolf, Fred Alan (1981) *Taking the Quantum Leap: The New Physics for Nonscientists*, San Francisco: Harper and Row.

Wolfram, Stephen (2002) *A New Kind of Science*, Champaign, IL: Wolfram Publishing.

Wood, Neil (1965) 'Introduction to Machiavelli's Art of War,' in Niccolò Machiavelli, *The Art of War*, New York: DaCapo.

Wylie, J.C. (1967) *Military Strategy: A General Theory of Power Control*, Annapolis, MD: Naval Institute Press.

Zukav, Gary (1980) *The Dancing Wu Li Masters: An Overview of the New Physics*, New York: Bantam.

INDEX

Printed in the USA/Agawam, MA
May 17, 2013

575401.116